BRAHAM MURRAY is a founding artistic director of the Royal Exchange Theatre Company. As a student at Oxford he became president of the Experimental Theatre Club and in 1964 his hit production of *Hang Down Your Head and Die* transferred to the West End and Broadway. From the Century Theatre, where from 1966–68 he was artistic director, he became a founding director of the 69 Theatre Company. Productions included *She Stoops to Conquer* and *Charley's Aunt* (with Tom Courtenay), *Mary Rose* (with Mia Farrow), *Endgame*, and the musicals *Erb* and *Catch My Soul*, all of which transferred to London. Other credits include *Uncle Vanya* (Tom Courtenay and Amanda Donohoe, Circle in the Square Theatre, New York) the world première of Tod Machover's *Resurrection* (Houston Grand Opera), *The Good Companions* (John Mills and Judi Dench), *The Black Mikado* (Michael Denison), *Andy Capp* (Tom Courtenay and Alan Price), *The Cabinet Minister* (Maureen Lipman) and *Lady Windermere's Fan* (all West End). One of the five founding artistic directors of the Royal Exchange Theatre which came into being in 1976, he has since directed over sixty productions including *The Dybbuk*, *Waiting for Godot* (Max Wall and Trevor Peacock), *Hamlet* (Robert Lindsay), *Maybe* (Vanessa Redgrave), *The Count of Monte Cristo*, *Peer Gynt* and *Riddley Walker* (David Threlfall), *Miss Julie* and *Hedda Gabler* (Amanda Donohoe), *Othello* (Paterson Joseph and Andy Serkis), *Hobson's Choice* (John Thomson, Trevor Peacock and Joanna Riding), *The Happiest Days of Your Life* and the world premières of *Snake in Fridge* and *Cold Meat Party* by Brad Fraser. He also directed the North American première of *Cold Meat Party* for Factory Theatre, Toronto. His recent productions for the Royal Exchange Theatre include *She Stoops to Conquer*, *The Importance of Being Earnest*, *Antony and Cleopatra* and *What Every Woman Knows*.

THE WORST IT CAN BE IS A DISASTER

The Life Story of Braham Murray
and the Royal Exchange Theatre

Braham Murray

First published 2007

Methuen Drama
A & C Black Publishers Limited
38 Soho Square
London W1D 3HB
www.acblack.com

ISBN 978 0 713 68490 2

A CIP catalogue record for this book is available from the British Library.

Typeset in SX Composing DTP, Rayleigh, Essex

Printed and bound in Great Britain by Caligraving Ltd, Thetford, Norfolk

This book is produced using paper that is made from wood grown in managed, sustainable forests. It is natural, renewable and recyclable. The logging and manufacturing processes conform to the environmental regulations of the country of origin.

For Jacob and Joe
who gave me a life

Contents

Foreword

Braham and I have been friends for over forty years. I was introduced to him by our mutual friend Casper Wrede at the first night of Casper's production of *The Father*, which starred Trevor Howard. 'Who's that dark chap over there?' I asked Casper. Braham had hair then.

It was Casper, a massive influence on both Braham and me, who suggested I play Lord Fancourt-Babberley in Braham's production of *Charley's Aunt* at the University Theatre in Manchester. He knew that after my heady success in the early sixties I felt I lacked experience and wanted to make a fresh start. So I went off, in December 1966, to Manchester and young Braham's tender mercies. And had a wonderful time.

Braham was a great antidote to Casper and also to Michael Elliott, the other great directorial influence on my life. I loved them both, of course, but they were very serious. Definitely heavyweights. Braham, more of a middleweight, if you will, was more extrovert. He wasn't afraid of having a good time – as many of the ensuing pages will attest.

I had dinner with him recently and went home feeling happy. He can be very uplifting, being an optimist. Readers of this book might feel that he has sometimes been overly optimistic and I can fairly say that in a couple of our joint ventures my pessimism turned out to be more justified than Braham's optimism.

But you can't win them all, and on a couple of occasions working with him has turned my life around: the aforementioned *Charley's Aunt*, of course, which started my connection with Manchester, and later, at the Royal Exchange Theatre, in a production of Molière's *The Miser* which made me feel like an actor again after a year or so in the doldrums.

Some of Braham's hair-raising experiences in the world of musical theatre I didn't know about and they make diverting reading. The story of the founding of the Royal Exchange Theatre is familiar to me, and Braham tells it well. It's a beautiful theatre. The philosophy behind it is simple: the actors and the audience share the same space.

Braham writes about the acoustic test of the new theatre prior to its opening. It was the first time the place had been filled with people. Several of us who were rehearsing the two opening plays (*The Rivals* and *The Prince of Homburg*) were to do a party piece. I went on after James Maxwell who delivered a glorious 'Ye elves of hills, brooks, standing lakes and groves'. As I walked into the space to do my bit, I suddenly found myself surrounded by what seemed like a wall of people. The shock made my legs tremble and I remember thinking that I was glad I was wearing trousers rather than tights, for I was about to utter Hamlet's 'How all occasions do inform against me' – my favourite of the soliloquies. Braham remembers it as 'Oh what a rogue and peasant slave am I'. Wrong soliloquy, but he gets the excitement right. We had learnt that the space was magical.

I'd like to add a post-script (literally) to Braham's story of when he went on for me one matinee, after Manchester's fog had descended on my vocal chords and rendered them useless. I don't think this goes amiss as it was clearly an exciting time in his life – for one thing his tights kept falling down. Braham tells us Ian McKellen saw his performance and ever after when he meets Braham he says in hushed tones, 'I saw your Romeo'. Well, having missed my Romeo, Ian some years later saw Braham's production of *Andy Capp* in which I played the eponymous Andy. Not my best performance ever, but Ian generously and mysteriously, as far as I was concerned, felt moved to write me a letter of congratulation. To which I was able to reply and express my gratitude, adding 'P.S. I bet you wish you'd seen my Romeo'.

I've enjoyed reading Braham's account of his life and the story of the Royal Exchange Theatre, and can't help but feel pleased to have been a part of that story. I'm rather hoping that as a reward for penning these few lines Braham will give me dinner again. He has been on a special diet for years now. The mainstay of it seems to be that you can drink quite a lot of wine with your evening meal. So his enthusiasms will be undiminished – for his latest project, for the rebirth of the brilliance of Tottenham Hotspur, for some new branch of Chinese medicine, for a life which is soulful as well as (moderately) materialistic. And I shall wander home, as usual, feeling the better for his company.

Tom Courtenay

Preface

This preface wanted to be written when I was about a quarter of the way through the book.

It is amazing that human beings survive as well as they do. From being in the womb, through the traumatic birth process and the first seven years of your life, you are entirely at the mercy of whoever is bringing you up. At seven, you become aware that you have a separate identity, but you are still dominated by your environment, which can never be wholly benign. At around about ten the titanic upheaval of puberty permeates your entire life, through the teenage years, as you struggle to come to understand the world and to be educated in an increasingly competitive society. At eighteen, if you're lucky, you have three years of higher education and for the first time the shackles come off. Then you are in the rat race, fighting for survival. Throughout the twenties, the white-heat years, you try everything, every substance, every experiment you can, and you thrash about to discover what you might be supposed to be doing with your life as you strive to earn a living. At thirty you begin to settle into a direction and by then you have probably started your own family, so the cycle perpetuates itself. Since it's only at about forty, with the first intimations of mortality, that you begin to know yourself in any profound sense it's a wonder that we do as well as we do.

When my agent, Penny Wesson, suggested I write my autobiography, I simply didn't want to. She didn't give up and suggested that during the summer, in my house in the village of Dunes in the Tarn-et-Garonne, I write a chapter and an outline, just to see. One fine French morning I thought, 'Why not?' I wrote three chapters very quickly, one funny, one serious and the all-important Chapter One. I showed them to my cousin Jaqueline Rose, a real writer. She liked them but insisted that I had to be more personal. I had kept myself out of the writing, she said, and if the book was to be of interest to anyone apart from theatre buffs, I would have to interest them in me. I refused to do that. I am a private person and I balked at the self-exposure and the possible exposure of the cast list of my life. I had been riveted but disgusted by the autobiographies of people such as John Osborne and Elia Kazan, and I didn't want to go down that path.

Weeks passed and then, on another fine French morning, I wrote about the early part of my life, again very fast. It was then that Methuen Drama commissioned me to complete the book.

The Russian thinker Ouspensky, in his book *In Search of the Miraculous*, says that when you find yourself in an intolerable circumstance and you don't know what to do, zoom out of yourself and observe yourself from outside yourself. Refer to yourself as 'he' and describe 'his' predicament. Then you will see clearly your situation and know what to do.

Writing the first part of the book has had the uncanny effect of introducing myself to someone whom I had never really known – a peculiar and somewhat harrowing experience. It is difficult by definition to be in touch with the seven-eighths of ourselves that is our unconscious. Dreams are one way; obviously writing about oneself is another.

I never wanted this book to be either ego-bound or merely theatrical reminiscences. Anyone's life should resonate with anyone else since we are all bound to grow up in the same pattern, if in very different circumstances. This book has turned out to be about a human being coming to consciousness. I am more eager than anyone to know where it will end.

CHAPTER I
Derek Destiny

There is 'a destiny that shapes our ends', of that I am convinced. I imagine I'm not alone in recognising the specific moment when Derek Destiny rises up and slaps you in the face to be sure you acknowledge it, not in its full enormity, but sufficiently to provide at least a centre to your life. I have 'rough hew'd' it over the years, but it has remained and been welcomed as an overarching guide.

The moment took place one night in March 1959 at the Lyric, Hammersmith. I was barely sixteen, a stage-struck teenager who went to see every – and I mean every – play on in London, sitting in the gods and marking them in my notebook out of ten. A friend of mine from Clifton College, where I was at school, David Stone, rang to say that he had read very good reviews of an obscure play by a writer called Ibsen, *Brand*, and that we should forsake the West End for the wilds of Hammersmith to see it.

We paid 2s. 6d. to sit on an uncomfortable wooden bench, and the play started. Patrick McGoohan was playing the driven priest Brand and in the first moment of the play he climbed from the stalls up on to the stage as if climbing a mountain. My heart sank. This was clearly going to be a trying amateurish evening.

Two and a half hours later I staggered out of the theatre on to King Street, Hammersmith, unable to speak, completely stunned. I was a quite unhappy teenager, the product of a broken home at the age of four, living with my mother and my grandparents in the Golders Green ghetto, sent away to a bizarre prep school aged eight to protect me from the narrow-minded environment of home, and now at the rather more enlightened public school, Clifton. I was lonely, confused, rebellious and introverted. This production had reached down into my very being. The play seemed to deal with the problems that I dimly perceived as mine. The emotional truth of the acting, especially from Patrick McGoohan as Brand and Dilys Hamlett, reached beyond thought to the heart. The production itself was stupendous. Years later when I stood on the tiny postage stamp stage of the Lyric, I could

1

not believe that here, Richard Negri and Richard Pilbrow had conjured up, not only a mountain, the fjords and a church, but had made me experience the avalanche that engulfed Brand at the final curtain. Unbelievably, I learnt later, this was Michael Elliott's first professional stage production. It displayed his unique mix of dazzling theatrical showmanship, piercing analytical intelligence and the ability to draw out of his actors emotionally true, powerhouse performances. I had never seen anything like it. It felt as if all these hugely talented people, including Ibsen whom I had never experienced before, had done this just for me. My loneliness was swept away.

Three major things happened as a result of that night, two of them immediately, the third somewhat later. The first was that my determination to make my career in the theatre was confirmed. If theatre could do this for me, it could do it for other people and I wanted to bring that about. This was not the reductionist, nihilistic theatre that ruled in London. This was theatre of life and hope. I don't think I realised this consciously – that came later – but I was drawn to it like water in the desert. Henceforth, all other theatre would be judged by this yardstick. It is still my yardstick.

The second result was that I wanted desperately to work with these people who had created this event. I had the programme; all their names were there. I made a vow that one day I would make this come about.

The third result was also momentous in a different way. I wanted to be an actor. When I was about ten, I was taken to see a comedy in the West End called *The Golden Wedding Anniversary*, starring Bernard Braden and Barbara Kelly. One of the parts was for a young boy. After the show I announced that I could do better than that. At my weird prep school I was made Captain of Drama. My first performance was in a play called *The Blue Ray*. As Captain of Drama I naturally gave myself the biggest part of the hero. One day into rehearsal, I realised that the smaller part of the German spy was better. Equally naturally, I ordered the boy playing that part to swap with me. A lesson learnt. At Clifton I had played Morry in *The Bespoke Overcoat* in the house play competition (we won) and then Antony in *Antony and Cleopatra* for the annual school play. Now it was time for the house play competition again.

I informed my housemaster, the remarkable Phil Polack, that I intended to play Brand for our house play. Polack went to the library and found William Archer's rhyming-couplet unplayable translation. He vetoed it. I wrote to Michael Meyer and asked if I might use his translation (it was just Act Five – it was a one-act competition). Meyer wrote back giving permission and saying how impressed he was at my ambition, adding that if I felt like it, he would be delighted to give me tea in London. In the face of this, Polack capitulated. Now this was *folie de grandeur* on my part. It was scarcely a role for a nice Jewish boy. The play is about a fanatical priest who is determined to save his flock, in the Norwegian fjords, from the decadence and corruption of the world. Initially his congregation become devoted to him, but as he demands more and more sacrifices of them, they turn against him and in the fifth act they stone him out of the village, up on to the mountain, where he dies in an avalanche. At the moment of his death a voice from the heavens tells him, 'He is the God of Love.'

The play was directed by an excellent chap called P. A. Leek. However, when it came to the stoning scene it became clear that he couldn't handle the crowd. As Brand I realised that the scene wasn't going to work if the crowd didn't do a great deal better. In a moment of intense frustration I took over the rehearsal and told them what to do. They were galvanised and the scene worked. At that rehearsal I knew that that was what I wanted to do. In the moment of taking over I felt totally fulfilled. I never wanted to be an actor again.

The production was a catastrophe. I was awful as Brand: big, hammy and empty. To cap it all, halfway through the climactic avalanche the tape recorder broke down, the avalanche stopped, in the ensuing silence I cried my last line, 'If not by will how then can man be redeemed?' to be answered in rich Yorkshire tones with, ''e is the God of Luv.' We didn't even get to the finals. My career as an actor, mercifully for the British public, was stillborn but that night in Hammersmith had brought about its third effect. Destiny had indeed revealed its hand.

CHAPTER 2

The (Un)Happiest Days of Your Life

The name started out as Braham Goldstein. Why Braham? My father, Sam Goldstein, wanted me named after his father Abraham; my mother, realising I'd be called Abe or Abie all my life, cut off the A (thank God) and called me Braham. Goldstein became Murray when my mother married again – Philip Murray. Actually, he was Philip Murray Zigman, but when he joined the Army in the Second World War, they suggested that the Zigman might not be helpful if he was captured by the Germans.

Anyway, at the age of eight Braham Goldstein was taken by his mother in a taxi to Paddington Station, put into a carriage with a horde of other boys and dispatched to Brockhurst School in the country near Newbury.

The reason, although not given then, was a good one. My mother sensed that the claustrophobic, narrow-minded atmosphere of my grandparents' home in Finchley, whither she had sought refuge after her divorce, might not be very good for me. It was a household where the subjects of sex, religion and politics were taboo, and where great emotion was never shown as if it were itself obscene. She was probably right, but since no explanation was given me I found myself that night sitting on my bed in Canada dormitory, helplessly, hopelessly wretched. It is the worst feeling I have ever endured.

There are three things I chiefly remember from Brockhurst: sex, anti-Semitism and Shakespeare.

The headmaster of this beautiful mock-Elizabethan pile was Mr Park. He had certain strict rules. No boy was allowed to put his hands in his pockets, no boy could be in a room with the door closed unless there was a master present (quite tough during winter nights) and no boy could sleep with his hands under the bedclothes. To enforce the last Mr Park would prowl the dorms with a torch in the early hours of the morning, catching any offender and causing him to place the offending limbs outside the sheets (also not so pleasant in winter).

No reasons were given for these and other similar rules, so that the boys happily discovered their own and their friends' genitals and indeed certain orifices (it was a long time before it became clear to me that they weren't weeing in each other's mouths). I, however, was the most degenerate of all. There was a rhyme going round the school which went:

> The ladies in Spain
> Do their wees down the drain.
> The ladies in Ceylon
> Do the same with nothing on.

I thought this very amusing and repeated it to a master. Hauled in front of the headmaster, I was told I was the rotten apple in the barrel. How, I was asked, could he face the other parents if he allowed such a corrupt influence to remain at the school. I had no idea what he was talking about and I think he must have realised that too, for I was permitted to stay.

On the last night of our last term the leavers each had a one-to-one talk in the headmaster's study. Mine went something like this: 'When you leave here you'll find another sort of chap and they're called girls. All I want to say to you is "never consort with prostitutes". Good luck.' My hand was shaken and out I went to face my public school, fully armed. That was the sex.

I was the only Jewish boy at the school and for the first year I was treated like an animal, and not a pet one. The abuse was both verbal and physical. I was prodded and pushed, by way of experiment, to see how such a strange creature would react. I assumed that this was normal. I had always known that I was Jewish; now I knew that made me dirty – a filthy Yid. It was an awful year. During the holidays I told no one but when the time came to go back, I had to be dragged screaming to the taxi, with my grandmother yelling at my mother not to make me go.

At the end of the long summer holiday the prospect of another year was so appalling that I broke down and told my Welsh nanny all about it. She reported it to my mother and an uncle was dispatched to talk to me. His advice was simple: 'The next time anyone insults you, hit them as hard as you can in the face.'

That term I was driven back to school, went up to my dormitory (Canada had given way to Australia) and started to unpack. A boy, one Mathias, came up to me. 'I've just seen your Jewish pig of a mother drive away,' he informed me. I hit him very hard on the nose. He fell down. There were copious amounts of blood. From that moment I was accepted into the life of the school. There was no further anti-Semitism and I made friends and played like everyone else. I still wonder what message to glean from this. A moment of violence brought acceptance.

I had an English master called William Robertson, known as Willie Fluff on account of a great mop of curly blond hair that sat atop his very tall, very thin, body. His jacket and trousers were always too small for him so that he looked like a scarecrow, and his arms were dipped up to the elbows in nicotine. Willie Fluff loved Shakespeare and especially *Macbeth*. English lessons largely consisted of him acting the whole play to us: witches, apparitions, thanes, kings and children. He was magnificent. I was swept into a world I had never entered before. From that moment I too loved Shakespeare and I never had any trouble with the language. Willie Fluff had given me a priceless introduction.

In 2003 I did a production of John Dighton's wonderful farce *The Happiest Days of Your Life*, set in a boys' prep school just after the war. I took my designer, Simon Higlett, down to Brockhurst, now run by Mr Park's grandson, because I wanted him to use the school as the starting point for the set. As I drove through the gates, a huge wave of nausea hit me. The school is now a most civilised place, with a girls' school in the old stables and a young committed staff, so different from the eccentric and completely unregulated masters who taught us.

I left Brockhurst with a love of Shakespeare, a very strange idea of the opposite sex and a toughness that was to prove a blessing in surviving my early years in the theatre, but a curse in other ways. Much later I identified this as the portcullis effect. Whenever I felt threatened it was as if a portcullis came down. If it preserved me in my professional life, it ruined my personal relationships. I was subconsciously determined never to be hurt again and that meant never allowing a woman too close. For this education my grandfather paid a small fortune, with extras such as awful food, uncomfortable beds, a bath once a week in shared water and freezing cold (no heating except tiny coal fires in the classroom). My mother's final pronouncement years later? 'Well, it made a man of you.'

CHAPTER 3

The Best School of All

In my first term at Brockhurst I was briefly in the church choir (briefly because I was tone-deaf and flunked the 'Sevenfold Amen'. Had my grandfather seen me in cassock and surplice, his alarm at my going to a non-Jewish prep school would have been even worse than it was. His bargain with my mother was that when I reached thirteen I would go to a Jewish school for my secondary education. The time had come and Carmel College, an all-Jewish public school, was chosen. However, Derek Destiny intervened. My mother persuaded him to send me, if I passed the entrance exam, to Clifton College.

Clifton was an English public school but it had a Jewish house, Polack's. The house had been founded at the end of the nineteenth century so that the cream of Anglo-Jewry could receive a public-school education and still practise their religion. They worked with the other boys, ate together (albeit kosher food) and, like the other boys, went back to their house to sleep and use their studies. They didn't go to chapel, they worshipped twice daily in their own synagogue, and they didn't attend school on Saturday or play games, unless they were selected for a school team, in which case they could decide for themselves.

Polack's had a considerable cachet in Jewish society. My grandfather was persuaded and I passed the exam.

Until that time my relationship to Judaism had been superficial. My grandparents were nominally orthodox. They kept a kosher home and observed high days, holy days and the Sabbath. They hadn't the slightest idea what the religion meant or what their rituals signified. Unlike fifty-two members of their family, they had left Poland in time to escape the gas chambers and they clung to their religion, fearfully guarding against a society of non-Jews who could turn against them as the Germans had done.

I was required to go to synagogue every Saturday morning for the four-hour-long service. There was some beautiful singing from the cantor, Rabbi Rosenfeld, sermons inveighing against marrying out of the faith from Rabbi Gellis, but mostly it was interminable prayers, which most of the congregation ignored, preferring to talk about the afternoon football matches; being north London they supported either Arsenal or Spurs. One Saturday, as my grandfather rattled through a prayer, I put my hand over the English translation and asked if he knew what he was saying. 'It doesn't matter,' he replied. 'It's the language of God.' I too could read Hebrew and went to chaider (the equivalent of Sunday School) but I was never taught to translate, nor was I given any religious instruction. Clifton was about to change all that. I began my lifelong interest in what it meant to be Jewish as opposed to following Judaism.

Being effectively deprived of a father (I saw him once a week when he took me to see Spurs, for which I bless him) Derek Destiny provided me over the years with remarkable substitute fathers. The first of them was the housemaster of Polack's, Philip Polack. He was the most civilised and civilising man I have ever met. Most of the boys in the house came from wealthy families who made their money in business. They tended to be materialistic and not a little arrogant. Polack was determined to provide a counterbalance to their behaviour. He was anti-Zionism and I'm not sure if he was religious, but he strove to nurture in each boy a wider understanding of his religion and his place in society. He officiated at all services, somewhat perfunctorily, but he introduced us through his sermons to a side of Judaism none of us had ever heard of: Moses Maimonides, Kabbalah and the great Sephardic poets. I particularly remember a text from Rabbi Hillel: 'If I am for me what am I? If I am not for me who will be? If not now, when?' That question of the balance between self-centredness and humility is one that every artist, every human being, struggles with.

The initial impact all this had was to make me, for an extremely brief period, more orthodox than my grandfather. He was rather taken aback during the holidays to find me every morning praying with the phylacteries bands on my forehead and left arm, and my grandmother had to wrestle with my now rigorous dietary requirements, which allowed for no breaking of the rules. The period was extremely brief. As I examined the English translations of the prayers, it seemed to me that they were all about praising and thanking God. There was no guidance, no teaching, no nourishment in them. My rejection of the religion was sudden and complete, but it marked the beginning of my quest to understand better what it is to be Jewish. The intensity of the quest erupted a decade later when I became a professional director, but that is to run on ahead.

Towards the end of my first year, Phil Polack asked me to come to his study. He had been watching me and he had the feeling that I was very unhappy. I was, but I could not have explained to him, or indeed myself, why. I gave what now seems to me a rather superficial reason: I hated authority. I hated the myriad of stupid rules and told him so. His reply was a milestone in my life: 'When you come up against a rule you don't like, think about it carefully. Think whether it's really important or not and if you really can't stomach it, break it.' That reply was the beginning of my conscious development. He had put me in charge of my life. He made me think for myself. If I chose to obey a rule, it was because I chose to, not because I had to. Life seemed possible.

At this stage my mother made, from her point of view, a fatal mistake, from mine another brilliant intervention. I was determined to be a barrister. The lure of the wig and gown, the wonderful words, 'May it please your ludship, members of the jury . . .' had me rapt. In those days unless you were right at the top, barristers found it hard to make a living. Relatives and friends were pulled out of the hat to put me off with stories of poverty and suffering. The advantages of being a solicitor – the security, the money – all these things were relentlessly hurled at me. I, of course, obstinately refused to listen, but something unstoppable was beginning in me.

If Willie Fluff had started my love of Shakespeare, two inspirational masters at Clifton cemented it. The English lessons of Tom Wells and Chris Watters were magical. The imaginative life of literature was unlocked to me. What was more, studying plays meant reading them out in class, not like Willie Fluff, who did all the parts, but everyone being given roles. The seduction of acting had begun in earnest.

Polack's house was never renowned for its prowess at rugger or cricket. Its record in the inter-house competitions was distinctly undistinguished. However, it regularly won the chess competition and, more to the point, the drama competition. Each house would produce either a one-act play or an act of a play. Mr Steadman, the school librarian, would choose the best three, and a distinguished professional would attend the final and name the winner during a critical speech. Aged fifteen I was given a leading role of an old Jew, Morry, in *The Bespoke Overcoat* by Wolf Mankowitz. I spent days in the East End picking up the accent. A friend of the family introduced me to the actor Bernard Spear, who helped coach me. We reached the finals. The head of the Bristol Old Vic theatre school, Duncan Ross, awarded us the prize and singled me out for special praise. All this was as nothing to the reaction of my art master, Bill Leadbetter. I couldn't paint and I couldn't draw. Art class was misery. Bill Leadbetter was a caustic Scot who made my life hell for an hour a week. The day after the finals he stopped me in a corridor, shook my hand and said, 'You're an artist too.' That was it. In the Easter holidays I gave my mother the news she had been waiting for: 'I don't want to be a barrister.' Delight. 'I'm going to be an actor.' Numb horror. But she'd shot her bolt. What could she do? I expect she thought I'd get over it, like a disease. My grandfather was appalled: 'Actors? They're all queers!'

The disease had taken hold. Morry was followed by Antony in *Antony and Cleopatra* and thanks to Phil Polack, who persuaded the conservative headmaster, Nigel Hammond, that sixth formers only would watch, Jimmy Porter in *Look Back in Anger* and Big Daddy in *Cat on a Hot Tin Roof*. I was as alive as I had ever been. My future was as an actor. Then came *Brand* and it all changed again.

I got in touch with Duncan Ross and asked him how I could become a director. He outlined three ways. Either become an actor and switch, or go into stage management and switch or, and this was best, go to Oxford or Cambridge, like the Peters Wood, Hall and Brook, where your work would be covered by the profession. My mother was delighted. At least I wasn't going to drama school and I would have the safety net of a degree when I failed as a director.

I finished my last year at Clifton by directing, in French, half of *Men in Shadows* by Sartre (the half I wasn't in), the masters in *The Bald Prima Donna* by Ionesco, also in French, and won the house play competition with Ionesco's *Jacques*. Of course, I didn't know what the hell I was doing. For *Jacques* I built myself a little booth at the side of the stage and during the performance shouted instructions to the cast like a football manager. I may not have known what I was doing but I was in seventh heaven.

Clifton was an enlightened school. It didn't cope with sex, which remained alarmingly and frustratingly on the back burner until Oxford, but it mitigated the anti-Semitism, and it extended and nurtured the love of Shakespeare.

Clifton has a hilarious school song written by Sir Henry Newbolt. I shall close this chapter by quoting the chorus:

> We'll honour yet the school we knew,
> The best school of all.
> We'll honour yet the rule we knew
> Till the last bell tolls.
> For working days or holidays
> And sad or melancholy days,
> They were great days and jolly days
> At the best school of all.

CHAPTER 4

Chutzpah

You have to understand that up to now you have been reading about a quiet introvert who listened a lot and said little. Now you have to deal with a lunatic, otherwise you won't begin to comprehend the next phase of my life or perhaps, indeed, the rest of it.

The release that directing gave me was liberating. It was a drug. There were many reasons, no doubt – megalomania, escape from life, creative expression, to name a few – but the result was pure adrenalin. I couldn't do without it and I would do anything to do it.

The first thing was to get into Oxford. English was my special subject. I had sailed through A level without stirring myself, but now I had to devote myself to the sheer magnitude of the Oxford entrance syllabus. There was an obstacle. To read English you had also, apart from a general paper, to do a Latin unseen. I hated Latin. I had squeaked through O level and forgotten it with relief. I hadn't a hope of passing.

I still can't quite believe what I did or that it succeeded. The subject my grandfather wanted me to take was Politics, Philosophy and Economics (PPE), because this would lead to a proper job (I suppose he felt I could already speak English well enough). To do the PPE exam you didn't have to do a Latin unseen; you were set a French unseen. I was fluent in French. I entered myself to read PPE.

In those days you took your exam at your preferred college. Mine was University College (Univ). During the first phase of the exam you were interviewed by the College dons en masse. Summoning up the last vestiges of my acting ability, I confessed to them that I had only entered myself for PPE because of family pressure, my heart lay with English Literature. Could I please, at this late stage, change subjects? The dons were impressed, nay moved, by this idealism. They agreed. Would it affect the papers I took? Ah well, I would have to take a Latin unseen. Was that a problem? I crumpled. It was a terrible problem. A hurried whispered conference. Don't worry, take the French unseen instead. If anyone didn't know what chutzpah means they should now.

I knew I would do all right in the exams, but competition was fierce, especially if you wanted to read English. The decisive factor was the interview you had with your potential tutor. I don't know why I chose Univ as my preferred college but Derek Destiny did. Peter Bailey, a great cuddly bear of a man, wasn't exactly another substitute father but rather a benevolent uncle. We talked about my likes and dislikes of English Literature, and he then asked what my extra-curricular interests were. Theatre. He perked up. You want to be an actor? I want to be a director. Game, set and match. Peter Bailey loved theatre and Univ had quite recently produced three successful directors: Ronald Eyre, Peter Dews and David Williams. Univ had therefore held a pre-eminent position in Oxford theatre, but that was a while ago. 'Have a glass of sherry,' said Peter. An offer he was to make many times over the coming years.

I had six months to wait until my first Michaelmas term at Oxford. I had inherited from Phil Polack strong anti-Zionist views. The creation of the State of Israel was putting more divisive barriers into a world which could ill afford them and the troubles it would cause were obvious. My grandfather, to whom, understandably, Israel seemed at last a safe haven where Jews could live without fear of persecution, offered to pay for me to go there with a friend, the same David Stone who had persuaded me to see *Brand*, for three months. The three months were to include a stay on a kibbutz.

I lasted three weeks. I felt no connection with Israel at all, and although I was moved by the sight of Jews going about the streets in their yarmulkes and prayer shawls, I was terribly aware of being in a country in a state of siege. The military was everywhere. In the cinema there would always be propaganda before the main feature and the new Israelis, the Sabras, had little to do with the European culture I adored. To cap it all I missed the Cup Final when Spurs became the first team to win the double in the twentieth century.

After two weeks in Tel Aviv staying with David's family, we took the bus to the kibbutz at Bet Ha'emek. We arrived in the middle of nowhere late in the evening, were greeted with no great enthusiasm and shown to our spartan wooden huts with their deficient mosquito nets. At five o'clock in the morning there was a knock at the door: '*Boker tov*' (Good morning). We went to the communal dining room and had bread, sugar and black tea. 'You me work.' We worked the vineyards till 8.30. 'You me breakfast.' Half an hour later: 'You me work.' At twelve o'clock: 'You me lunch.' At 12.30: 'You me work.' At four o'clock: 'You finish.' Now we anticipated what we had come for: folk singing and dancing, group discussion etc. Of course not. Everyone disappeared, worn out, until dinner. After dinner surely our ethnic induction would start. Well, there was a showing of *Baby Doll* in the schoolroom attended by half a dozen pioneers who fell asleep during the first reel. Next morning at five, '*Boker tov*.' But today there was a *khamsin*, the dry hot wind from the desert that was intolerable to work in. I felt ill and retired to my room. It was decided that I would be excused vineyard duty and instead work in the kitchen for a day. My job was plucking chickens, a totally awful chore. However, plucking with me was a beautiful girl, clearly Israeli with her dark-brown skin and big brown eyes. This was it. The famed free love of the Sabras was about to make everything all right. I enunciated very carefully, 'Where do you come from?'

She answered nasally, 'Golders Green. Where do you come from?' The next day I left the kibbutz and within a week I was back in London.

I filled in the remaining time before Oxford doing several jobs including, notably and ineptly, serving on the ladies' glove counter at Selfridges, but living for the evening and the theatre. I was anti-Israeli, anti-Judaism, but I had chutzpah.

CHAPTER 5

A Lunatic at Oxford

– i –

I hated Oxford while I was there but I loved it in retrospect. Eighteen to twenty-one is a fearsome time for everyone. With everything unresolved in you, you are required to make the transition from child to adult. If you are lucky enough to be in higher education, at least you are shielded from actually having to make a living. In those days (1961) the state paid you quite generously to survive these years. But you are with thousands of other inchoate adolescents living their own troubled existence. With them you experience having, for the first time in your life, all the major restraints lifted. I mean, of course, primarily sex and booze. This was the beginning of the sixties and we had all been brought up vaguely in the last gasp of Victorian morality. You drank at lunchtime and you drank and drank and drank at night. You drank at staircase parties and you mixed your drinks according to what bottles you could lay your hands on, and after you had had as much as you could of whisky, gin, beer and rough Spanish burgundy, you threw up anywhere you could get to. You fell in love two or three times a week and suffered the tortures of the damned as your untutored inept bungling got you nowhere with the beauties you had ogled during lectures. In those days all colleges were single sex.

At that time very little work was actually required of you. Lectures were voluntary and you had one tutorial a week with your literature tutor and one with your Anglo-Saxon tutor. For literature you had to produce an essay, for Anglo-Saxon prepare passages of *Beowulf* or some such text for translation. Thus your days were largely unregulated and therefore, unless you were a swot, you were likely to fall into any temptation going, once you had recovered from your hangover.

I was saved from complete dissolution by the fact that I had come to Oxford to direct plays. There were two tiers in the theatrical hierarchy: college and university societies. The two university societies were the OUDS (Oxford University Dramatic Society) and the ETC (Experimental

Theatre Club). These societies did two minor (three-night) productions and one major (a week) a year at the Oxford Playhouse, which usually housed a professional company, Frank Hauser's Meadow Players. The college had a competition for freshmen called Cuppers, and did their own productions, mostly outdoors in the summer, but every now and again, if they had a sufficiently strong project, at the Playhouse.

If you were an actor the process was simple; you auditioned at college or university level and, according to your talent and the taste of the director, you were cast. For a director it was much more difficult. You had to persuade the committee of the given society to let you do the play of your choice or sometimes of their choice. To get that first production was very hard, to get a production at the Playhouse was practically impossible before your second year, and even then you had to have a spectacular success at college level.

You had three years to make your mark. Would-be politicians joined their political clubs and tried to speak at the Union, journalists fought for posts on the university newspapers, *Cherwell* or the magazine *Isis*; everywhere the ambitious were pursuing their aims with a cut-throat savagery, fuelled by the extremely short time limit. After all, the last term was for taking Finals, so effectively you had two and a half years only.

I prepared to hurl myself at Oxford theatre. There were two other freshmen in my year who wanted to go into theatre as actors. They were Michael York (then called Johnson) and Michael Elwyn (then called Emrys-Jones); we were the Three Musketeers. Most of the plays I did during my time were bound up with one or both of them. In the first term only acting was open to me, so I appeared in the college Cuppers and with the two Michaels in the college production of *Serjeant Musgrave's Dance*. But my aim was to get a production as quickly as possible. I bombarded the OUDS and the ETC. I harried the committee members. I danced with the women; I even remember flirting with Esther Rantzen. I went to every theatrical event, talk, party I could find. With the OUDS I got nowhere. The president referred to me with some reason as 'that little fucker Murray', but the ETC seemed interested. I was pitching for an American play I had seen in London called *The Connection* by Jack Gelber. It was a free-form play about druggies and included in the cast a small jazz band. I should emphasise that at this phase of my life I chose plays instinctively. I didn't think about them, I just reacted to them and then did them, again instinctively. I loved the play and it seemed to chime in with the committee who were aware that they were being criticised for not living up to the experimental E. (Their major production that term was *Peer Gynt*.) They agreed to produce an extra ETC minor in the Easter term, not in the Playhouse but in a church hall in north

Oxford: St Margaret's Hall, Polstead Road. I had a production in my second term and for a university society.

I don't remember much about it except that Miles Kington played bass in the band, Pat Crumly saxophone, the actor playing Cowboy, Dick Celeste, later became a Democratic presidential candidate and Leech, the character who took a controversial fix on stage, was played by another Univ actor, John Watts, whom I have worked with many times since.

When the production was announced, another Univ man whom I had not met before, Brian Gurnett, approached me. His goal was to go into advertising, so could he do the publicity for the production? What he did was to get a story into the national press about a supposed drug ring among Oxford undergraduates. There may well have been, but this was entirely fictitious. It had the desired effect. Although the venue was an obscure church hall, the first night was packed and a member of the audience obligingly had a fit when Leech took his fix. This, too, managed to make the papers. Not only because of the publicity, I hope, the production was a box-office success. A surprised ETC committee had made both a bold decision and a profit. The reward was instant. I was awarded the ETC major in the Playhouse for the following term.

— ii —

Michael Meyer, the translator of *Brand*, had driven through dense fog to be at the first night of *The Connection*. Two years after he had invited me to tea, I rang him and accepted. Now that I was bent on being a director, he was the only person I could think of who was connected to the professional theatre. Rather than tea, he invited me to the Savile Club for lunch. He swiftly became my second substitute father.

Michael's father had founded Montague Meyer, the timber merchants, who later became Meyer International, so Michael, who was a bon viveur in the Falstaffian mode without the dark side, could have led a totally hedonistic existence. He did the opposite. His translations of Ibsen and Strindberg introduced a new generation to these geniuses. They have never been bettered, nor have his definitive biographies of these two masters.

At that moment he was riding high. Following *Brand*, he was embarking on a further translation and his *Peer Gynt* was soon to be produced at the Old Vic, where the 59 Theatre Company team had come together again, under the leadership of Michael Elliott, to run the theatre.

My mother assumed he was gay, which couldn't have been further from the truth, otherwise why would he take such an interest in a seventeen-year-old like myself. He was a nurturer of potential young talent. I was one of many whom he generously encouraged. Our relationship lasted until his death in 2000 and proved decisive in introducing me, in the fullness of time, to Michael Elliott and Casper Wrede. He promised to see any production that I did at Oxford and *The Connection* was the first. He was impressed and, as I understood it, he began to talk to Michael and Casper about me from that moment.

Theatrically we were kindred spirits. He invented two famous clubs, 'The Wild Horses' Club' and 'The Can Do No Wrong Club'. Members of the former were actors whom wild horses wouldn't drag him to see; the latter actors and directors whom the critics, for reasons best known to themselves, had conferred untouchable status on however awful their work. On one memorable occasion he phoned me to say that he had been to the National Theatre where he had witnessed the Annual General Meeting of The Wild Horses' Club. On another he informed me that a production starring our least favourite actor was, 'worse than one could have hoped for'. We were of the Elliott–Wrede school, everything was judged against that criterion.

Michael was also a substitute father in a more obvious way. I had rebelled against my background. The milieu in which my grandparents and parents moved was narrowly Jewish and almost exclusively connected to business. I wasn't exactly left-wing but I railed against what I saw as soulless materialism. I behaved unspeakably badly to their friends, and my poor mother and stepfather became the focus of what I can only with shame call something akin to hatred. I spent as much time as I could away from home, seeking instead the company of my doctor uncle and aunt who seemed to lead a far more relaxed existence. I was ruthlessly cruel to my mother and stepfather to the incomprehension of my friends who, quite rightly, adored them, but I now see that I was fighting for my independence. I had no idea who I was but I was sure of what I didn't want to be.

Michael Meyer was Jewish, although you wouldn't have guessed it apart from his name and, like Phil Polack before him, he encouraged the rebellious streak in me while putting it in a wider context that slowly robbed it of its venom. It was as well that he was Jewish, otherwise I could have been almost accused of anti-Semitism, although in truth I didn't, until I reached Oxford, know many people who weren't Jewish, so it was merely the middle-class business ethic that I hated.

Indeed, Oxford released me from the schizophrenic existence that I had led from the age of eight, first at Brockhurst and then at the Jewish house of Clifton. At Oxford I felt free of labels and for the time I was up there the issue of Jewishness disappeared. When it reappeared years later it was in a very different guise.

17

– iii –

Again, I have very little recollection of rehearsing *The Hostage*. I had loved its energy in Joan Littlewood's production and so I did it. I knew what I wanted and I shouted and stormed at the actors until I got it. Although I was deeply into the works of Stanislavsky, I had no real directing method. The OUDS had a professional director once a year, to direct their major Shakespeare production. This year Peter Dews, who was responsible for the marvellous BBC television series *The Age of Kings*, directed *Henry IV Part I* (Oliver Ford-Davies was a superb Falstaff) and I gathered from the cast that shouting and storming was what directors did. Well, it seemed to work. This was probably because the cast were amateurs and were grateful to have someone who seemed to know what they were doing, and *The Hostage* was a big production with its quasi-musical form. In such a large cast some of the actors were rather basic but some were superb. Michael Elwyn brought the house down as Monsewer with his rendition of 'The Captain and the Kings', Michael York was very touching as the innocent Cockney soldier and the brothel owners were expertly played by Ian Davidson, who later became a successful comedy scriptwriter, and the beautiful Canadian Nancy Lane, who is now a distinguished professor at Cambridge. Anyway, it was a pretty massive success.

Now there was no stopping me. Under a new president, the OUDS asked me to direct the OUDS minor at the Playhouse. It was to be a production to mark Lope de Vega's four hundredth anniversary. The play chosen was his most famous one, *Fuenteovejuna*. It would open in the Michaelmas term of 1962.

– iv –

There was one major problem looming. Officially I was at Oxford, on a state grant, to study English. It wasn't that I didn't want to do my academic work, it was that I was so obsessed with theatre that my brain simply wouldn't engage. Directing is an exhausting process both physically and mentally. The actual rehearsals require hour after hour of intense concentration and when you're not actually rehearsing, the play never leaves you, even in your sleep. Rehearsals started in the afternoon so as to leave everyone free to attend lectures and tutorials, which were always in the morning. So you rehearsed all afternoon and sometimes evenings as well, continued your exploration of drinking and sex afterwards, woke late the next morning, missed all lectures (the theatre was a much better way of meeting women) had coffee in the Broad at about eleven, went to the pub for a pint and started rehearsals again. Work simply wasn't on the agenda.

Peter Bailey was understanding itself. Delighted at my successes, he didn't mind if the weekly essay wasn't forthcoming; indeed, I remember him being quite put out when I, for once, did produce an essay on *King Lear*. He listened to my effort, his response: 'Bloody good play! Sherry?' A year later I cast him in one of my productions: tutorials became extra rehearsals.

My Anglo-Saxon tutor was a different matter. He was C. R. R. Tolkien, the great man's son, and as fascinating and erudite a person as you could wish for. It is one of my great regrets that I took no advantage of his wisdom, but theatre meant that another dead language after my abhorrence of Latin was anathema. He was never openly angry but eventually he dumped me. He was right to do so. I was handed over to another tutor, whose name I don't remember, who was authoritarian and unpleasant. He threatened to make life very difficult for me until one day he was late for a tutorial. After waiting for half an hour, I left and reported the matter to Peter Bailey. There was no further trouble.

There remained the little matter of first-year exams called prelims. Cambridge makes you take an exam in each summer term, thereby ruining your summer and keeping the academic pressure on you all the time you are up. Oxford prelims took place in the Easter term. If you failed, you took them again in the summer. If you failed again your university career was over. Once you had passed them there was nothing further till Finals.

If you read English, you had to do three papers. One on the first two books of Milton's *Paradise Lost*, one on Anglo-Saxon grammar and one, oh horror of horrors, on two books of Virgil's *Aeneid*. Milton was no problem – I knew and liked *Paradise Lost* – but the others might as well have been Swahili exams. The prelim came right after *The Connection*. I failed spectacularly.

The problem was that the resitting took place immediately after *The Hostage*. I managed to put it out of my mind during rehearsals. I had to pass. I had an OUDS production in the Michaelmas term and I had to do it. In the end I memorised the English translation of the *Aeneid* so that I could trot out whichever passage came up, provided I recognised enough of the Latin, and most of *Sweet's Anglo-Saxon Primer*. I passed spectacularly. That was the last academic work I ever did at Oxford.

The graph was moving inexorably upwards. I had conquered the ETC; now I would conquer the OUDS. I had a rival star director, a Texan Jew called Michael Rudman, who had done a well-received production of *A Month in the Country* for his college at the Playhouse. He had his group of actors headed by David Aukin, the TV and movie producer, and Annabelle

Leventon, the actress. Despite the fact that we were both Spurs supporters the rivalry was intense and bitter, far bitterer than anything I have encountered in the professional theatre, where we both ended up. Three years to make it in a closed society bred ruthlessness. Oxford theatre was split into two camps. That Michaelmas term you were either in my production of *Fuenteovejuna* for the OUDS or Rudman's production of *The Good Woman of Setzuan* for the ETC.

Fuenteovejuna, literally the 'sheep well', was the name of a village under the tutelage of an autocratic nobleman who ruled with great cruelty and exercised the droit de seigneur with unfailing regularity. The villagers rose up against him and killed him. At the trial, when each witness was asked who killed the commander, the answer was always the same: 'Fuenteovejuna did it.' This play about collective responsibility had been interpreted variously as a Marxist tract and as a right-wing piece (because the king and queen sorted it all out). The OUDS rightly thought it was imaginative scheduling and I was the director of the moment.

I have said that in those days I chose a play I was instinctively attracted to and did it. In this case I was offered a play to direct and I accepted because it hadn't occurred to me that there was a play written that I couldn't direct successfully. To my lunatic energy there had now been added arrogance. I had never known failure; I was omnipotent.

Rehearsals started. The cast was led by the two Michaels as ever. I rehearsed the way that had always worked: a version of Stanislavsky with much shouting and screaming and a great deal of improvisation. Rehearsals seemed to be going well and confidence reigned.

Fuenteovejuna was quite a short play so we presented it in a double bill preceded by Ionesco's *The Lesson* with John Watts as the Professor. With Ionesco I was on home territory and I knew that it was very, very good.

On the first night *The Lesson* was superlative. The audience was wound up tight as a drum by the time the curtain rose on *Fuenteovejuna*. The production started with a mime dance that briefly depicted the story of the play. I didn't know then that this is a sure sign that the ensuing production is likely to fail because the director has said everything he wants to right at the beginning. Anyway, it was an effective mime and all was well. The first scene proper consisted of a rather long self-introduction by the villain: 'My name is Don Gomez de Guzman, Gran Maestre of the order of Calatrava,' etc. etc. etc. The audience listened politely. The next scene was set in the village square and the set for that was a sheep well. This sheep well came on from the wings on a track operated by pulleys. On it I had placed two or three of the village maidens looking jolly and happy with life.

The sheep well trundled on on cue but stuck halfway through its journey, with a jolt that caused the village maidens to cling on with some alarm. The operator of the pulley, David Wright (later to write *Hang Down Your Head and Die*) was determined to get the sheep well to its right position, rather than leaving it where it was. He took it off again, with the maidens still aboard, then propelled it at great speed back towards the centre of the stage. By now the audience were howling with laughter.

Lope de Vega wrote with a simple storytelling innocence, quite unlike Shakespeare, and his work is difficult to translate. The translation was horribly twee and awkward, a problem I had completely ignored in rehearsal because I didn't realise that it was a director's job to ask for changes. The audience began to find almost everything funny. Simple lines like 'Let him enter' were greeted with the gales of laughter usually reserved for brilliant farces.

When the villagers finally revolt, it is the women who lead the rebellion. 'Rise up, women of Fuenteovejuna' is the battle-cry, and on that cue half a dozen undergraduates, brandishing cudgels, invaded the stage. The theatre was bedlam. I ran out of the auditorium and was comprehensively sick in Beaumont Street.

I went backstage afterwards, certain that the next night would be all right. I told the cast not to weaken, that it was a fine production, that all would be well once the sheep well was functioning properly on the following night. In truth it was an awful production. Stanislavsky and Lope de Vega didn't mix. I had totally failed to appreciate what the text, however badly translated, required but I wasn't prepared to admit it that night.

The next day Don Chapman in the *Oxford Mail* was scathing about the show and I had to face the fact that I had produced a major flop. I crawled miserably to the Playhouse for the second night. How could I face the cast? How could I face the OUDS who were certain to lose money in the face of empty houses.

As I came down Beaumont Street I saw that the 'House Full' notices were up. It was a miracle. I was vindicated. Great art would always triumph over philistines. I went backstage and broke the good news to the cast.

Once again *The Lesson* went very well. As the curtain rose on *Fuenteovejuna* and the mime sequence started the whole house rocked with laughter. When the first scene started – 'My name is Don Gomez de Guzman' – the laughter was incessant. I tapped the shoulder of a member of the audience in the back row. 'What's going on?' I asked.

'Oh,' he replied, tears streaming down his face, 'we were told if you wanted a really good laugh come to the Playhouse to see *Fuenteovejuna*.'

On the last performance the Spanish Ambassador came. He was

delighted. 'Ah, you cheer and boo just like the Spanish audience,' he said, beaming.

It was my first disaster and I still can't bring myself to think about it without a feeling of humiliation and horror. Of course, disaster is crucial to any director's career, it is the great teacher. I didn't know that then and, when Rudman's Brecht was a smash hit, my wretchedness was complete.

— v —

I had to direct again as soon as possible, that I knew. Unless I was prepared to do an outdoor production, the summer term was out. I was still acting; Maestro Servandoni in Peter Ustinov's *Blow Your Own Trumpet* directed by my Clifton chum, Brian Block, who had directed me in *The Bespoke Overcoat*; and I was to play Brabantio in the OUDS major production of *Othello* (Oliver Ford-Davies in the title role) but that wasn't the point.

Fortunately, the Univ Players (my college society) said they would produce *A Man for All Seasons* by Robert Bolt in the Playhouse for the Easter term. John Watts agreed to play Sir Thomas More. He was superb, his mixture of integrity and tough cunning seemed to me to put Paul Scofield in the shade. It was a strong cast: Michael Elwyn was Cromwell; Michael York, Henry VIII; Paul (now Justice) Collins, Norfolk; Peter (newscaster) Sissons, Roper; and my tutor Peter Bailey was Cardinal Wolsey.

Rehearsals took place mainly in John's sister's flat in London. This was not a place for screaming and shouting; moreover, *A Man for All Seasons* is a quiet play, probably the first one I had done, so the rehearsals were calm, thorough and therapeutic. The play may have dated now with its pseudo-Brechtian device of the Common Man, but it worked a treat then. In fact, it was probably director-proof. The critics generously saw this as a return to form and I was rehabilitated.

— vi —

I said at the beginning of this chapter that I hated Oxford. To my mother's despair I was continually trying to leave. In spite of all the theatrical activity, I was very unhappy. It wasn't Oxford's fault, I would have been unhappy anywhere, but I couldn't see that.

I had failed to lose my virginity. Because I had a few, very attractive, long-lasting girlfriends I had a reputation as a Lothario, but that was a long way from the truth. I was cursed with an innate sense, bred from Golders Green, Brockhurst and Clifton, that my sexual urges were dirty and not commensurate with love, so I shouldn't sleep with any woman I cared about and anyway, she wouldn't want to sleep with me. Sometimes through my fear, sometimes through theirs, nothing finally happened.

Theatre had been a good way of displacing the libido but now I was facing the rest of the Easter term and the whole of the summer with no theatre at all for the first time. A black reaction set in. Theatre was useless, a shallow façade that I had been wasting my time on. Therefore my life was useless because I had given myself over to it completely.

One weekend I went down to London to see the Losey–Pinter movie *The Servant*. It was a nihilistic, negative movie, brilliantly made. As I drove back to Oxford my depression reached a new intensity. The road ran alongside a cliff. Suddenly I turned the wheel and rammed the car at full speed into the cliff. The car bonnet concertinaed up to the windscreen. I got out unscathed. 'Oh,' I said, 'I see!' The life force came flooding back. Derek Destiny had taught me an unforgettable lesson about how easy it was to self-destruct. I have never contemplated suicide since. Maybe you have to be brought to the brink to see that the dark side of life is part of the thrill and fascination of living. It is to be embraced and subsumed, which is perhaps as good a way as any to describe the power of great plays or, indeed, any great work of art.

Three things happened in rapid succession to mitigate the weeks without a production. *A Man for All Seasons* was invited to the Dublin Festival in August to play at Trinity College and I was elected president of the ETC. Of course, I had wanted to be elected president of OUDS, but *Fuenteovejuna* had put paid to that. Not only that, but Michael Rudman had been elected. I would have to make do with the ETC, which was after all my natural home. I didn't realise it but this was one of Derek Destiny's trump cards. Within a year I would see how lucky I was.

— vii —

The third thing was that I got my first professional job. I had written to George Devine at the Royal Court, asking him to consider me as an assistant. With typical modesty I described myself as 'probably the most talented young director in England today'. This was the Royal Court in its heyday, the vanguard of the new English theatre. The directors who worked there on a semi-permanent basis included Lindsay Anderson, Tony Richardson, Bill Gaskill, Anthony Page and John Dexter, all of whose work I knew, marked out of ten and respected to varying degrees with one or two exceptions. It was a formidable list by any standards, even my arrogant own.

I was granted an interview with George Devine. I can't remember a single thing about it; I was probably numb with shock. It must have gone all right, though, because to my astonished joy, I received a letter asking me to be John Dexter's assistant for his revival of Arnold Wesker's *Chips with Everything*, which was to play a short season at the Court before going via the Golders Green Hippodrome to Broadway. All this fitted in with the long summer vacation before the Dublin Festival. Moreover, they were going to pay me £10 a week. I was actually going to be paid for what I loved doing. That miraculous realisation has never really left me.

John Dexter took me to lunch at Tolliani's in Soho. This compact bull of a man was revelling in his newfound fame and determined to enjoy its trappings. He was about thirty-five and had served a long apprenticeship, and now everything was paying off. He was charm itself. Although I wasn't yet under contract, he invited me to attend auditions at the Phoenix, which I jumped at.

When people heard that I was to assist John Dexter some winked and said, 'Watch out!' If I was naïve about heterosexuality, I was even more so about the homosexual world. From the comments that were being passed in the stalls of the Phoenix, it dawned on me that talent wasn't the only criterion by which the actors were being cast.

Be that as it may, a very talented company assembled in a church hall near Sloane Square to rehearse, including Alan Dobie, Gary Bond, Corin Redgrave, Frank Wyllie, Derek Fowlds, George Layton and George Innes. I should have been thrilled to be in rehearsals but I was bored stiff. I was a director and if I couldn't direct I didn't want to be around. However, this was the first, and indeed the last, time that I could observe a professional director at work. Dexter had done the play before, so there was nothing for me to do and he seemed as bored as I was.

Dexter's great talent was spatial. He knew how to place and move actors on stage. He knew how to place furniture. He was the physical director par excellence. The famous 'coke-stealing' scene from *Chips*, which was without dialogue, was entirely invented by him. The staging, like the rush-hour kitchen in a restaurant scene in *The Kitchen*, was breathtaking. He didn't seem much concerned with psychology and personal relationships, and his relationship with some of the actors was brutal.

A famous ploy at the beginning of rehearsals would be to confront a young actor with the question, 'What are you?' The actor was then badgered until he answered, 'I'm a cunt.' Only then were rehearsals to proceed, the proper relationship between actor and director having been established. He mortifyingly pried into their sex lives and I believe a significant proportion of the all-male cast found their way into his bed. He was, in short, for all his brilliance, a bully. Watching him did me no good at all. It rather confirmed my ideas of how a director was supposed to behave.

Often during a run-through he would beckon me out into the foyer to have a cigarette. Thus he missed large chunks of the play, which didn't seem to hamper him giving copious notes to the actors afterwards. 'Oh, I know what they did,' he said. At any rate he was very pleasant to me, the show opened smoothly at the Court, played its week in Golders Green, to the great delight of my family, and was due to set off to Broadway.

My contract ended at that point. I bade Dexter farewell and thanked him. He thanked me and asked what I was doing in the summer, and I told him about the Dublin Festival. He invited me to visit him afterwards in Chichester where he was rehearsing his production of *Saint Joan* with Joan Plowright, prior to it going to the National Theatre, where he was now an Associate. 'Sit in on rehearsals, see the *Workhouse Donkey* (John Arden's play with Frank Finlay) and you can stay in the Directors' Cottage where there's a spare room. Make a nice break for you.' I eagerly accepted.

After the successful visit to Dublin, I duly motored down to Chichester in my old Ford Prefect, sat in on rehearsals, was taken out to dinner, watched the play, had a few drinks at the bar and was then told by Dexter that we should get back to the cottage as he had an early call the next day. I had noticed that whenever I was introduced to actors or anyone connected to the theatre, there was the suggestion of a smirk and the odd raised eyebrow. I took no notice. As I say, I was very naïve.

As we neared the cottage Dexter said, 'Oh, by the way Eleanor Fazan is sleeping in the spare room, you'll have to share a room with me.'

'Oh,' I said. The room was large and bare except for a double bed and bedside tables. 'Oh!' I thought. He went off to wash. I opened my suitcase. He came back. 'Oh,' I said, 'I've forgotten to pack my pyjamas.'

'Ah,' he said, 'you can share mine. Would you like the top half or the bottom half?' Panic. He was bigger than me. Pull up or pull down?

'Top half.' Oh shit, that's wrong. He gave me the top half. We got into bed.

'I'm just going to flick through tomorrow's scenes. You can look at this.' He handed me *The Royal Hunt of the Sun*, the next play he was doing at the National. We read for about ten minutes. 'Right. Early start tomorrow. Lights out.' Phew!

I felt a hand crawl across my thigh. What do I do? This is John Dexter,

25

Associate Artistic Director of the National Theatre. I gingerly picked up the hand and put it back.

'Oh, sorry.' He rolled over. I rolled over. The hand came back. Repeat performance. A good long gap. I tried to sleep. The next thing I knew there was a full-on assault.

'I'm not like that,' I shouted hysterically. 'I'm engaged.'

'Oh, sorry.' He rolled over and went to sleep. I did not. I forced myself to stay awake all night.

The next morning the alarm went off and he shot out of bed, washed and went downstairs. I crawled out of bed, washed and blearily stumbled down to find he had cooked a full English breakfast: eggs, bacon, the lot. 'Sorry, John, I'll just have a coffee, I'm not feeling too good.' A pause.

'*They* usually make breakfast for *me*!' Then he named someone who had been in a play of mine at Oxford. '*He* did,' he said.

On reaching the theatre I phoned my girlfriend in London. I asked her to come down to Chichester and be at the stage door for the end of rehearsal. 'When I come out, insist on my going with you and don't give up however much I protest.' She did and I escaped. There is a pay-off to this story but it has to wait a year.

– viii –

As president, I was determined the ETC would finally live up to its experimental tag. What could a group of university students do that professionals couldn't? The commodity we had was time, time to create a show of our own and produce it. We decided to take a theme, research it and, through improvisation, develop it into a rough script. We would involve actors, writers, composers, anyone who might be interested. The show would be a total theatre show with songs, dance, mime, anything that was appropriate. Joan Littlewood's *Oh What a Lovely War* had just hit London and I had seen it about six times already. That was my inspiration.

The theme I wanted passionately was capital punishment, which was still practised in Great Britain in 1963. The committee of the ETC agreed the theme. It had obvious theatrical possibilities from Punch and Judy to folklore.

We held the workshop sessions in the evenings, as people were rehearsing Michaelmas term productions during the day. The research led by David Wright, he of the sheep well pulley, yielded fascinating riches, Jo Durden-Smith (the television programme creator, *Johnny Cash at St Quentin* etc.) was a mine of information on songs from 'Geordie' to 'Strange Fruit' and we unearthed two remarkable but totally different composers, Greg Stephens and David Wood (the children's play author). Greg composed in the tradition of the folk ballad American style, while David wrote in the comic Gilbert and Sullivan–music-hall style. The research material fell into roughly three categories, the Establishment through the Royal Commission, the judges and Parliament, the victims and various opinions of the people at all levels of society. We decided that the format of the show would be the circus: the ringmasters as the Establishment, the strongman as the Hangman, the white-faced clown as the Condemned, the carpet clowns as the vox pop and the female assistants, who in every circus invite the audience to applaud, as those who cover up the gruesome reality of executions.

It was an exciting time, at the end of which David Wright was given the task of shaping the vast amount of material into a script that could go into rehearsal in the Easter term, for the ETC had committed to *Hang Down Your Head and Die* – for that was its name, misquoted deliberately from 'Tom Dooley' – being a major in the Playhouse.

– ix –

Everyone was rehearsing their own shows for the Michaelmas term and that included me; I had to make up for all those months not directing.

The Oxford University Operatic Society did a major production in the town hall every year. The orchestra and chorus were undergraduates, the principals, conductor and director professionals. That year they were mounting Verdi's *Sicilian Vespers* with László Heltay conducting and Brychan Powell and Emile Belcourt from Sadler's Wells leading the principals. This time they broke with tradition and asked me to direct. It was an honour and very flattering so, despite being tone-deaf, unable to read or indeed follow music, and having very little knowledge of the form, I accepted.

Before that I was scheduled to direct Ionesco's *Rhinoceros* for the Univ Players. I had taken *The Lesson* to the NUS drama festival in Loughborough and now I wanted to enter a full-length play for the competition. The production was to be done in a church hall off the Cowley Road and, if the NUS adjudicators chose, it would appear in the finals at Aberystwyth at the turn of the year.

Ionesco had been my favourite playwright since Clifton days. He was there to *épater les bourgeois* and so was I. *Rhinoceros* was my revenge on the Golders Green middle class. Michael Elwyn played Berenger and

27

Michael York played Jean, the character who turns into a rhinoceros on stage. He did this superbly and without make-up. Being a handsome actor, he was to be snapped up by Zeffirelli, Joe Losey and the movie industry, but I knew him as a remarkable character actor. Ah well, there's still time.

The production was heavily stylised with much freezing in clichéd positions to echo the deliberate banalities of the text. The cast had to be drilled to perfection, and screaming and shouting was back in spades. Looking back, I don't know why they didn't thump me but they didn't and the production was duly selected for the finals.

— x —

I was due to go straight into rehearsals for the opera, but rehearsing all day and doing the workshops in the evening took their toll. I had a minor breakdown, was put under sedation and recovered in time for the bulk of the rehearsals.

Fortunately, I had plotted the very large chorus in great detail to coincide with the score and my assistant had been able to give the notes and drill them before I arrived. The principals had not yet arrived; they had already been in a production of the opera and I was to have them for one week only.

I had neither been to the opera a great deal nor much cared for the productions. They seemed old-fashioned and heavy. Nobody minded about the appalling acting with its ridiculous gesticulations. The music was all that counted and to hell with what the opera was really about. It was like going to the theatre as I imagined it to be in the Victorian era.

The opera was about the Sicilian peasantry rising up and overthrowing their tyrannical masters (echoes of *Fuenteovejuna*). Sicily is, of course, a volcanic island dominated by Mount Etna so the production was imagined like a volcano. The set was on two levels. The masters acted on the upper level and the chorus, dressed in molten lava colours, were below. Their revolt was like a volcanic eruption which invaded the upper level and took over the whole stage. The result was a stylised production which suited the very large chorus. They didn't have to be individualised, they had to be drilled: more screaming and shouting than ever before.

The production the principals had been in had been conventional, with much clinking of beer glasses, thrusting forward of chests, hurling of arms in the air and spreading of legs wide apart. However, they were prepared to listen to this twenty-year-old upstart and found that by being stiller and expressing the real content of the text they actually sang better.

The evening was highly praised and Anthony Besch, the director from

Sadler's Wells, was impressed enough to offer me a job directing there. I was proud of what I had done and was very flattered and excited. In principle I accepted but DD had other plans.

— xi —

There was no let-up. In the Christmas vacation *Rhinoceros* went to the NUS Festival. In the vast theatre in Aberystwyth it took the festival by storm, except for Harold Hobson, the *Sunday Times* critic who awarded the prizes. While heaping praise on us he gave the trophy to a feeble production of *The Three Sisters*. As we came out of the hall, we came face to face with the winning college clutching the cup. It rolled out of their hands and into the gutter. We passed in silence. The following Sunday Hobson eulogised the production and years later, when asked if he regretted any of his judgements, he said only that he should have given the prize to Univ. How little it matters now; how much it mattered then.

CHAPTER 6

Hang Down Your Head and Die

When asked to account for the incomparable Spurs double team of 1960–61, Danny Blanchflower said that the right player filled every position: eleven stars playing together as a team. The same thing might have been said of the company assembled to rehearse *Hang Down Your Head and Die*. Michael Elwyn and Jo Durden-Smith played the Ringmasters, Richard Durden the actor, Jo's younger brother, played the Strongman, and the Carpet Clowns included David Wood, Robert Hewison (the *Sunday Times* drama critic), Roland Oliver (actor), Dickon Reed (ex-director of drama at the Arts Council) and the massive voice of the equally massive Bob Scott (now Sir Robert of the Commonwealth Games). Greatest in present-day luminosity were the talents of Michael Palin, and Terry Jones who played the Condemned Man. The women of necessity had less rewarding parts, but they included Adèle Weston (now Geras, the author), the high-flying academic Vivian Ault and one actress still in the profession, the daughter of the Persian Ambassador to Brazil, Jasmina Hamzavi (now Daniel). The band was conducted and orchestrated by the, alas, now dead Iwan Williams and the whole production staff, led by the documentary producer Tony Summers, were all tiptop. The set was designed by Michael Ackland whom I had met at Clifton when he was Head of Design at the Bristol Old Vic theatre school.

Rehearsals, like all rehearsals, had their ups and downs. Although officially it was called a revue, *Hang* was more like a full-scale musical and was therefore very demanding. Feelings ran high about the material and on one occasion Jones and Palin appeared with a totally rewritten second act, which I had to reject with my heart in my mouth. We survived that crisis and proceeded.

About halfway through rehearsals there came a massive bombshell. In those days theatre was still subject to censorship by the Lord Chamberlain's office and we had duly submitted our script. When it came back there was a blue pencil through two-thirds of the show. Quite simply, it was impossible to continue.

The cuts were of three different kinds. Anything about the sordid details of executions was not allowed, anything that seemed to belittle government or the judiciary was not allowed (the Conservatives were still just in power under Sir Alec Douglas Home) and, most extraordinarily, no quotations from dead people that might cause offence to their living relatives were allowed, even the vile fascist Professor Joad or Shaw, at his most lunatic, advocating euthanasia. It was a pretty clear case of political censorship. Capital punishment was the law of the land. Capital punishment must be protected.

Being now an expert on capital punishment, I knew that Gerald Gardiner QC (Lord Gardiner) was one of its leading opponents. Having obtained the right to appeal in person against the Lord Chamberlain's Office, I phoned him for his help. He was outraged and offered to come with David Wright and me to the hearing. For good measure he arranged to bring Lord Willis and Kenneth Robinson, soon to be Minister of Health in the next Labour government.

On the appointed day, advised by Gardiner, David and I turned up at the office of the Assistant Controller, Lieutenant-Colonel Eric Penn, who effectively was in charge of censorship. When we were shown in I asked permission to bring in three extra persons. He refused. I explained that they were Lord Gardiner, Lord Willis and Kenneth Robinson. He panicked. 'There aren't enough chairs,' was his comeback. I suggested that other chairs might possibly be found from other offices and this was done. Our three champions appeared. Slowly we began to work through the script. Penn's answers were clearly specious. Gardiner sat silently at the back of the room. Finally he spoke: 'This is clearly a case of political censorship. At the next election there will be a Labour government and I shall be Lord Chancellor. I shall abolish your office. I suggest you listen to these gentlemen.' We returned to Oxford to continue rehearsals while we awaited the outcome.

We also made sure that the national press got hold of the story. They went to town. Photos appeared of the prettiest girls in the cast who were being victimised by the big bad Lord Chamberlain and when the script came back with almost all the cuts restored, they carried our triumph too. You couldn't have bought such publicity. *Hang Down Your Head and Die* was now the most eagerly awaited show in Oxford for years.

There was one cut Penn would not reinstate. It was a re-enactment of the execution of Julius and Ethel Rosenberg. He would allow us to read out a newspaper eyewitness account of the execution, but not to act it out. The horrific fact of the execution of this couple is that it took three jolts of electricity, each lasting roughly fifty-seven seconds, to kill them. What we did instead was to have the Carpet Clowns sit in a semicircle looking at a bentwood chair while the account was read out. When the narrator reached the first jolt he fell silent for fifty-seven seconds. It had a devastating effect on the audience. Each night some people had to leave the theatre. It worked far better than our original intention. Thus Lieutenant-Colonel Eric Penn became a member of the creative team.

The opening night fell on 12 February, my birthday. I will never have a better birthday present. My family was there, Michael Meyer was there, the Oxford theatre establishment including Michael Rudman – who had just had a comparative failure with *Twelfth Night*, his OUDS major – was there and so was the right-hand man of the West End impresario Michael Codron, Dickie Eastham. At the end of a rapturous evening he approached me backstage and asked if I was interested in a future for the show? If so, Michael Codron would come and see it later in the week.

The reviews were sensational, the two-week run quickly sold out and Michael Codron came. The General Manager of the Oxford Playhouse was Elisabeth Sweeting, a splendid lady who knew all there was to know about the commercial theatre. Her instruction was simple. I wasn't to say anything to Michael Codron. He was famous for his silences, which usually led to his prey begging him to produce his play with the result that Codron was able to extort a very favourable deal. We sat in silence for what seemed like an eternity. Finally he spoke: 'What would you like to do with this?'

'I don't know.' Endless silence.

'Would you like to take it to London?'

'Yes.' That was it. We were booked into the Comedy Theatre for the duration of the Easter vacation. It was all like a dream.

The dream got better. The first night in London was also a wonderful performance and reception. All the newspaper offices were in Fleet Street and we knew that the reviews came off the press in the early hours of the morning. We were determined to be there. On our first round none of the papers was out, but the doormen were obviously infected by our nervous enthusiasm. Finally we came back to the *Daily Mail* for the second time, the paper of the fearsome critic Bernard Levin. As we neared, the doorman was holding up the review. The banner headlines read 'These People Do Honour to the Theatre and Themselves'. I don't think I can remember a moment like it. The dream had become a fairy tale. We were so young and it was all so unexpected. Critic after critic confirmed our success, from Milton Shulman to Harold Hobson. Anyone who was anyone came to see the show. We won Best Revue in the *Variety* critics' poll and I was voted third-best director with Bill Gaskill, after Stanislavsky and Laurence Olivier. I was on a royalty too. It amounted to about £80 a week, a lot of money in 1964. This was the life. I had always thought I was God's gift to the theatre; now I was sure of it. I knew it all. I had nothing to learn.

Apparently there was more. Unbeknown to me, backstage on the first night there was an American lady called Marion Javits, waving a cheque-book and yelling, 'Who owns this show? I want to buy this show. How much?'

Michael Codron was unimpressed. 'The show is not for sale.' The next day she appeared in his office. He explained that as she had no experience as a producer, he had no intention of selling to her. Would he do so if a genuine producer were to become involved? Yes, he would. Within two days Roger L. Stephens, Broadway impresario and ex-cultural adviser to Kennedy, flew in and agreed to produce. I knew none of this. The story of what happened when I was told is the subject of another chapter. Suffice it to say that *Hang Down Your Head and Die* was scheduled to open on Broadway in the autumn of 1964, with rehearsals starting in September.

I drove back to Oxford for my last term, the term in which I was to take Finals. Finals? The thought was appalling. I hadn't done a stroke of work for nearly two years. If I shut myself away and worked myself to the bone, I might just scrape a Third or Fourth. And for what? I was launched. I was going to New York. I was the hot young thing.

On the advice of the ever sympathetic Peter Bailey I sought a meeting with the Master of the College. Lord Redcliffe-Maude was a formidable and impressive man with whom I had had little or no contact. I knew that when he was up he had been a leading actor with the OUDS, which was the only encouraging thing about the encounter. I told him I wanted to leave without taking Finals and leave immediately.

'As Master of this college I must tell you I deprecate your behaviour. You have come here to study at the taxpayers' expense and have abused the system.' He paused. 'As a person, I consider you have achieved what you came here to do and the college has prepared you for your career. Jolly good luck.' And he shook my hand. He informed the Middlesex County Council, who had given me the grant, that the purpose in coming to Oxford had been fulfilled and that the grant should not be repaid.

I was free. I motored out of Oxford. And, by the way, Oxford had fulfilled my other wish. I had lost my virginity.

CHAPTER 7

'You're Such a Talented Young Man'

Halfway through the run of *Hang Down Your Head and Die*, Michael Codron phoned me. 'Would you like to direct the show on Broadway?' he asked. Ever mindful of Elisabeth Sweeting's advice I muttered without enthusiasm, 'Yes.'

'Well, you're going to. I've sold the show and you're going there in September.'

'Fine.' He must have been nonplussed. Had he seen what I was really feeling . . . but I had been taught to keep quiet. Marion Javits, one of the producers, was in town, staying in a Mayfair flat. Michael had arranged for me to go and see her that very evening.

I arrived at the flat and rang the bell. The door opened and there was this mind-blowingly beautiful woman in the Jacqueline Kennedy mode. She was exquisitely dressed and coiffed, and had a sensational cleavage that plunged and plunged. 'You must be Braham Murray. I am so pleased to meet you. You are such a talented young man.' She gestured for me to sit down on a long, low sofa. 'Drink?'

'Scotch, please.' I'm sitting in this sumptuous apartment and this gorgeous woman is pouring me a substantial Scotch on the rocks. Like a film soundtrack I can hear the ice cubes going tinkle, tinkle and the whisky going glug, glug. She comes over, gives me the drink and slides on to the sofa next to me. It's like the movies. It's all going to happen just like in a dream. I was numb with excitement.

'I was in Arkansas the other day.'

'Ah.'

'I went to a waxworks museum there and they had waxworks of Red Indians scalping white men.'

'Ah?'

'I want to know if this is because of a genetic inheritance of the Red Indian or the results of the psychological repression induced in the Red Indian by the white man.'

'Ah!'

'I thought we could treat of this in the show.'

'Uh huh.' The excited numbness was being invaded by less pleasant feelings.

'My husband is Senator Jacob Javits of New York. He is a prime mover of the Civil Rights Bill.'

'Ah!'

'I think we should also deal with the issue of civil rights in the show.' I mumbled something about the death penalty having been exercised disproportionately on blacks in America as an important point but that was about it. She rushed on and I soon rushed out.

Codron was great. He negotiated a contract that meant that no more than a certain percentage of the script could be altered and every change would be agreed by myself and David Wright.

When you're young you don't heed warnings. I was going to Broadway, not taking Finals, all kinds of people were showing interest in me, I had money in my pocket and I could enjoy the four months before I was due to start casting in New York.

Apparently there was more good news. Peter Bridge, then at his peak as an impresario, wanted to try out a new revue at the Edinburgh Festival with a view of bringing it to London. Revue is defunct now; in those days it was still big. It meant sketches by various different writers, not linked thematically, interspersed with song and dance. I was too young to remember Johnny Cranko's *Cranks* or Robert Dhéry's *La Plume de Ma Tante*, but *Pieces of Eight* and *One over the Eight*, with contributions by Pinter and N. F. Simpson, I had seen and enjoyed.

This revue was to feature two very clever comic mimes, Julian Chagrin and George Ogilvy. Hence the awful title *Chaganog*. Vivian Ellis wrote a song for the show:

> Chaganog Chaganog
> Oh what a name for a horse or dog
> Nobody seems to know
> Why that's the name of our show
> What does its title mean?
> Is it perhaps obscene?
> Chagrin, Ogilvy
> Chaganog could it be?
> At any rate it isn't me.

Actually the mimes were brilliant. Chagrin, who remains a great friend, was very tall, with a face like a bemused parrot, and Ogilvy was very small, like a baby panda. Then there were the dancers Sheila O'Neill and David Toguri, plus the comedienne Patsy Rowlands. It was my first professional job and it would open at the Lyceum in Edinburgh as a late-night show the day before I was to fly to America.

That was not all. A script arrived from one Michael Dorfman who had presented Marcel Marceau in London several times. The script by Ned Sherrin and Caryl Brahms was called *Oom-Pah-Pah*. It was a translation of a long-running Parisian hit *Les Pupitres*, which means the music stands. The idea was simple. A second-rate orchestra runs out of money and disbands. The musicians wander around Paris using their instruments in weird and witty ways to earn a sou or two. For instance, a trombonist would imitate a hooter (illegal in Paris) while his friend the trumpeter dressed as a gendarme would simulate a police siren and extort fines from innocent motorists. What I didn't know was that the show had been tailored for the extraordinary talents of a French comic called Raymond Devos who is still going strong. No doubt he made the material work. The script I read had a certain charm but was devastatingly unfunny. I was twenty-one and this was a West End show to come back to after New York, and no one was advising me. Not for the last time in my career I decided it was brilliant. I would get Sherrin and Brahms to rewrite it and all would be well. I accepted. I met with Sherrin and Brahms who were thrilled to be working with such a 'talented young man'. They agreed to rewrite and send the script to New York.

Dorfman wanted the French designer Bernard Daydé to design. He flew in and we met in his hotel room. He produced a tape recorder, 'I 'ave 'ere a tap recordère. On zis tap recordère I 'ave Peter Brook, I 'ave Franco Zeffirelli and now I will 'ave Brahm Muerray.' I was much flattered. We agreed that the set would be the podium and music stands of the orchestra, which would then reconstitute themselves as the rest of the scenery required. The podium would become tables and chairs, the music stands would shoot up to become lamp-posts or fold out to become doors and so on. Daydé was charming and funny. I was delighted. It was agreed that a model of the design would be sent to New York so that I could prepare the production, which would go into rehearsal soon after my return.

I had to cast the show before I went and what a cast I assembled. Joe Melia, Al Mancini (star of *That Was the Week that Was*), Harry Towb, John Bluthal (*The Vicar of Dibley*), George Murcell and the comediennes Rosemary Martin and Joyce Grant. I persuaded them to take on trust that the script would be brilliant, that we would be improvising a great deal and they should on that basis commit. They did.

I rehearsed *Chaganog* and went to Edinburgh. The first night seemed to go very well. We caroused for what was left of it and I caught a flight to the USA from Glasgow the next day, very hung-over but very happy. What a six months! West End, Edinburgh Festival, Broadway, West End and I was only twenty-one and a half. Who said showbiz was tough?

CHAPTER 8
New York

Pre-rehearsal

As I stepped on to the tarmac at Kennedy Airport, two men in dark suits, to the amazement of my fellow passengers and of myself, escorted me to a black Lincoln, passport and customs were waved aside and, flanked by two policemen on motorcycles, I was driven to Marion Javits's New York apartment, courtesy of Senator Javits.

David Wright had arrived a few days before me. He had also been met at the tarmac but had been taken to Governor Harriman's residence in upstate New York. There, very jet-lagged, he had swum, in an outsize pair of borrowed swimming trunks that he had great difficulty in keeping up, in the Governor's pool, surrounded by the political élite of America, fielding such questions as, 'And tell me, how is Harold doing?' Harold being our new Prime Minister, Harold Wilson. Perched on a bar stool after his dip, he was given a jumbo-sized gin and tonic and promptly fell off the bar stool. He took to his bed. In the middle of the night he felt nauseous, failed to open the window, which was securely locked, tried to find the toilet, stumbled into someone's bedroom by mistake, set off the alarm and found himself throwing up in the corridor surrounded by the entire household.

My welcome was modest in comparison. When I arrived at the Javitses' apartment, also jet-lagged, Marion was entertaining the Huntingdon Hertfords. I found out that she was invariably entertaining someone. After they left, she handed me two closely typed sheets of paper. She had sent a letter I had written to her to a handwriting analyst and this was his character reading. I read it cursorily, laughed at the fun of it and handed it back. I didn't realise how it would be used against me.

The first thing she told me was that she had decided the show shouldn't be presented on Broadway (the first syllable spoken with an elongated sneer: Brooooadway). Brooooadway wasn't right for such a controversial show, we would do it off-Broadway. This meant that tomorrow we would start looking at off-Broadway theatres that might be suitable, which was fine by me. Apart from that she had appointed a designer, Fred Voelpel; the Stephens office had set up auditions and we had about three weeks to prepare everything before rehearsals started.

Those weeks were a nightmare. There was no suitable off-Broadway theatre. They were too small and ill-equipped to deal with what was in effect a medium-sized musical. Marion got more and more annoyed. 'Says right here in the handwriting expert's report. "He is ambitious and idealistic and not always realistic." Says right here, "He can be obstinate and dig in his toes."' However, others persuaded her I was right. Her solution was unusual. In the middle of the Broadway theatre district stood the empty Billy Rose's Horseshoe Saloon on Forty-sixth Street. She decided to take it over and convert it into a theatre that would suit us. It must have cost a fortune, but then I had heard her on the phone to Republicans that she wanted to invest in the show. It was the nearest thing to political blackmail you can imagine. The Mayfair Theatre was born.

Roger Stephens was nowhere to be seen and it was obvious that this was Marion's current plaything. She wanted a hand in everything, in every appointment, every artistic question, everything. The only salvation was that she quickly became bored with auditions so I was saved that horror.

All this was taking place in New York, which I was experiencing for the first time. I loved it and hated it. It was and remains a city with the most pulsating energy flowing through it twenty-four hours a day. It was also a city of celebrity hype. I was 'The new Orson Welles' (*New York Times*), I appeared on chat shows. I met Tennessee Williams at Elaine's, Hal Prince, Stella Adler. The introduction was always the same: 'This is that brilliant young . . . etc. etc.' There is no quiet in New York, there are no trees, no birds, only the skyscrapers forming avenues for scurrying, scavenging human beings. It was, I thought, the gutter of the world, but it was a place I wanted to conquer.

I was staying at the Hotel Meurice up by Carnegie Hall, my first posh hotel. One morning the phone rang. 'What are you?'

'I'm a cunt. Hello, John.' It was John Dexter.

'I'm taking you out tonight, dinner and a show.'

We went to see Bea Lillie in *High Spirits* and dined at Sardi's after a drink with Alec Guinness at the bar (forgive me I'm still only twenty-one). 'I'm staying at the Algonquin. You can walk me back to my hotel.' At the corner of the street he stopped, turned. 'It's all right, I'm not going to try and make you tonight,' and off he went. He had some redeeming features.

Somehow I managed to survive those terrible weeks. David Wright and I clung to each other, mostly over a whisky bottle, seeing the new shows and movies as they opened. Marion had other protégés. One of them was the great documentary maker Emilio di Antonio who made *The Bay of Pigs* and the definitive movie about Senator McCarthy. He was often present at our contretemps as she tried to rewrite the script. One day when we were alone he said, 'Don't you realise what you have to do? She wants you to fuck her!' At that moment I nearly threw in the towel. I'd prefer to have done it with a rattlesnake. He was deadly serious. 'She's pissed off with you because you haven't fucked her.' Then she would have to stay pissed off.

Finally, somehow, we reached the eve of rehearsals. I was lying in bed in the hotel unable to sleep, very nervous and very alone. At two o'clock in the morning the phone rang. It was the Company Stage Manager. Company managers were to come and go so frequently that it is difficult to remember which one this was but I think he was called Michael. 'Braham, this is Michael. Your friend Michael, who likes you very much. Michael has a message from Marion Javits. When he gives you the message you are not to shout and scream at Michael because he is your friend. He is only giving you Marion's message.'

'What?'

'Marion thinks she is spending too much money on this show, so she says you cannot have a musical director and you cannot have a choreographer.'

'But . . .'

'Do not shout and scream at Michael, he is only relaying the message.' I got dressed and took a cab to the Javitses' apartment. It was now three o'clock in the morning. Marion answered the door fully dressed and as gorgeous as ever, but I could no longer appreciate it. She had other cuts to make. 'What is this sound man? What is a sound man?' I explained that he controlled the sound. 'Oh. Oh, another thing. What is a board?' I patiently explained it was where the lights were controlled from. 'Oh, well, I guess you can have one of those.'

Then we got down to the nitty-gritty. After a long argument she conceded that a band had to have a conductor, so I was allowed an MD, but on the choreography she stuck. Her argument was that I was billed as the choreographer in England. This was true, I had moved my undergraduate ladies in various numbers in a rudimentary way. In New York I had a chorus line of six professional dancers. There was no way I could cope with them or they put up with me. She wouldn't listen. 'Either you choreograph the show or pack your bags and go back to England.' It was now at least four o'clock in the morning and I was exhausted. A sensible man would have said fine, I'm off. I didn't do that, I reckoned I could use one of the dancers as an assistant and get her to supervise the routines. I capitulated. The interview wasn't over.

'My husband has something to say to you.' And in walked Senator Jacob

Javits, the Republican Senator for New York and prime mover of the Civil Rights Bill, at 4 a.m. fully dressed. He started a peroration as if he were addressing a political rally. 'I have heard it bruited abroad that you have called my wife an "amateur".'

'Ah, you mean amateur in the English sense of the word – a patron of the arts,' I tried. I might just as well not have been there. He went on with his harangue, turned and left the room. That's how I spent the last night before rehearsals.

Opening and Closing

In contrast to the preparation period, rehearsals were a joy. *Hang Down Your Head* was a great show and I had the confidence of a director who had nothing to prove with it, as it had been a great success in London. I also had a superb cast who were as fully committed to the subject matter as the Oxford one had been, with the surprising exception of one Joe Chaikin who left early on because he didn't want to be part of an ensemble company. (Joe went on to found Open Theatre based on those very principles.) The cast also began a learning process in me. They were professionals with their own honed talents and they could bring surprising things to the material in a way that inexperienced undergraduates couldn't. They didn't need so much shouting and screaming.

I had solved the problem of the choreography by asking the one English member of the cast to help me out. She had been a dancer in *West Side Story* and now lived in New York. She was a striking auburn-haired lady called Virginia Mason; we became an item. I have almost left out any reference to girlfriends to this point but if I'm writing seriously about destiny, I cannot ignore perhaps the single most important, troubling and unfathomable strand of my life. If you accept, as I do, the idea that all relationships are, at least in the initial stage, a transference – in other words that you see in the object of desire that which makes you feel whole, irrespective of whether she actually contains those attributes or that they are the attributes you really need – then the women in your life will tell you more about your path and yourself than almost anything else. The only important relationship so far had been with Jasmina Hamzavi, who had been in *Hang Down Your Head and Die*. It was my second year and at the beginning of each new year the university societies put on a Freshman's Fair so that the freshers could join those of their choice. I was on ETC's stall when this dazzling vision of beauty passed by. As has happened several times in my life, I knew that girl was someone I had to know and I had to go up to her and ask her for a date.

I was drama critic for *Isis* (I know, I know, forgive me) and I asked her to the theatre. This was the beginning of a relationship that in its initial stage, when we thought we might be in love, lasted on and off for five years. It was never satisfactory in that we couldn't do without each other – or I couldn't do without her – but when we were together it never worked properly physically. The simple truth, as I realised much later, was either that if it had it would have been the end of any artist in me and/or it was never meant to be like that. It is now a deep soul relationship that has lasted all my life. It continues to be sustaining at the most unexpected moments and has taught me how much more complex relationships are than Hollywood would have us believe.

Anyhow, that one was in an off period. I had also, as I said earlier, finally lost my virginity, but in such an unsatisfactory way that I couldn't see what all the fuss over sex was about. I had no inclination to try again . . . until I met Virginia. The first time we made love the heavens opened, and I mean the heavens. I was in paradise. It was so good that I didn't want to get out of bed the next morning. It was the first and last time I have ever been late for rehearsals. Given the horrors of Marion Javits and New York, Virginia saved my life. I left my hotel and moved in with her. If sex with her was like this, I wanted to be with her for the rest of my life. We became engaged.

Once I had persuaded Marion that it wasn't a good idea to have backers sitting in rehearsals from day one, they proceeded smoothly. The cast showed me the other sides of New York, such as Harlem, where Robert Jackson, a black member of the cast, chaperoned me, and the Bowery with the hideous charabanc-loads of the rich coming to look at the wretches lying drunk in the gutter to make themselves feel good. We arrived at the previews in pretty good shape, or we should have done. Marion had fired the Production Manager just before the get-in, so what should have taken a weekend took over a week. The previews and first night had to be delayed.

Finally they started and were just great, except for note sessions with Marion, which were so ludicrous that eventually I had to have my American agent pass the notes between us. We would sit in a line and Marion would start: 'Would you please tell Mr Murray that Jordan Chaney's knickerbockers rode up in the teeter-totter scene and I found his hairy knees objectionable. Please see to it that they are shaven so as not to reoffend.'

'Please thank Mrs Javits for her note.'

All seemed well and we arrived at the last preview day. I was rehearsing the company when Marion came down the aisle and sat behind me. 'I can't hear Robert,' she hissed.

'OK, Marion, in a minute.'

'Are you going to do something about it?'

'Wait till I'm finished rehearsing, then I'll listen to you.' She left the auditorium.

The Front of House Manager was called Moish Baruch. When we met on the first day of rehearsals his comment was, 'Jees, dere making dem young nowadays!' Now Moish was at my shoulder. 'Braham, you'd better scram. She called de cops and told dem you are trespassing.'

Sure enough a large archetypal New York cop appeared at the back of the auditorium. I adopted my best British accent: 'I say, there's no need for all this, you know' and walked as steadily as I could out of the theatre and back to Virginia's apartment.

After what seemed ages, there was a ring at the door. The umpteenth Company Manager was standing there. 'Oh boy! Oh boy! Oh boy!' He pushed past me into the room. 'Drink?' I poured him one. He drank it. 'Oh boy! Oh boy! Oh boy!' He put his hand on my shoulder. 'Oh boy! Oh boy! Oh boy!' He walked to the door. He opened it and turned. 'Oh boy! Oh boy! Oh boy!' He left.

Eventually the phone rang. It was Roger Stephens's secretary. I was to be allowed to take rehearsals on the opening night and attend the show.

I turned up on the first night to a typical Broadway opening-night scene: crowds outside the theatre, mounted police. It was all very exciting again. I walked into the foyer to be confronted by the enormous figure of Roger Stephens: 'Let's have a drink.'

'I don't want a drink.'

'Yes you do.' We left the theatre and found a bar down the street. He ordered two Manhattans. We drank them. He ordered two more. 'We've had it,' he told me. Apparently Marion had wanted the first night to be a special one for her Republican friends, where she could hold court in her new gown, which had been photographed for and appeared in the *New York Times*. Stephens had talked her out of it and persuaded her to do it at a preview, but because the first night had been postponed she had managed to rearrange it. A Republican reception on the first night of an anti-capital-punishment play was not a clever idea. As Stephens put it, 'We're fucked.'

Back at the theatre, Marion was holding court. The show began, the auditorium was practically empty, people drifted in through the first act and the atmosphere was icy. After the show Marion was giving a cast party. I thought it best to miss it and Stella Adler invited me back to her apartment to have a few drinks and watch the first reviews on TV.

The reviews were very good and word came that the *New York Times*, while not a rave, was not at all bad. The phone rang. The cast implored me to come to the party. They promised to look after me. I arrived at the restaurant and opened the door. The cast had lined up to make a corridor and as I came down the stairs they started to sing to the tune of 'Bye Bye Birdie', 'We love you, Braham, we do. We love you, Braham, we do.' I cried, they cried, Marion gnashed her teeth.

I was due to fly back the next day as *Oom-Pah-Pah* beckoned. Stephens asked me to call at his office. He was complimentary. He wanted me to direct *Stephen D* in the next Broadway season. The reviews were good enough for a decent run and they'd fly me back every three months to look at the show. The phone rang. He picked it up. 'What? Uh huh! Uh huh!' He put it down. Marion Javits had rung to say, 'The shit Braham Murray isn't going to get another cent from me. I'm closing the show immediately.'

We rushed round to the theatre, knowing that the actors would be arriving for the second night. They were all on the stage, tears rolling down their faces, singing songs from the show. Marion was sitting in the auditorium saying how sorry she was. I went up to her. 'Marion, if you value your life, leave the theatre now.' She did. I flew out that evening.

There is a coda to this. The cast so loved the show that they held monthly reunions where they sang the songs and had a good time. They regularly let me know about these evenings. One day I got a letter from two of them, James Rado who played a ringmaster and Gerome Ragni who played the Condemned Man. Inspired by the free form of the show, they had written their own musical and it was to be performed in a tiny off-off-Broadway theatre. I wrote a friendly, condescending letter back. A few months later I got another letter. The show had been a success and was going off-Broadway next season. The season after it was on Broadway. It was called *Hair*. A few years later Rado and Ragni flew over to London for the opening of *Catch My Soul*. They posed with me for pictures for the press. 'This is the guy who inspired *Hair*,' they said. Funny, they didn't mention royalties.

CHAPTER 9

A Thing with Music

I flew back to England, tired, upset but not demoralised. It hadn't been my fault, the production had been good, I was still the whizz-kid. Now rehearsals for *Oom-Pah-Pah* were imminent. There were problems.

Sherrin and Brahms had indeed sent a script to New York, but not a word had been changed except that a sketch had been added for Al Mancini, which he had already performed on TV. No set had arrived from Bernard Daydé.

Michael Dorfman elicited a response from the writers that I shouldn't worry as they would attend rehearsals and work with us through improvisation. Over Daydé there was a problem. 'I've lost Bernard Daydé,' Dorfman announced.

'Lost him?'

'I phoned Paris, he's not there. They tell me to phone Vienna, but he's not there. They say to phone Milan. He's not there.' With a week to go to rehearsals and a further four weeks to opening on the pre-London tour at the Bristol Hippodrome, this was disastrous. I told him I had better talk to the Stage Manager about how to mark up the rehearsal room. 'What Stage Manager? We don't have a Stage Manager.'

'The Company Manager, then.'

'We don't have one.' Dorfman had presented Marcel Marceau and *Black Nativity* in London but these were shows already in existence. He had never produced a show from scratch.

Virginia, whom I was missing badly, was to be my assistant and I went to Heathrow to meet her. In those days you saw the passengers coming down a great escalator as you stood behind a vast glass window. I was beside myself with excitement. Virginia appeared at the top of the escalator. I knew immediately: 'Wrong'. It had been like a holiday romance and it had been wonderful, but it wasn't going to be for the rest of my life. I was going into rehearsal for a West End show with no script, no set and an assistant my engagement to whom I was going to have to break off at some point soon.

No point in detailing the rehearsals. Sherrin and Brahms never turned up once. George Murcell left by mutual consent and Joyce Grant walked. The rest of us soldiered on refusing, as professionals do, to face the hopelessness of our situation and praying for a miracle.

Halfway through rehearsals Bernard Daydé appeared. 'Don't woree. I 'ave 'ired a warehouse and I will make ze set myself.' He showed me his delightful model and disappeared to make good his word.

The Bristol opening was a tight schedule. Get-in on Sunday, tech on Monday, dress rehearsal and open on Tuesday. Virginia and I went down on the Saturday to prepare for the Monday tech. On Sunday I went to see the set. Daydé, in an immaculate white tracksuit, was surrounded by bemused Bristolian stagehands and a lot of wooden rostra. 'Let me show you ze set. Zis little rostrum, he becomes a shair. Let me show you 'ow 'e becomes a shair.' The rostrum was a square box. He lifted the lid. '*Voilà.*' Now it was a square box with an upright lid.

'It's not very chic,' I offered.

'It's not very chic, but it's very funny! Zis rostrum 'e become a table. Two men come to one end, two to the other end. Zey lift it up. One man brings down ze legs from underneath, another from the other side etc. *Voilà* a table!' That was six people to turn one bit of set into a not very exciting table, and all the scene changes were to be done by members of the cast.

'What about the music stands?' I asked.

'Ah, *les pupitres*. You know we said *les pupitres* would go fiss, fiss, fiss in the air to become a lamp-post and fft, fft, fft to become a door? This is not possible. So for example I make very big music stand when you want a lamp-post and so on.' I saw the lamp-posts in the corner. The idea was that the girls would bring them on stage, but they were so huge I doubted a fifteen-stone navvy could have managed one.

'How will they get them on?' I asked.

'Oh, it's very easy. You put one 'and 'ere and one 'ere to find the point of balance. You lift ze lamp-post forward, take three paces back and run on and you put it down.'

The technical was everything I expected it to be – appalling. One scene was set by the Seine with steps coming down from the bridge above. The joke was that the balustrade was made up of jugglers' clubs and that, at a given moment, all the cast would dismantle and juggle. The clubs would never stay in place and time and time again they would crash around the theatre one sketch too early. The *pièce de résistance* came when the six girls had, as instructed, to bring on the lamp-posts to loll against. They faithfully tried to follow Daydé's instructions. Lamp-posts broke in two, lamp-posts crashed into scenery and ripped backcloths, it was a miracle lamp-posts didn't do someone a fatal injury.

The technical plodded on and on. Monday gave way to Tuesday. There was no possibility of finishing, let alone having a dress rehearsal. I promised the cast I would make a speech to the audience to get them on our side. I did my best and went to join Virginia to watch the show.

Any pretence at optimism gave way to that dull sick feeling when you know you are watching a fully-fledged, unredeemable disaster. There was a sketch about an anarchist conspiracy to blow up something or other. The poor actors were dressed up in black capes and berets. One of them, Charles Lewsen it was, had to utter the line, 'Things can't go on like this.' At which point a voice from the rapidly dwindling audience shouted, 'Too bloody right, mate.'

Ned Sherrin's opinion? 'Very funny people doing very funny things. I enjoyed it.' We never saw him again. Dorfman made half-hearted promises about finding new writers but we knew we were doomed.

The publicists in their wisdom had billed the show as *Oom-Pah-Pah*, 'A Thing with Music'. The local press seized on it with glee. An empty Bristol Hippodrome is a lonely place to be when you're on stage every night in a flop. There was still the rest of the tour to do. Al Mancini and Joe Melia came up with the idea that we should jettison the entire show and put together a revue of our own based on the various sketches that the cast had been in. This we did and Nottingham audiences, where the show finally died, had a better time of it than the Bristolians and Geordies before them. Even my mother hated it.

Worst of all, *Chaganog* was about to open at the Vaudeville. It had been a great success in Edinburgh and I had been asked to expand it for the West End. I had already committed to *Oom-Pah-Pah* so I couldn't do it. Quite naturally they didn't want to wait until the new year and so they went ahead with another director. After all, it was a very simple show which was surely director-proof by now. Not if you overloaded it with a ridiculously expensive set like a golden bookcase with parrots and geegaws all over it, and camped the whole thing up so that its wonderful humour was swamped, it wasn't. The show was panned and came off very quickly.

I still wasn't taking it all too much to heart. I shouldn't have done *Oom-Pah-Pah*, but it wasn't my fault that the show was so awful. First New York then this and a broken engagement had left me battered but none the wiser.

CHAPTER 10

Three Strikes and You're Out

I've always empathised with Parsifal, riding into King Arthur's court on a donkey with a dunce's hat on his head, saying, 'I can do it, I can do it.' I had not learnt to think about myself, all I could do was to go on until something gave. I was still only twenty-one.

The turning point came in 1965, and the first half of that year offered three very different possibilities. Peter Bridge had been deeply upset by the failure of *Chaganog* in the West End and realised that my production had been better than the version at the Vaudeville. He decided bravely, but foolishly, to revive it. I was to re-direct it at the Hampstead Theatre Club and, if it worked, he would take it back into the West End. It did work and it was to go via Brighton to the St Martin's.

Then came the real life-saver. John Harrison asked me to direct *The Winter's Tale* at the old Birmingham Rep. The fact was that, for all my idealism, I had never directed a serious play and certainly never a Shakespeare. Of course, it never occurred to me to say no, even though *The Winter's Tale* is one of the late plays, notoriously difficult to pull off. It is astonishing to think that Shakespeare, having written the greatest plays in our language – the four tragedies and the sublime comedies – suddenly threw all he knew out of the window. He wanted to express something new: the possibility of regeneration in spite of the most profound hardships. To do this he experimented with new forms and new ways of using the language. *The Winter's Tale* is an early staging post on that voyage. I write with hindsight. At the time I simply read it and said yes.

It actually dawned on me that this was a challenge that I might need help with. Nevill Coghill agreed to give me a 'tutorial' on directing Shakespeare. Coghill was an Oxford don who was an authority on verse speaking and indeed directed the OUDS major Shakespeare in Worcester Gardens every summer. His 'tutorial' in verse speaking was a revelation. He made me turn to Act Five, Scene Three where Paulina conjures the statue of Hermione to come to life:

> Music, awake her; strike!
> 'Tis time; descend; be stone no more; approach;
> Strike all that look upon with marvel. Come,
> I'll fill your grave up: stir, nay, come away:
> Bequeath to death your numbness; for from him
> Dear life redeems you. You perceive she stirs.

He had already explained the break halfway through each line called the caesura, and end-stopping, which meant you also took a break at the end of every line, less when there was no punctuation, more where there was; now he told me to read. I rattled through the first line and a half. 'No, no, a semicolon is a pause, a colon a bigger pause, a full stop a bigger pause. Leave in all the pauses.' I reread those lines with pauses and I realised what he meant. The statue doesn't come alive immediately. It takes so long that Paulina starts to doubt that it will. It is a being coming painfully and slowly back into the world after years of 'death'. 'Apply these rules to the whole play and you will see how Shakespeare gives his actors instruction as to how he wants it played.' He despised the Royal Shakespeare–Peter Hall Classics Illustrated verse speaking as boring and lifeless, almost as much as he despised what he called 'The Kottomites', the followers of Jan Kott whose radical reinterpretation of Shakespeare, especially in Brook's *Lear*, was all the rage. The rest of the verse-speaking mystery, he believed, took care of itself if you had a feel for the poetic value of the words. Even the question of the iambic pentameter, with its five stresses in each line, would take care of itself if you observed the caesura, the end-stopping and the punctuation, because it would then come naturally to the actors, even as it did in Shakespeare's day. He was absolutely right. It takes about half an hour to teach a cast how to speak the verse so that it is more alive and resonant than I have ever seen on the Stratford stage.

Anyway, since it never occurred to me that Shakespeare needed doing in a certain way, or indeed to wonder what the play was about, I did a simple straightforward production that told the story. I had an excellent cast led by Prunella Scales as Hermione, with Oxford friends such as Michael Elwyn playing the smaller parts. The production was a great success with the critics and, to John Harrison's surprise, with the audience. The play ran for three and a half hours, too long for last buses in Birmingham in 1965. I was worried that the auditorium would start to empty at about 10.15. In the event no one stirred until the statue of Hermione finally moved, when there was a stampede for the exit.

I was still unconscious of what I was doing but very conscious that rehearsing Shakespeare was the most exhilarating experience I had ever had. It was connecting with an extraordinary energy centre that fed you endlessly and called from you reservoirs of invention you didn't know you had in you. John Harrison's offer had put me finally on the right road.

Chaganog opened in the West End, received excellent notices and promptly closed. It was a hopeless task to entice audiences after its first failure but once again I was not to blame. Life seemed somehow to have steadied itself.

Now I was asked to go up to Nottingham to see a new play at the Playhouse called *Collapse of Stout Party* by Trevor Peacock, starring Bill Fraser, the big television star of *The Army Game* and *Bootsie and Snudge*. Laurence Olivier Productions wanted to remount it in the West End and if I liked it I could direct it. I went to see it. It was about a lady who was too fat to get out of her top-floor flat. It was a satire about bureaucracy as all the local services including the Fire Brigade (Bill Fraser) sought to work out what to do. I watched it, and on the basis that the audience was laughing a lot and I would obviously be able to do it much better, I agreed.

I went to meet Trevor Peacock and realised he had crossed my path once before. When I was about sixteen and wanted to be an actor, a friend of my mother's, the society bandleader and agent Alf Van Stratten, had got me a holiday job at Sommerfields Agency in Golden Square who dealt with TV celebrities and sportsmen. They also had a script department, run by one Al Berlin, in which I chiefly worked. One day this amazing satyr-like creature burst in to read a sketch he had written about throwing old ladies in wardrobes off the Cliffs of Dover in an Olympic-style competition. This was Trevor Peacock, who was at that time writing continuity scripts for *Six Five Special*, which was being produced by his friend Jack Good. Five years later he was not only a playwright but a songwriter, whose composition 'Mrs Brown You've Got a Lovely Daughter' was Number One in the States, and a fledgling actor who had made his début for Michael Elliott at the Old Vic in 1961.

Murray Macdonald, the Executive Producer for LOP Productions, had put together an extremely starry cast including Gladys Henson, Kathleen Harrison and Richard Pearson. It was the first time I had worked with established West End stars at this level and I imagine I was out of my depth. However, they had their performances all ready (the ones that had made them West End stars) and I made sure they didn't bump into each other. They seemed happy.

We opened out of town at Wimbledon and things did not go well. The principal reason, it seemed to Trevor and me, was that Bill Fraser was playing farce while everyone else was playing comedy. Bill's character didn't come on till the end of Act One and until that point all was well. After that the audience stopped laughing. We went to Murray Macdonald and asked that Bill be replaced, only to be told that Bill had put up most of the money for the show, so that was out of the question.

Trevor rewrote the second act, we re-rehearsed in Oxford and proceeded to the Golders Green Hippodrome where my mother ensured a very favourable audience on the first night. The next day Murray Macdonald phoned to inform me that Bill had decided that I was too inexperienced to get the right laughs out of the text so he was going to take rehearsals forthwith. If I liked I might attend these rehearsals so that I could pick up some useful tips from the master. Amazingly, I did attend. Bill assembled this very experienced cast, informed them of his reservations about their performances and promised to show them how to get more laughs.

Richard Pearson was first up. 'Now then, Dickie, you have this line, "Good morning, Mrs Tune. And how are you today?"' Richard Pearson admitted he did. 'You're not getting a laugh from it.' Richard again admitted that this was true but that it hadn't occurred to him that it was a laugh line. Bill demonstrated how to get the laugh. He was a very large man with a face like a bullfrog. He started by winding his voice up higher and higher – 'Now-then-Mrs Tune' – then plunging it lower and faster – 'Andhowareyoutoday' – at the same time rolling his eyes, stretching his lips with his fingers and letting out gasps of air. Richard tried to emulate this somewhat half-heartedly. Kathleen Harrison was next. 'Now then, dear, how would you like your tea? With sugar and milk? Now-Then-Dear-How-Would-You-Like-Your-Tea? Withsugarandmilk?' It was Bill's way of getting laughs, it wasn't theirs and they openly rebelled. Bill retired hurt and I was reinstated. However, the play did not survive the tour and closed in Brighton. For the third time, once in New York and now twice on pre-West End tours, a production had blown up in my face – and I was engaged again, of course, this time to a member of the company, Pat Maynard, who is now happily married to a judge in the West Country after an earlier marriage to Dennis Waterman. The engagement didn't last long. This was down to my uncle who clearly thought it was a mistake and encouraged us to go on a motoring holiday to Italy. He reckoned that the navigator–driver tensions would ruin all but the most durable relationship. I suppose he was right.

It still hadn't occurred to me that I was doing anything wrong. If I was offered a show, I saw no reason not to do it. I simply didn't make choices. I went on the adventure, however risky or foolhardy. Mad producers, inadequate scripts or miscast actors were all part of the game.

The phone rang. Bernard Delfont was to produce a new West End

Musical called *Passion Flower Hotel*, Trevor Peacock was to write the lyrics, would I direct? A voice said 'No' and I put down the phone.

I had heard this voice before in New York – I had been offered a contract by the Hollywood producer Joseph E. Levine for three years. The first six months I would learn film directing, then I would direct a film a year. For this I would be paid, in 1964, $800,000! The voice had spoken then and it had said the same thing, 'No.' On both occasions it took me a moment to understand that the voice had come from me. There is a wise old soul in all of us who always knows what to do if we keep in touch with him. If I had gone to Hollywood I would have been lost either through success or failure, and the West End was no longer the place for me if I was to have a chance of a real future in the theatre. On the table by the phone was a copy of *The Stage*. I turned to the 'Situations Vacant' page. There was an advertisement for a new Artistic Director of Century Theatre which, in addition to continuing to tour in its own put-up theatre in the north west, was to become the resident company at the new Stephen Joseph-designed University Theatre in Manchester. This was the key moment that changed my professional career for ever. I sent off my letter of application.

CHAPTER II
Century Theatre

I knew vaguely what an artistic director did; I knew nothing about Century Theatre. An artistic director chose the plays. That's what Casper Wrede had done at Hammersmith, deciding to bring European drama to London; that's how Peter Hall had made his name at the Arts, introducing Lorca, O'Neill and Beckett to London; that's what Olivier did at the National and that's surely what I could do.

Century Theatre was a remarkable creation. It consisted of three huge pantechnicons which, when unfolded and joined together, made up a 300-seat auditorium. Accompanying these pantechnicons were a fleet of caravans, which provided the dressing rooms and accommodation for the company. This theatrical circus toured the towns of the North that did not have a theatre, playing three-week seasons in Preston, Burnley, Rawtenstall, Rochdale, Bolton, Lancaster, till the summer came when it ended up via Windermere in Keswick for a three-month season. It was a brilliant engineering feat, nothing quite like it has happened since and it spawned permanent theatres in Preston, Bolton, Lancaster and Keswick.

The University Theatre in Manchester was equally unusual. It was the brainchild of Stephen Joseph, who pioneered the strange concept of theatre in the round, which inspired Peter Cheeseman at Stoke and Alan Ayckbourn at Scarborough (where the theatre was named after him). The University Theatre was not in the round but was an adaptable space that could play on the proscenium or on a large or small thrust stage, or an open-end stage. None of this interested me very much. A stage was a stage was a stage; give me one and I'll put a play on it.

Anyway, I went for my interview and got the job. It seemed par for the course for me at the time but now it seems as amazing as anything that had happened in my short professional career. I was twenty-two, easily the youngest artistic director in the country; indeed, I'd be surprised if there has been a younger one since. I suppose my jet-propelled start in the theatre still carried some allure for the interviewing panel who probably had not caught up with the out-of-town flops of my recent past. I can't remember the interview but I have always been a good bullshitter and Century Theatre was such an obscure company, paying so badly, that they probably thought they had made a catch.

My appointment wasn't to start till the late autumn but the company was playing in Windermere so I went up to see the 'Blue Box', as the touring theatre was known. It was quite a shock to see the set-up in a car park by the lake, but no matter, I assembled the company and told them that when I took over I would make Century into a company with a national reputation. I don't think they believed me. Here were a group of actors being paid £18 a week, who not only had to tour in remote and obscure parts of the north west, but also had to drive the pantechnicons and help put up and strike the theatre. As they looked at me they must have thought like Moish Baruch, 'Dere makin' dem young dese days.'

I was to take over the company in Plymouth in September where it was playing a season at a conventional theatre, the Athenaeum. The last play in that season was to be my first production, which would then play in the new University Theatre. Then there would be a new season at the University Theatre followed by a short conventional tour and finally in the early spring we would start the Blue Box tour, gradually building up a repertoire of six plays for the Keswick residency. I was grateful to have a few months to put it all together. I may not have been aware of why I did plays but I was a pragmatist. I knew I would have to assemble a company of actors who would withstand nine months on the road and I would have to persuade the Board of the theatre that they should no longer require the actors to be long-distance lorry drivers. I realised it would be hard enough to form a company without that obstacle.

I don't know how I chose the first season but I elected to open in Plymouth with Shaw's *The Philanderer*, which would go to Manchester. Then *Macbeth* and *See How They Run* would play the next Manchester season before touring. Then the Blue Box season would have *The Philanderer*, Machiavelli's *Mandragola*, a double bill of Ionesco's *The Chairs* and Pinter's *Dumb Waiter*, *Private Lives*, Ann Jellicoe's *The Knack* and finally *Uncle Vanya*. There was, after all, a captive audience in Keswick with nothing else to do in the evenings, so I could afford to be ambitious. I would direct everything bar *Mandragola* and *The Knack*. I had quite unconsciously provided myself with what I desperately needed: to learn how to direct. This course of plays was the best training I could have devised.

CHAPTER 12

A 'Secret'

Before I was due to go to Century I directed one more play. The experience was in a very different way of great significance.

Peter Bridge had read a play called *The Secret* by Robin Hawdon. It had caught his fancy and he wanted to try it out at the King's Lynn Festival. Would I direct it? Yes, I would.

The actual play was not the point. I thought it was a clever pastiche of *Waiting for Godot*. I cast it with a couple of chums: Derek Smith, who had been my Autolycus at Birmingham; and Anthony Newlands, who had been in *Collapse of Stout Party*, augmented by the Festival Director Michael Burrell and a young actress called Emma Stuart. We had a lot of fun until the author came to see a run-through and informed me that what I had seen as a comic send-up was a deeply serious philosophic play. In the circumstances all I could do was to suggest he went back to London, which he did.

The point was that as part of my contract the festival found a family who were prepared to put me up in their house and feed me an evening meal. My family, whose name I forget, had a very comfortable and prosperous farm. They were a charming couple with two delightful children. I did my best to behave properly. I didn't swear, washed under the armpits and didn't praise Harold Wilson. The first three weeks of rehearsal passed pleasantly enough. Then, on the Friday (I went back to London at the weekends), the lady of the house knocked on my bedroom door. She was frightfully sorry but the harvest was starting next week and various friends were coming down to help them out. That meant there would be no room for me. I thanked her for her hospitality, packed my bags, shook her hand and drove off to King's Lynn.

When I arrived at the theatre Michael Burrell was waiting for me with a look of extreme tension on his face. 'I'm so sorry,' he said. I explained that that was fine, I wasn't at all upset. 'What did they tell you?' he asked. I told him. Then he told me what they had said to him.

At some point they had realised I was Jewish and they wanted me to leave because they didn't want their children to be 'contaminated'. It was a devastating moment. For years now I had not been conscious of being Jewish and not since my prep school had I encountered anti-Semitism in any shape or form. It was unreal to be despised, or indeed feared, for no reason and it started a lifelong process of trying to understand the fear in people that leads them to stigmatise their fellow human beings because of their race. More than that, it made me conscious again of being Jewish and want to find out what that meant.

I remembered a conversation I had had with my grandmother. She had said she wouldn't have wanted a daughter of hers to marry a black man. I was outraged. 'How would she feel', I asked, 'if her daughter wanted to marry a non-Jewish man and his parents objected because she was Jewish?' A look of amazement was followed by, 'Who wants to marry one of them?'

I had rejected the religion but that was obviously not enough. I was a Jew. The Jews were called God's chosen people. If that was so, they existed before he chose them. So who were they and why did he choose them? If I was going to be hated, I wanted to know why. It was the beginning of a quest that continues to this day.

CHAPTER 13
Artistic Director

Being an artistic director was the dawning of a new kind of consciousness in me. If I look at the list of plays I chose for the first year's work at Century, I see that they were all a celebration of life. They had a humanity that fed the positive side of being. This was why I had rejected so much of contemporary theatre and why I started to think again of those men who had been responsible for *Brand* six years earlier.

I began to bombard Michael Elliott and Casper Wrede with letters asking them to come and direct at Century. Michael, after his definitive *As You Like It* at the RSC with Vanessa Redgrave, was at the height of his fame, being wooed by Olivier at the National and the BBC, who wanted him as Head of Drama, while Casper had forged a career both on TV and in the movies. Not surprisingly, they didn't find my offer tempting.

I assembled a company for the first year. Michael Elwyn left a lucrative job in a new soap on TV called *The Newcomers*; I recruited Roger Swaine and Emma Stuart from King's Lynn; I found a hugely talented Australian actress, Rosalyn de Winter; Peter Childs from Birmingham; Pat Maynard (whom I was no longer engaged to); John Watts; and, later in the year, Sam Walters and Auriol Smith (Mr and Mrs Orange Tree). While at Clifton I had met and had a schoolboy crush on the beautiful Ann Beverley, who was a trainee designer at the Bristol Old Vic, and I asked her to design the year. She and her husband, John Bloomfield, working under pretty awful conditions, performed that miracle for me.

Before going to Plymouth to start rehearsals I made my very first trip to Manchester to see the University Theatre. On tour with pre-West End shows, I got as far north as Nottingham, and there the management paid for me to stay in the best hotel in town, and the hotel and the theatre were all I knew of England outside London. North of Watford was a foreign country.

I was in for a shock. Manchester, in those days, was a depressed city, at least ten years behind London. The sixties hadn't happened; indeed, parts of the city were still bomb-sites from the Second World War. The University Theatre was on the University campus, far from the city centre in a particularly run-down area, and the General Manager of Century had booked me into the Verdene Hotel near it. My room at the Verdene was dank, lit by one central light bulb. It was too cold to undress and I lay on my bed in utter misery. I wanted my mummy. I had made a terrible mistake.

It was a relief to get to Plymouth and rehearse. I have no idea how good or bad the productions were that year. At the time, of course, I thought them marvellous. *The Philanderer* just about happened. As they carried the set from the lorry to the theatre the heavens opened and I spent the rest of the night helping to repaint the scenery. However, we had enjoyed rehearsals and the play seemed to go well.

We arrived in Manchester, had a good notice in the *Manchester Evening News* and nobody came. Not only was the University Theatre off the beaten track but it was a university theatre. Century was only to play three short seasons a year, while the various university societies filled the majority of the time. When I say societies, I don't just mean the Drama Department under the eminent directorship of Hugh Hunt, but the French Society, the German Society and whatever group could afford to pay the rent. The public, who already had the famous Library Theatre to go to in the centre of town, had no incentive to visit a theatre that appeared to be for amateurs. What to do? It seemed that our tenure would be very short.

Destiny entered in a very unlikely guise. The next play up was *Macbeth* and for this the basic company would have to be augmented. That same friend of the family, Alf Van Stratten, who was an agent as well as a bandleader, rang me. He had signed up the new Miss World, Ann Sydney. She was interested in being an actress. Was there a small part she might play in my company? I nearly dismissed the idea when a thought struck me. Would she consider playing the Third Witch? She would indeed. The very beautiful and delightful Miss World duly arrived and, as I had foreseen, most of the national press with her. Every tabloid carried the before and after shots: Miss World–Witch. The theatre was packed out. People knew who we were. *See How They Run* was added to the repertoire and the two plays went out on a distinctly Number Two tour.

If Manchester had been a shock, Darlington in February made it seem like Nirvana. The digs we could afford were ghastly. It became clear that we were not the only occupants of our shared rooms. While we were out during the day, night workers were using our beds. Admittedly it meant that they warmed up the linen in the otherwise freezing rooms. Darlington, Whitby, Redcar, Consett, how would we survive?

When I was at Clifton we were not allowed home at half-term. Our parents had to book in at an expensive hotel and we were allowed to see them during the day. Since we were not permitted to go to the cinema, the time passed very slowly. The one oasis was Horts, Bristol's leading restaurant. There I developed a love of good food and indeed wine. Touring was not much different from boarding school and the trick was to find a decent restaurant wherever you went. In Darlington it was a quasi-Greek restaurant called the Blue Lagoon. Just knowing you could eat passably once a day with a good bottle (which was easier to achieve) made life bearable. The right restaurant has been part of my life ever since. Michael Meyer was a friend of Sir Raymond Postgate, the founder of *The Good Food Guide*, and he was on the Board. I became an inspector for the *Guide* and eventually the north-west food correspondent for the *Independent*. The *Guide* was part of my survival kit.

We did, of course, survive, but what would I do in the next season at the University Theatre? Miss Worlds don't fall into your lap every day. This time Destiny arrived in the more familiar shape of Michael Codron. He had presented Joe Orton's *Entertaining Mr Sloane* with great success in London and sent out his next one, *Loot*, on a pre-London tour with a glitzy cast headed by Kenneth Williams and directed by Peter Wood. As well as causing huge outrage to Respectable of Worthing, it had flopped badly because the production had been misconceived. The set was highly stylised in black and white, instead of being the 'everyone's front parlour' that Orton had wanted. Further, Williams had been unable to sustain a proper acting performance in the role of Truscott. The result had been a laughter desert. Codron still believed in the play and wanted to revive it at Hampstead with me directing. I explained why I couldn't but offered to put it on in Manchester as our next production.

I met Joe Orton outside Baker Street tube station. Quite contrary to the lurid impression that the papers had given of him, he was charming and rather shy. We sat in a coffee bar and discussed the play, which for once I had genuinely loved, and he agreed to let me do it. I suppose it was his only chance so he took it.

For a while he made some radical alterations to the script, notably condensing it from three acts to two. I would visit him in his Islington flat to discuss the changes while his frankly terrifying companion, Kenneth Halliwell, sat like a bloated spider in the corner.

My old friend the Lord Chamberlain had made some pretty savage deletions, which I was determined to have reinstated. When I turned up at Lieutenant-Colonel Eric Penn's office his reaction was, 'Oh, not you again!' He capitulated pretty quickly. Joe was delighted.

I persuaded Julian Chagrin to play Truscott and he was quite hysterically funny, so funny that it was almost impossible to get through rehearsals. John and Ann Bloomfield designed the set that Joe wanted and the show was a success. A couple of critics from London came up and gave it good reviews. Everyone was pleased.

In truth it couldn't have been that good. I realised the play was in part a satire on the police force, but I had no idea about its sexual content. In spite of my adventure with John Dexter, I didn't really understand the bisexual nature of the two boys, Hal and Dennis. I had cast Michael Elwyn and Peter Childs in the roles, who were as resolutely heterosexual as could be. When I came to do the play again decades later with Derek Griffiths as Truscott, I was mortified at what I had missed in 1966. It is sobering what directors can get away with.

Never mind, Oscar Lewenstein decided to take it to the West End. The problem was that because of the controversy that had dogged its original production, no theatre would risk it. As it was reported to me by Lewenstein, Charles Marowitz at the Jeanetta Cochrane would chance it but only if he could direct it. That may just have been an excuse but I knew Joe was happy to go with me. I was young and naïve, so I readily relinquished my rights in the play's future. The rest is history. *Loot* was a big West End hit and a brilliant play was saved from oblivion. I am pleased I was the one who saved it initially, and it was the first feather in the cap of Century nationally.

Now we began to rehearse for the Blue Box tour. I have no intention of going into detail about the productions. They may or may not have been good but I was learning my craft at a rate of knots. I suspect my direction was a little bit pedestrian but perfectly adequate. If anyone said that about me now I'd go and shoot myself.

Those six months on the road were thrilling. Playing to audiences who were effectively theatre virgins was electrifying. On the first night, in Burnley, of the Ionesco–Pinter double bill, the audience refused to leave the auditorium. They had been captivated, especially by *The Chairs*, and they wanted to talk about it, to know what it meant. When I asked them to tell the story as they had seen it on stage, it became clear that they had understood it perfectly, they just hadn't trusted themselves with such an alien style of theatre. For three weeks we became a focal point of the community. Later that year the local council decided to fund a brass band rather than have us back for another year. We knew nothing of this but sitting in our digs in Manchester, we switched on the ITV national news to see crowds marching through the streets of Burnley waving placards saying 'Bring back Century'. Neighbouring Nelson and Colne stepped in and booked us instead. To have an audience that affected by theatre – unforgettable.

In Rawtenstall at a performance of *Private Lives* I was taken aback to see a party of Lascar seamen entering the auditorium. Downtown Rawtenstall was not noted for its nightlife and the seamen had thought we were a cinema. They were stunned when the curtain went up and they were confronted with their first live theatre show and Noël Coward at that. One of them could speak English and he began a running translation, not particularly quietly. The result was delayed reactive laughter, which made it very hard for the actors and indeed the native audience. That is what it was like: a raw immediate reaction quite other than the more conventional audience we were used to. We all loved that tour and worked very hard.

The last production to enter the repertoire was *Uncle Vanya*, which was due to open in Keswick. The final run-through was scheduled for the afternoon of the World Cup Final. Given my love of football, you will realise how committed I was when I tell you I refused to cancel the run. Thus I missed one of the great events in English sporting history.

Once all the plays were in performance the rest of the summer was idyllic. The Lake District is one of the most beautiful places in the world and we were free to explore it and the many great restaurants it had then, and still does. The theatre was packed every night and the pleasure of working with a permanent company over such a long period was very rewarding. It's the first and last time I have had that luxury. But the year was nearly up. How was I going to put Century on the national map and how was I going to get Elliott and Wrede to work with me?

CHAPTER 14

The First Link

Michael Meyer triggered the solution. He suggested that since Elliott and Wrede showed no interest in coming to Manchester, I should invite their wives or friends to come and act there so they'd have to come up to see them. He thought that, for example, Dilys Hamlett would be interested in coming if the play was right. I for my part had realised the company that was playing in the Blue Box was not right for the University Theatre. They were a young company of necessity, and if we were doing, say, *Uncle Vanya*, Telyeghin would have to be played by a thirty-year-old in a wig and old make-up. That would not do in Manchester and if we were going to make our mark we would have to move the company up a notch.

I proposed to split Century in two, one company for touring, one for the Manchester University residency. My Board was dead against it. Not only would it be expensive and risky but I was accused of making Century 'too professional'. I went to see the Director of Drama at the Arts Council, Joe Hodgkinson. In those days the Arts Council was very informal, a long way from the bureaucratic nightmare it became. I was used to popping in to see 'Uncle Joe' who was a fan of mine. He had a place in the Lake District and liked what he had seen that summer. In those days you could say 'We're a bit short of money' and a cheque would arrive without any fuss. I explained the problem to Uncle Joe. 'Leave it to me,' he said. He attended the next Board meeting and said quite bluntly that if they didn't do what I wanted he would withdraw their funding.

In a fit of madness I had promised the Board that I would guarantee the season against losses, which might amount to £10,000. Between that and the Arts Council, the Board buckled. I should also add that the Chairman of the Board, Cecil Davies, backed me to the hilt. Heroes should be acknowledged.

When he heard of my guarantee Michael Meyer, with typical generosity, took over the pledge. We were set.

The season I chose was *Long Day's Journey into Night* by O'Neill and Michael's own play *The Ortolan*. Both were one-set plays and could cross-cast, so they were relatively cheap. The O'Neill I had seen at the Bristol Old

Vic while at school and it had been one of my great experiences. *The Ortolan* was more Ibsen than Ibsen and was a little thank you to Michael.

Dilys Hamlett agreed to play Mary Tyrone and the lead in *The Ortolan*. By making that act of faith she became the crucial link in the chain that finally brought about my dream. I was overwhelmed. I had seen her as Agnes in *Brand*, Solveig in *Peer Gynt*, in the West End in *A Passage to India* and now I was going to work with her.

By this time the company had found a base to live near the theatre. Called the Carousel Hotel, it was fairly basic but was run by two splendid ladies, Sheila and Joan, who made us feel at home. When we were at the University Theatre we practically took over the whole place. It was aptly called the 'Carousel' as the walls were paper thin and breakfast time was always interesting as people covered up or openly flaunted the events of the previous night.

I met Dilys the night before the first rehearsal and we struck up an instant rapport. She became my leading lady for many years. With her Garboesque beauty, her talent and her bravery she was one of the finest actresses I have ever worked with and one of the most interesting. She was also Casper Wrede's wife.

Derek Fowlds, he of *Heartbeat*, played Edmond and Helen Mirren made her professional début as the Maid. The problem was the actor playing Tyrone. This is a hard part to cast in any circumstances; at an unknown theatre in Manchester it was practically impossible. An agent I knew, Barry Cross, recommended his client Michael David. His CV was impressive. He had played Horatio to Paul Scofield's Hamlet and had been a leading man in various West End productions. What Barry had neglected to tell me was that he had become mentally ill during the break-up of his marriage and had had a lobotomy. This meant that he had no worries. Rehearsals were impossible. I was reduced to standing next to him on stage and forcing him to emote, move, shout – in short to act. I think it was the last time he appeared on stage and his mental state deteriorated thereafter. Nevertheless, with Dilys and Derek on fine form we got away with it and started to rehearse *The Ortolan*. I was totally exhausted. I had been doing nearly a play a month for a year and I had another very minor breakdown. Oh, and I got engaged again, this time to my Deputy Stage Manager, Stella Donelly. She was a delightful Irish lass who also doubled as a masseuse.

I recovered, *The Ortolan* went on and predictably did not draw an audience. Michael Meyer never told me how much of the guarantee he had to pay. The season had been an artistic success and we were beginning to establish ourselves properly in Manchester but to my, and Dilys's, chagrin Casper Wrede had not come up to see the production. The company disbanded, but then came a phone call from Dilys inviting me to come and have dinner to meet Casper at their home in Barnes. The next huge step was about to be taken. Since they're about to enter the story, this is the time to introduce the group I was so keen to work with.

CHAPTER 15
How the Group Came into Being

Casper Wrede was a Finnish baron – the seventh son of a Finnish baron. At fifteen he fought as a sergeant in the Finnish Army against the Russians. When he was eighteen he went to Oslo University in Norway, there he met Armund Höhningstadt. Höhningstadt, a much older man, became his mentor. These two extraordinary men formed an extraordinary relationship which will always be at the heart of what is now called the Royal Exchange Theatre Company.

Armund taught that just as every person is on an individuation process so is every race, every country, every continent and finally the whole world. To understand what state this process was in he had an astonishing knowledge of religions, myths, legends, folklore and art. He saw how mankind expressed its knowledge of the mysteries of our existence, how that understanding developed for the good or the bad, and therefore sought to understand the precise moment of that development so that it could be directed towards the good. He spoke of the gods, Christian, Jewish, Muslim, Greek, Norse, what you will, as if he were on nodding acquaintance with them. It was up to you whether you took them literally or as human projections.

He saw our civilisation as being at the end of a 2,000-year cycle spiritually. Each great religion, as it comes into being, has a profound effect on its time, taking mankind forward. Thus the Jewish religion with its belief in a single invisible God was replaced by Christianity with its revolutionary understanding of the higher ego, the concept of love and above all the existence of God in man: 'I am within you and without you.' No more the Jehovah God of 'thou shalt not' ruling through fear. Now mankind could be in charge of its own destiny.

Armund saw that the power of Christianity was now declining. That its hold as the spiritual regulator was weakening. That we were living in a time which would become increasingly degenerate as we lost all sense of that wise voice within which told us how to live. He saw all too clearly that time in which we now live.

He believed that as one spiritual impulse declined, another was being born: degeneration was always followed by regeneration. A Martian visiting Britain in February would see a grey, barren land. If you told him that within three months, trees, flowers, the sky, everything would be transformed he would ask, 'But where is all this going to come from?' The answer would be that it is already happening, under the earth. And so it is in February, the activity under the ground is phenomenal, preparing for spring. Then when it comes to fruition it does so suddenly and dramatically.

Imagine the Roman occupation of Jerusalem. If you had said to this wretched people ruled over by an omnipotent foreign power that in ten years' time they'd all be gone and a whole new concept of religion would spread like wildfire across the known world, they'd have laughed. Yet that is what happened. It is difficult to grasp the sudden explosion of Christianity in an age when there was no television, no media of any kind.

Armund taught that this was where we now stood. We could not see what was to come but we could be sure that it would come. Our job was to hold on to all that remained powerful and positive from the declining civilisation, to keep the ground fertile for the new impulse when it came.

This is, of course, a simplification of his teaching. It was supported in extraordinary detail by his analysis of mankind and his gods throughout history.

What Casper wanted to know was what he should do, what anyone could do, to further this end. Armund's reply was astonishing. The power to change things lies in everyone and rarely in so-called leaders in the political world. Politicians follow what is actually taking place, they maintain power by gauging what the *Zeitgeist* demands. The people who have always led have been the artists. They have been the visionaries and, through their art, have directly influenced the hearts and minds of civilisations. In our time one art form was more important than any other: the theatre. With the decline of religion, theatre was the only place where people came together in a community and experienced the mysteries. He invoked the memory of the ancient Greek drama festival when, for three weeks, the entire population of Athens, including the slaves, sat in the theatre from sunrise to sunset because they knew that the greatest minds of their time would lay before them, through the stories of their people, their understanding of the titanic problems that we all face in our lives.

The two men, who knew nothing of the theatrical world, did their research. England was the centre of world drama. Casper must go and study theatre in England. The most famous theatre in England was the Old Vic and by chance the great French director Michel Saint-Denis ran a school there for just three years. Casper applied and was granted a place on that course.

It was packed with people who would form the nucleus of the group who worked together for years and finally found a permanent home at the Royal Exchange. They included Richard Negri, the inspired artist who designed the Royal Exchange, Litz Pisk (movement director) who together with George Hall (composer) ran the golden days of the Central School, and the actors and actresses: Dilys Hamlett who married Casper, Avril Elgar who married James Maxwell, who later became an Artistic Director of the Company, Rosalind Knight who married the as yet unknown to the group Michael Elliott, Eric Thompson, Phyllida Law and so on and so on.

Saint-Denis's theatrical style perfectly expressed Casper's spiritual aims. Such was the ethos of those three years that, in 1956 when they left, they founded a small company called the Piccolo Theatre based in, of all places, Chorlton-cum-Hardy in the suburbs of Manchester. The company was run on a shoestring and survived only one season.

In those days the OUDS or even college productions at Oxford regularly employed professional directors for undergraduate performances. Casper directed *Hippolytus*, where he met Jack Good of rock 'n' roll fame and, more significantly, indeed crucially, a new play by Michael Meyer, that same *The Ortolan*, at the Oxford Playhouse, which had in its cast the young Maggie Smith. After one performance, a long thin undergraduate with a piercing nose and ears like a radar system sought him out. He had been mightily impressed by the production, declared that he wanted to be a director and wished to work with Casper. This was Michael Elliott, and so the dynamic relationship that was to propel the group on to the national scene was formed.

In those days there was no National Theatre and the RSC was confined to Stratford, where it produced Shakespeare exclusively. There was no outlet for European drama in London. Casper decided to launch a new company to correct that lack. With the help of Laurence Harbottle, the theatre lawyer and champion, he raised the money from a businessman, James Lorrie, and in 1959 the 59 Theatre Company was launched at the Lyric Hammersmith. It presented *Danton's Death* by Büchner, translated by James Maxwell, Strindberg's *The Creditors* and Ibsen's *Brand* both translated by Michael Meyer. It also gave the world première of Alun Owen's *The Rough and Ready Lot*. The following year it showed James Maxwell and Dilys Hamlett in *Little Eyolf*. Casper was the Artistic Director, Michael the Associate Artistic Director, Richard Negri the designer, the actors from the Old Vic School were the nucleus of the company and there were notable additions in the shape of Richard Pilbrow as Lighting Designer and Ronald Harwood as an ASM.

The season was an enormous success but the company had no subsidy and so it too had to disband. Casper and Michael formed a formidable partnership in television. Their reputation grew so that when Michael was asked to become Artistic Director of the Old Vic in 1961, he invited Casper to join him as Associate Artistic Director and the group, including Litz Pisk and George Hall, re-formed, strengthened by new blood: Leo McKern, Catherine Lacey, Lee Montague, Fulton Mackay and, making his acting début, Trevor Peacock. Once again the season was a success with Michael's production of *Peer Gynt* with Leo McKern (and Wilfrid Lawson as the Button Moulder) the high spot.

For the third time the company was short-lived, this time because the National Theatre was formed by Laurence Olivier, and while its new theatre on the South Bank was being created, it took up residency at the Old Vic. Once again the group disbanded. This time it would have to wait eight years before its next and rather more permanent incarnation. However, the inspiration and ideals of Armund were now firmly fixed in a wide band of artists. George Hall and Litz Pisk went on to run the Central School of Speech and Drama, and Richard Negri became Head of the Theatre Department at the Wimbledon School of Art. A new generation of artists would have these ideals handed on. Casper went into movies and Michael became one of the most respected theatre directors of his generation. Both men continued to work in television and Ronnie Harwood left stage management for a distinguished career as a writer. Richard Pilbrow founded Theatre Projects and became not only a pre-eminent lighting designer but the world's leading theatre consultant. Jack Good brought rock 'n' roll to Britain and Eric Thompson became famous for *The Magic Roundabout*. All the actors found their careers blossoming and their reputations enhanced. The group was lying fallow but it was gaining strength for the next phase.

CHAPTER 16

First Meetings at Last

He didn't come to see *Long Day's Journey* but I was invited to their elegant home in Barnes to have dinner with Dilys and Casper Wrede.

In his youth Casper had been the archetypal northern European. He was slim, blond, his good looks were almost feminine and he had been a sprinter for Finland. When I met him in his late thirties he had broadened and his hair had darkened but he still had an aristocratically imposing face. They were a handsome couple. He had a total grasp of English, albeit heavily accented. His voice was high-pitched, almost strangulated, and he had a habit of pausing during sentences, emitting a hint of tortured 'emem' noise and peppering, and even disconcertingly suddenly ending, his pronouncements with the phrase 'You know . . .'. Frequently people didn't know and were baffled by what he was actually trying to convey. This meant he was the despair of some actors who could never understand him but beloved of others who could follow his often inspired pronouncements. Once I remember him having a conversation with Michael Elliott which perfectly illustrates what I mean. Michael had asked him what he thought of Alexander Knox for the lead in *When We Dead Awaken*. 'Yes . . . it's . . . emem . . . you know . . . very . . . emem . . . a bit like that when he . . . you know . . . but then it can be absolutely . . . you know . . .' Michael leant forward. 'Could you say a bit more, Casper, I don't quite understand.' Gigantic pause and we both awaited elucidation. Then, 'No, no, I'm quite wrong!'

Anyway, this was my first encounter with him and the evening passed pleasantly enough. He asked about my plays. I told him I was doing *Charley's Aunt* next, but I had lost my Fancourt-Babberley as Julian Chagrin, who was to have played it, had had to withdraw. At about eleven o'clock I prepared to take my leave. Casper insisted we have a cup of tea first. I demurred. He insisted. We had tea. The conversation – I now realise deliberately – turned to religion. This was the first serious topic of the evening.

It ended in a furious row. Having rejected Judaism, I had turned against all the Western religions. They seemed to me simplistic and narrow, especially the idea of the God portrayed in Christian religious paintings of an old man with a white beard. I was more attracted to the Greek gods, the Norse gods, the Yoruba gods and indeed Buddhism. Casper insisted that all these different gods including Jehovah, God the Father and Allah were real. I insisted they were not. Casper became very angry. To him it was crucial that we realised there was something outside us, an otherness. I had no difficulty with that but I held that it made no difference, whether one believed it or not, as to how one should behave as a human being. Finally mustering his considerable powers of forcefulness he thundered, 'You are young! You are ignorant! And you are wrong!'

I shouted back, 'You are old! You are ignorant! And you are wrong!' The evening was at an end. I departed and drove back to Golders Green.

The next morning the phone rang very early. 'Casper here. You are doing *Charley's Aunt*. How would you like to have Tom Courtenay as Lord Fancourt-Babberley?' Tom *Billy Liar*, *The Loneliness of the Long Distance Runner*, *Dr Zhivago* Courtenay? If only . . .

'Yes.' I laughed. 'Great.'

'Be at the Savile Club at one o'clock. That'll be fine.'

Completely bemused, I went to the Savile Club as directed, and there were Casper and Tom Courtenay, and he seemed eager to come to this little-known company, playing in a backstreet theatre in Manchester, and be in *Charley's Aunt*. After leaving RADA, taking over from Albert Finney in the West End run of *Billy Liar* had catapulted him into the movies, but his ambition was to be a proper stage actor and this role was just what he wanted.

This astonished me then and still astonishes me now, but less so as I have come to work with him and know him over the years. The actor is the one being theatre cannot do without, because without the actor nothing can happen. Everyone else is dispensable, even directors (!) and writers because the actor can improvise. The actor is the high priest who transmits the mystery to the congregation. He is the storyteller. If the theatre has the power to stir people's hearts for good, it is the actor who has the potential to be a force for good. The actor is an artist but, unlike the painter, the composer, the writer, he must practise his art in public. Unlike other artists, he faces great temptations. Ours is a profession split between an art form and the entertainment industry. There is little money to be made from theatre unless you are starring in the West End; there is a great deal of money to be made in the movies and TV. An actor's idealism is sorely tried and very few can resist the lure of big money, even when it means taking on roles that are the very opposite of nourishing or important. Ideally an actor should be as dedicated as any other artist. Only that way can he develop and fulfil his artistry. To be a great actor one must also be a considerable human being. Tom Courtenay is almost unique in my experience in his integrity and his determination to do that which fulfils his talent. He has continually faced the temptation to opt for the easy life: he has never yielded to it.

The public didn't believe that Tom Courtenay was coming to the University Theatre. 'Is he any relation to THE Tom Courtenay?' the box office was continually asked. Once they were convinced, the show was immediately sold out.

Manchester was becoming a better place to be, especially gastronomically. It had been a gourmet desert but one night down an unprepossessing side street called Bloom Street, Michael Elwyn, Peter Childs and I had seen a sign saying Shish Kebab House. We descended to the basement and there was an exotic room, like a black silk tent, with tapestries on the wall, glamorous lighting, music and of course the smells. Here we sampled the most stunning Middle Eastern food I have ever tasted. It turned out to be an Armenian restaurant, presided over by the larger-than-life figure of George Mardorossian, with his wife, mother and brother-in-law. It became known to us as 'George's' and was a haven which become the Century Theatre's club. Later Michael Meyer came to eat there, it appeared in *The Good Food Guide*, made George a deal of money, so he relocated to Didsbury, buying a hotel and re-creating the same amazing atmosphere. Until 1978, when he left for the sun and relaxed tax regime of Arizona, he played host to countless companies. There has never been his like again.

Century Theatre was a very humble company. There was no such thing as a casting director. You auditioned those who had written to you, phoned imploringly to agents and cobbled together such casts as you were able to. Tom seemed not to mind this a bit. Indeed, he brought with him that fine character actor Jimmy Cossins and besides, Helen Mirren had stayed on to play Kitty and cause havoc among the male members of the cast. I was back with Jasmina and just managed to stay out of the fray. Tom was absolutely superb as the Lord; the show went well. Century Theatre was now on the national map and Tom said he would like to come back to work with the company again.

As far as I remember Casper didn't come to see this production either. With hindsight he must have been monitoring me deliberately from afar to have some idea of what consciously or unconsciously I was really about. First Michael Meyer, then Dilys and now Tom had been the scouts. There was to be one more before the next and defining stage was reached.

CHAPTER 17

'I Am a Jew'

It's said that a man's life goes in eight-year cycles and certainly 1967, when I was twenty-four, was the beginning of a new cycle. I had decided to start the year at the University Theatre with *The Merchant of Venice*, for the simple reason that it was on the O-level syllabus and that meant full houses. Dilys agreed to come back to play Portia, Helen Mirren to play Nerissa and, prompted by Michael Meyer, I asked James Maxwell to play Shylock and prompted, I suspect, by Casper, he accepted.

Max, as everyone called him, was in fact an American. His father was a distinguished professor at Clarke University. Years later when he played Big Daddy in *Cat on a Hot Tin Roof*, the *Sunday Times* in a favourable review called him 'that most English of actors'. He had disliked America, disliked academia and had fled to England, where he had indeed become as apparently English as you could imagine. He had a deep, melodious, refined baritone voice, ideally suited to the classics and, after his time at the Old Vic Theatre School, he had made a fine career both on stage and television. He was possessed of a very active mind and an encyclopaedic knowledge of literature and music, which he disguised behind a languid and tolerant drawl that put everyone at their ease. Unlike Casper, whose fault was that he knew he was always right, Max gave the impression that he wasn't sure of anything much. This was, I think, to cover up an impatience with lesser mortals, which he disliked in himself, and a terrifying temper which, thank goodness, I only saw at full blast on a few occasions and only once was the object of. He was easily the match of Casper and Michael intellectually, but he was first and foremost an actor. He loved acting, he loved actors and in the group he was the guardian of acting against the tyranny of direction.

I still directed entirely by intuition and instinct. Since my background obviously made me very sensitive to the Jewish side of the play, I got on very well with Max. I had one insight born out of Nevill Coghill's advice, and that was about the fifth act of the play, in which Shylock does not appear and which is set in Portia's Belmont and concerns itself entirely with the future of the three sets of lovers after the traumas of the trial.

This act is often seen as anti-climactic but I realised that it was, for Shakespeare, the climax of the play. One evening after rehearsing it I returned to the Carousel Hotel and Max was there. He told me he had slipped in to watch me and thought it was going very well. 'After all, it's a cardinal cross play,' he said. I asked what he meant. He explained, 'Aries, Libra, Capricorn, Cancer. Portia is Aries; Bassanio: Libra; Antonio: Capricorn; Shylock: Cancer.' I had had one brush with astrology in my life when I was threatening to leave Oxford in my second year. My mother had, in desperation, paid to have my horoscope read by Katrina who did the daily horoscopes in the *Evening Standard*. Her reading was to the point, 'You are thinking of making a big change but it seems very ill-advised. The course you are already embarked on will in the long run be very important to you.' I had been momentarily stunned, then inspiration struck me. 'How much did my mother pay you to say that?' I asked. Katrina confessed; so much for astrology. Now here was this erudite man spouting the same kind of babble.

When I asked him what he meant, he explained the chief characteristics of the signs and in so doing he gave me an extraordinary analysis of the inner workings of the play. I pressed him further. He explained that at one time the finest minds of the Chaldaeans analysed the world through astrological symbols. The twelve houses were archetypes and all great plays were archetypal, therefore they were subject to this kind of analysis. Later that year, when I was preparing *Romeo and Juliet*, I asked him to give me the astrological breakdown of the play in the hope it might save me study time. He said that too was a cardinal cross play. Romeo is Aries, 'More like the lightning which doth cease to be ere one can say it lightens'; Juliet: Libra, 'The orchard wall is high and hard to climb'; the Friar: Capricorn, with his spiritual aspirations; and the Nurse, the earth mother, Cancer. Many, many years later when I did *Othello* I remembered that he had said Othello and Iago were the higher and lower levels of Scorpio, Othello the eagle and Iago the scorpion; while Desdemona and Emilia were Taurus, 'I nothing but to please your fantasy'. Both these interpretations were devastatingly accurate. Pragmatically I had now to take astrology seriously however much I resisted the idea.

The other moment I remember, also guided by Coghill, was when Shylock is asked by the Doge if he accepts that he must become a Christian. Shylock replies, 'I am content.' Coghill had taught that Shakespeare always means what he says. If Shylock says 'I am content' he means it, however unpalatable that might seem to a modern audience. Max agreed and that's the way he played it.

Now it almost doesn't matter if the production was good or bad – Max and Dilys were outstanding – what matters is what happened when I came to see it a week after it opened. Up to a first night, a director is so fired up with excitement and fear, so determined to will the show to success, that he can't always see objectively what he is doing. It's why it's good to have someone you can trust watch a late run to give advice. After a first night the adrenalin goes and a director can feel completely cold about the production, as if he's disconnected from it. That is why some directors, certainly me, find going back to see it again almost distasteful, like a lover when the passion has cooled.

I dutifully but reluctantly went back to see *The Merchant* in the second week of the run, completely unprepared for the revelatory experience that was waiting for me. The play was about me! It was about my Jewishness, my emotional and cultural difference from the society in which I lived, and about the importance of love. It seems blindingly obvious now, but I realised then that plays have a meaning; that the choice of plays and how they are cast, designed and directed are critical to that meaning being formed, and that I as a director was always expressing myself in my work.

This was the dawning of real consciousness. Henceforth my attitude to directing was completely changed. Eventually that would bring rewards but initially it also brought about a self-consciousness that could be hampering. Casper had said – which I hadn't fully understood – that one could only express in one's work what one had lived through and resolved in one's life. That now became a terrifying challenge. I had bulldozed my way through my private life; I hadn't resolved anything. Finally Max had said that the play was about the opposition of the Old and New Testaments. When Shylock said 'I am content', what he meant was that he had received a mercy from Portia that he had no right to expect by the Old Testament code; I needed to read the Bible. I needed to understand.

At last Casper and Michael Elliott came to see my production. I didn't know they were coming and I wasn't there. I received a phone call at the Carousel Hotel: 'Casper here. When are you coming to London?'

'Tomorrow.'

'Come directly to Barnes. We'll expect you at ten o'clock.'

I was on a very early train.

CHAPTER 18

Accepted

The meeting started at 10 a.m. and went on into the night, with no break for food. As I recall I hardly said a thing throughout. Casper did most of the talking but Michael was potently present. It was my first real encounter with him. His father was Canon Elliott, the famous wartime preacher who had people queuing round the block to attend his church, St Michael's in Chester Square. He was a charismatic, inspiring man with great oratorical gifts. He was also someone addicted to power and towards the end of his life became mentally unbalanced. Michael had inherited all the positive features of his father and was scared of inheriting the negative side. He combined the presence of an archangel with what people called an extraordinary 'bedside manner' so that when he fixed on you, you were made to feel very special. When you crossed him he had a ruthlessness that was breathtaking.

So this Anglo-Scot and this Finn told this Jew that they were prepared to accept him as a colleague. They said they would unofficially work alongside me in Manchester, helping to form policy and choose seasons. It was like Arsene Wenger and José Mourinho offering to work with some rookie manager at Accrington Stanley. They seemed old to me but they were young men in their mid- to late thirties who, particularly in Michael's case, could have chosen to work at or run practically any theatre in the land.

I had planned the spring season at the University Theatre; they had already thought about the autumn and winter. Michael wanted to direct *The Playboy of the Western World* with Tom; Casper wanted me to read a new play by a writer he was championing, Gerard McLarnon, called *The Saviour*; and it was suggested that I do *Romeo and Juliet* with Tom as Romeo. I had promised to put Century on to the national map and this ensured that it would be.

Why did they take this huge step? Ever since the end of the Old Vic season they had harboured the dream of coming together again somehow and their disillusionment with the established theatrical scene meant that, despite the many offers that Michael had had, they didn't want to work in London. I was a kind of unconscious messenger.

There was a very important added attraction. They were opposed to the proscenium arch. When the Romans separated the audience from the actors and confined the drama (or the gladiators) to a slit at the end of the room for us to peer at, they cut off the participating relationship of the audience. The Elizabethans restored it, but only for a short time. To them the proscenium arch was dead. Richard Negri, who had designed *Brand*, now ran the design course at the Wimbledon School of Art, and with him they were experimenting with different theatre forms. Lo and behold I was running a company in a completely adaptable theatre, suitable for all kinds of staging.

This was the outer layer of the meeting and could have been dealt with in an hour or two. The kernel was talking about what they believed in. The content was much as I have outlined in my chapter on the group but they expanded it and explained the type of plays, actors, people in every aspect of the theatre they wanted to work with and, equally to the point, those they wanted to avoid like the plague. They had a totally inspiring messianic zeal and it reached into every part of me. I had finally found my family. In theatrical terms I was now about seven years old. I began to understand the level of commitment it would take to be a really good director. I realised how unconscious I had been of what I was doing and that if I were to earn the right to have a meaningful career as a director, everything from choice of play to casting, design and staging would have to be subjected to a rigorous discipline so that the audience could be properly nourished.

It was difficult to believe that only a couple of months ago I had sat in this very house and told Casper, 'You are old. You are ignorant and you are wrong.' I had now to endure for many years to come what any child with remarkable parents does. I accepted everything they said as gospel. It was a long time before I became my own person again. Naturally I wasn't aware of this at the time and I haven't regretted it since. That was how it had to be.

They were as good as their word and we met frequently in Barnes or at Michael's flat in Compayne Gardens, West Hampstead. We were a family. I went back to being the listening child of my youth.

CHAPTER 19

The Last Century

Before our first season working together there was the small matter of the spring at the University Theatre which coincided with the second tour of the Blue Box.

The Blue Box tour was still pretty ambitious: *The Rivals*, *The Importance of Being Earnest*, *Who's Afraid of Virginia Woolf?*, *Waiting for Godot*, *Little Malcolm and His Struggle Against the Eunuchs* and *The Lady from the Sea*. I had to find directors for everything but *Little Malcolm* because I was doing both productions in Manchester. The standard remained high and James Maxwell cut his directing teeth with the Ibsen.

In Manchester, Dilys came back again to do *Private Lives* with Francis Matthews and I had my first encounter with *Waiting for Godot*. The phone rang. 'Casper here. That . . . er . . . you know . . . in *Godot* . . . em . . . Estragon. There is a wonderful actor, Trevor Peacock. You should have him.' Three times couldn't be a coincidence. He came and we have been best friends ever since.

My second *Private Lives* built on my first, played à la Strindberg and therefore very funny and *Godot*, with Anton Rodgers partnering Trevor and Wolfe Morris as Pozzo with Derek Fowlds as Lucky, was a peculiar triumph. It was peculiar because none of us had any idea how to do it. We persevered day after bemusing day, trying to be sensitive to the play's music but, inside, becoming increasingly desperate. Then suddenly, at the dress rehearsal, something clicked and the production took off. Just when I was trying to apply myself to directing more consciously, I had to put all that aside and rely unconsciously on intuition. There are no rules.

The wear and tear of directing two plays, as well as producing the beginning of the Blue Box season, was too much and Casper and Dilys nursed me through another minor collapse. I was still blundering through life seeing nothing but theatre. The sixties were now nearly over and I had hardly noticed it. When I read about that time and look at the pictures, it is a foreign country to me. I had substituted the theatre for life. It is a very natural thing to do. The plays are about the great issues of living, so that it is easy to think you are living life to the full, simply by doing them. It is a dangerous illusion. It certainly stunted my real growth.

Jasmina was in the company in Keswick when I directed *Little Malcolm*. It was our last attempt to make our incomprehensible relationship work. Desperate not to end it, I suggested we become engaged and then we would have to solve it. Sensibly she declined. She was right, four engagements one on top of another would have been a little much. We finally parted. It was the portcullis effect in spades.

There were rumblings too from the Board of Century Theatre. Many of the directors had been founders of the theatre and they had fond memories of the early days of camaraderie, driving trucks, putting up the theatre, everybody helping everyone else. They accused me of making the company too professional and they were particularly worried about using actors such as Tom Courtenay. This was not in the spirit of Century Theatre. I contacted Joe Hodgkinson at the Arts Council and told him what was going on. Again he came to a Board meeting and told the members to back me or they'd have their grant withdrawn. They accepted the ultimatum and I was allowed to continue, but the discontent was obvious and wouldn't go away.

They could not have been happy with the first of three productions in which Michael and Casper were unofficially involved. Gerard McLarnon, whose play *The Saviour* I was to direct, had had a chequered career. His play about the Troubles in Belfast, *The Bonefire*, had been directed by Tyrone Guthrie and created massive controversy in Ireland, then John Blatchley had directed *Unhallowed*, which was a success. Laurence Olivier Productions then presented *The Mcrory Whirl* in the West End. The critics were outraged by what they saw as its obscenity, and LOP publicly apologised for it and withdrew it immediately. Gerry, nearly twice my age, had like me been bowled over by *Brand* and got to know the group as a result. He was like a good-looking, nay striking, Irish version of Hugh Griffiths with a dramatic nose and piercing eyes. As we got to know each other he became like an elder brother and I became his main director.

The Saviour was set on a remote island where a suspect brotherhood had a community centred on what, on the insistence of the Lord Chamberlain, was a deconsecrated church. The action of the play took place after the bombs had dropped, and a group of shipwrecked representatives of the aristocracy and ruling class of England had fetched up there. It was a relentless attack on the English Establishment and the sixties generation that had rebelled against them. Gerry saw both parties as different sides of the same corrupt coin. He was, of course, right and we are living with that legacy. At the time he managed to alienate almost every faction of the audience and the critics, with the honourable exception of Ian Watson in

78

Plays and Players, panned it. The auditorium was horribly empty night after night.

The cast were momentarily shaken by the ferocity of the reception but rallied to give defiantly committed performances for the run. I remain proud of having directed it. I wonder what the reaction would be now.

The production was also important to me because it introduced me to the person who in the fullness of time would be responsible for the biggest revolution in my private emotional life. Casper had discovered a designer at the Wimbledon School of Art whose career he wanted to further. Johanna Bryant was a tall blonde, with a beautiful open face and an infectious laugh who immediately became, and still is forty years later, my main designer.

The director–designer relationship is of crucial importance. By the time rehearsals start they have worked together for months, translating into physical reality the ideas and passions that will motivate the production. Ideally your designer has the same world-view as you and a complementary theatricality. Most directors are allied to one special designer, and a trust and shorthand build up over the years. Johanna was and is that person for me.

She designed the next production for Michael Elliott, *The Playboy of the Western World*. This had the best Christy Mahon, Pegeen Mike and Widow Quinn I have ever seen in Tom Courtenay, Bridget Turner and Dilys Hamlett, but partly because of some erratic casting in the minor roles it never quite gained the power that I was expecting from the director of *Brand* and *Peer Gynt*. Nevertheless it firmly cemented the company as of national interest.

Now everything came together at once. Michael and Casper decided it was their moment to come back into the arena publicly. The Board of Century had had enough of me. Hugh Hunt, fed up with Century's attitude and impressed with our achievement, invited us to form a new company to be resident at the University Theatre and gave Century notice to quit.

There was one last production for Century Theatre: *Romeo and Juliet*. Several events that took place during the rehearsal and playing period were probably more important than the production itself.

Although I had calmed down as a director, I was still a martinet. Discipline, I had learnt from Dexter and Dews, was important. If an actor was late for rehearsal, I would call a halt and berate him or her in front of the whole company. Berate is perhaps too mild a word – I'd tear them to pieces.

In the second week of rehearsal Bridget Turner, who was playing Juliet, was late. Everyone knew that she and I were great chums and it was clear that they were all on tenterhooks wondering if she was going to get the treatment. She wasn't just late, she was very late, she was over twenty minutes late, and realising that I would lose face if I didn't treat her as I had treated the others, I prepared for my onslaught.

Eventually she came through the door. 'Stop the rehearsal,' I said sternly. Everyone was silent.

Before I could launch into my tirade, Bridget spoke: 'Braham, I know I'm late. I am mortified at being late. If you shout at me I won't be fit to rehearse and we will waste the rest of the session.' I was dumbfounded. Of course she was right but until that moment I had never really considered what an actor might be feeling and that it might help or hinder the creative process. An actor was there to carry out the director's will and that was that. At least I now understood that an unhappy actor might not work as well as a happy one. It was a step in the right direction.

The next thing was that my stepsister Irene, whom I had not seen for a long time, interrupted rehearsals to tell me that my father had died. At a Jewish funeral the son must say Kaddish (the mourner's prayer) for his father. The funeral was the next day; I had to be there. I had had barely any relationship with my father for many years but this seemed an imperative. I took half a day off, grudgingly.

First I had to go to the flat where he lived, to see the coffin before it went to the grounds. Women do not go to the burial, they stay and prepare the food and drink for the mourners. The coffin leaving the flat was their farewell. As I entered I was introduced to the rabbi, who shook my hand warmly and cut off my tie from the knot. I was put out: it was my best tie. I remonstrated but apparently it was symbolic of the rending of the garments. The coffin was carried out amid very un-European scenes of wailing and women hurling themselves on it to say goodbye. We rode to the burial grounds at Bushey.

Apparently the son has to wheel the coffin to the place of burial. It was like being part of an avant-garde French film. Looking over my shoulder I saw, to my amazement, what appeared to be the mourners playing some form of Grandmother's Footsteps. It was later explained to me that whoever was nearest to the coffin would be the next to go. Finally the coffin was laid to rest but the surreal farce wasn't over. The grave was to be filled by the mourners. Unsuitably portly businessmen huffed and puffed until the job was done.

Afterwards, back at the flat, the ritual of sitting shivah was begun. For seven days the close relatives sit on chairs with cut-off legs and are visited by friends and relations to be given comfort. All the mirrors are covered to prevent anyone seeing the reflection of evil spirits and the mourners must not wear anything that could have come from a living creature, for instance leather shoes. I lasted one night and never came back.

The connection with the final acts of *Romeo and Juliet* are obvious and the production was fed with the experience. What was distressing for me personally was my complete lack of distress. This was my father but I didn't feel a thing; this was death but I didn't feel a thing. All I felt was a further alienation from my heritage. The desire to escape into theatre became even stronger.

The final incident happened during the run of the play. It was a Wednesday, a matinée day. The phone rang. It was an extremely hoarse Tom, barely able to speak. He'd lost his voice. He couldn't appear. There was only one solution other than lose the show and the box-office income, so I took it. First I put on the green tights, then I summoned the cast so that they could get over their laughter. I was going to play Romeo. I had had to stand in for sick actors before, notably for Michael Elwyn when I had to give my Elyot Chase in *Private Lives* for a week, which must have been a bizarre experience for cast and audience alike. But this was different.

The performance was a waking nightmare. Although I, of course, knew the play very well, I had to carry the script. The first obstacle was the wall. It was described in the text as 'high and hard to climb', and so, in Johanna's design, it was. Tom had balked at it and I had goaded him until he had reluctantly agreed to master it. I was 'hoist by my own petard'. Carrying the script and granted my physical ineptitude, it seemed to take for ever to get over. Eventually I arrived on the ground, bruised and grazed, to play one of the greatest love scenes ever written. Finally I settled down. During the scene Juliet is called inside and Romeo has a short soliloquy, 'O blessed, blessed night'. This I knew, so I abandoned the book and delivered the soliloquy with as much passion as I could muster. Then I heard Juliet's voice, 'At what o'clock tomorrow shall I send?' I hadn't a clue and in the dimly lit scene it was very difficult to find my place again. By the time I had and answered 'By four of the clock', the audience, who were being kind, were mercifully trying to stifle their giggles. On we went to the fight scene. Being the Gloucestershire nearly Junior Foil Champion, I had arranged the fights myself so I knew they should be no problem. They wouldn't have been if I had secured my tights properly. Trying to look dashing while desperately attempting to prevent your tights from falling to the ground is not easy. I failed. On the play went until the scene where Romeo, having spent the night with Juliet, has to leave with the dawn. I had set this on a high level and had persuaded Tom to jump lithely down, before doing a long exit off the thrust stage and through the audience as Juliet watches him. I jumped, sprained my ankle and the long exit became even longer as I limped miserably off.

The final blow came after it was all over. Ian McKellen had come from London to see Tom's Romeo and he had caught mine instead. To this day, whenever I bump into him he puts his hand on my shoulder and whispers in my ear, 'Saw your Romeo.'

That afternoon was another step forward in my education as a director. I had caught a glimpse of the negative side of what it could be like to be an actor. I began to adapt my rehearsal style, not just to make the actors happy as Bridget had taught me, but to understand what they might need. It was still a long way away from what I now think a director should be but it was a beginning.

What of the production itself? I think it had the virtue of clarity and was probably richer than my past attempts at Shakespeare but, although I had been thrilled by Zeffirelli's great productions at the Old Vic, it was too conventional and it fatally lacked the right spark at the centre.

In my state of strange emotional detachment I had not paid any attention to the necessary chemistry between the two lovers. I had never experienced love at first sight, the *coup de foudre*; my relationships had been like Romeo's love for Rosaline. I had never felt that madness that rates the loved one more important than death. *Romeo and Juliet*, although one of Shakespeare's most popular plays, is hard to pull off. How many times have you seen that kind of chemistry on the stage? Even in the movies it is rare and when it does happen the film becomes a classic like *Casablanca*. Indeed, it wasn't until a recent production by my son at the Exchange with Andrew Garfield and Gugu Mbatha-Raw that I had seen the play really work. That is why, if you trawl through reviews of the play, you will find it has hardly ever been successful. Get that right and you're home and dry, get it wrong and however good everything else is you won't succeed. In Tom and Bridget I had two wonderful actors and wonderful they were, except in that one aspect, the crucial one. Not their fault, my fault; an example of how one's life influences one's work.

Despite all this the theatre was packed, the audiences appreciative and I left the company on a high note. I shall always be grateful to Century. I think we used each other to our mutual benefit. I began to learn my craft and they gained a reputation that solidified at the Dukes in Lancaster and later, when the old Blue Box finally ground to a halt, at the Theatre by the Lake in Keswick. But that was over and my real dream was about to be realised.

CHAPTER 20

The New Group

Years later I asked Casper why on earth they had agreed to work with me. I was young, volatile, arrogant and pretty inexperienced. His answer was simple: 'Well, my dear, you know . . . you were knocking on the door so hard that if we hadn't opened it you would have knocked it down.'

Their proposition to me was simple: if I would be the front man in Manchester they would set about forming what they wanted to call the 69 Theatre Company, to preserve the continuity of the group. It is a measure of the austere nature of my new colleagues that they looked completely blank when I laughed at the name by suggesting that it would be remembered at very particular moments in people's lives and in very strange positions.

The externals of what then happened are easier to describe than the internals. They set about the task with great energy. Michael, who was on the Arts Council, persuaded them to subsidise the company as a bridgehead, the goal being to have a major theatre company in Manchester. This is no insult to the Library Theatre, which has only 300 seats. They asked Laurence Harbottle, the theatre lawyer, to be the first Chairman. This remarkable, urbane, dry, kind, witty man loved the theatre and devoted, indeed still does devote, much of his time to unremunerated services to companies or projects he believes in. It was he who had been instrumental in funding the 59 Theatre Company by introducing Casper to the business-man James Lorrie. It was an excellent choice and he was an excellent Chairman, unobtrusive, masterly at handling a Board and always supportive. I brought in my old Oxford friend Bob Scott to be what was then called Administrator and the wagon began to roll.

A group of Manchester businessmen, headed by the stockbroker Peter Henriques and supported notably by Edward Bacon and Bernard Terry, committed themselves to raising money to support the company. Their enlightened and totally disinterested (they had no power in the structure) encouragement linked the company directly to the community from the word go.

In addition to all this Michael and Casper persuaded the Edinburgh Festival to present our inaugural productions at the 1968 festival at the Assembly Hall. Tom Courtenay would play Hamlet, directed by Casper, and Michael would direct Ibsen's great late play *When We Dead Awaken* with Wendy Hiller. Talk about sticking your head over the parapet!

In order to understand why the company was received with open arms, you have to understand that British theatre was very different then from how it is now. If you lived outside London you were, as a theatregoer, treated like a second-class citizen. The major touring theatres were either trying out productions prior to the West End or presenting West End hits, with distinctly inferior casts, after their run had finished. The rep theatres, the cornerstone of the profession, were where young artists learnt their craft, stepping stones to the greater glory of London.

Michael and Casper wanted to create a theatre outside London with national standards. It must be remembered that Michael had been asked by Olivier to be his Number Two at the National and then succeed him, but Michael had declined. Now we take the regional centres like the West Yorkshire Playhouse or the Sheffield Crucible for granted. Then they did not exist. But there was another innovative idea that came from Casper. All three of us had been Artistic Directors in our own right – Casper at 59, Michael at the Old Vic and myself at Century Theatre – and we all knew how tough it was. Most artistic directors that were any good had great success in their first year, lived off that success in the second year and then either had a nervous breakdown or joined the BBC in the third year. Running a company, choosing the plays, dealing with the politics and directing plays was a twenty-four-hours-a-day, eight-days-a-week job. As Tyrone Guthrie said, 'Have you noticed what a bad director you've become?'

Casper's idea was that since we were so like-minded we should form a group theatre. Practically, we could share the workload, especially releasing the director who was in rehearsal to do his work uninterrupted by office chores, and critically the group would benefit from three very different human beings creating a richer repertoire than one man could. Moreover, it was unlikely that all three would run out of ideas at once, so that there would always be enough energy for the company to renew itself.

To this we agreed, although initially there was not enough money to pay all three of us. As the resident in Manchester I would have a meagre salary and they would take a nominal fee of £1 per annum. It meant that all of us would have to seek work outside the company to make a living, but since we were only able to do at most six shows a year at the University Theatre, it seemed a reasonable proposition. Later, when the Royal Exchange came into being and a full-time commitment was required, all the advantages and disadvantages of the group would become apparent, but initially it proved almost one hundred per cent beneficial.

The idea was that whoever was right at any given time would be the leader at that moment. It was the opposite of Communism. By pooling our strengths, we would be able to mitigate each other's weaknesses and create something greater than any one of us would have been able to do. In effect it was replicating the process of rehearsals. A group of actors, designers, together with a director and author, respecting each other's talents, work together, leaving their personal problems outside the rehearsal-room door, to produce, with luck, a work of art for an audience. The more I have seen this concept in practice the more I am convinced that it is a paradigm not just for running a theatre but for society as a whole.

The group has to be like-minded and they have to respect each other's differences. The problem, as we were to find out, was that putting three such huge egos together was bound to create its own difficulties.

Michael and Casper had been close colleagues for years, both in the theatre and in television, but they envied each other. Casper envied Michael's public success as a director, which he also suspected was sometimes achieved by a less than pure approach to the plays, and Michael envied Casper's ability to be the thinking spiritual leader of the group. Their rivalry was as intense as their collaboration. Where did I fit in? I felt myself, rightly, to be the most junior, so much so that I allowed things to happen that I would never have tolerated from anyone else. For example, when Casper came to see *Romeo and Juliet*, he went backstage to congratulate the actors and then emerged to inform me that he had given some of them notes. This is something no director should ever do to another, but I meekly accepted. A couple of years later he actually called a rehearsal of one of my shows, *Catch My Soul*, which was on its way to London, without telling me, then made me watch his attempt to change things he didn't approve of. The actors were astonished at my behaviour and they were right, but I was completely in awe of him. Michael took advantage of me in more material ways but that comes later. My advantage was that I had an innate grasp of the practicalities of running a company, especially in matters of finance but also politically, which I kept under wraps for a while because that was Michael's forte.

On my birthday, 12 February 1968, the company came into being officially in the presence of Laurence Harbottle at Richard Pilbrow's home in Hampstead. It was the fitting beginning for the fourth cycle of my life.

CHAPTER 21

Filling in Time

Suddenly the frenetic rush of the past few years came to a halt. I had practically nothing to do. I was used to overseeing twelve productions a year for Century, directing about ten of them and running two companies. The first two productions for the new company were already settled. The earliest I would direct again would be in December 1968, a whole year after *Romeo and Juliet*. It should have been a time for stocktaking but as it is said, 'Nature abhors a vacuum'.

One day in spring I went down to Oxford to visit my cousin Gillian Rose who had just gone up to St Hilda's. Apart from girlfriends, I have been blessed all my life to have close relationships with remarkable women. Gillian was one of the most remarkable. She became an eminent philosopher before she died tragically young of cancer. During those last years she wrote a singular autobiographical/philosophical book called *Love's Work*, which is still much read and is an intensely moving testament to the immortal spirit of the human being. We were emotionally very akin: both from broken homes; both in search of a haven; both, I realise now, deeply scared of our own potential vulnerability. Intellectually we were miles apart. She was a Marxist Freudian, whereas to me those two renegade Jews epitomised in their reductionism everything that was going wrong in our Western society. Gillian and I were as close as brother and sister.

I went to find her in her rooms and she introduced me to my first wife. I knew I was going to marry her the moment I saw her. It wasn't love at first sight, it was wedlock at first sight. I can't really explain it. Clearly something in me was itching to get married. I had been through three and a half fiancées in three years. When I look back at those three, Virginia, Pat and Stella, I have no real memory of them except as warm, kind, sexually attractive women. It doesn't take a therapist to explain that. I didn't consider any of them as people in themselves. I treated them, I now realise, callously. When the projection phase was over, as with Virginia coming down the escalator, I simply ended the relationship. When they ceased to exist as my fantasy, they ceased to exist for me. My only comfort is that we were all young and searching, and that they were all – and I use the work in its most potent sense – 'good' people.

Lindsay Stainton was beautiful. She was a slender blonde with large eyes and a discerning youthful charm. She was also brilliant. She was qualifying as a barrister, would eventually take a First in History, painted, and played the oboe in the National Youth Orchestra. I returned to London, sent her a postcard asking to meet her again. She agreed and very, very soon we were engaged. This time, although I had a good go at it, there was to be no escape. The portcullis didn't come down.

There were problems. Lindsay's father was Keith Stainton, the Conservative MP for Sudbury and Woodbridge, and her mother Anne was descended from the Denbighs and the Cliffords, the oldest Catholic aristocracy in England. Lindsay was not yet twenty-one, which was then the age at which you could get married without parental consent. Lindsay thought her mother would be an ally so she told her first and we met for lunch near the House of Commons. Her advice was that I should go to the Commons, ask for Stainton and request permission to marry his daughter.

The thing about directors is that no matter what they are going through, they always keep part of themselves detached, storing away even the most traumatic events for future use. Part of me enjoyed this bizarre encounter with the formidable, thickset MP.

Clearly Stainton needed a Jewish son-in-law like a hole in the head. Suffolk was a very conservative county and it might not go down well with his constituents. Mrs Stainton appeared more conciliatory: 'Oh, Jews can be very clever, you know. We have one of them on our Board.' They both had to bow to the inevitable. I absolutely refused the idea of a church wedding and it was decided that we should hold the ceremony in the crypt of the House of Commons. It was grand enough and it was an inter-denominational venue. The wedding would take place in the autumn.

I think we wanted to get married for the same reasons even though we were not conscious of them. We both wanted to break all the old familial contracts and make public our new beginnings. Lindsay came from a very troubled family. The tensions between her father and mother were extreme. He actually came from Belgian peasant stock and his wife had grown rather to look down on him. He had a major drink problem and the marriage had nearly broken up over it. Lindsay was the oldest of six children, the second trio being years younger than the first. Her father, according to Lindsay, ran an odd regime at home. He lived in one half of the house where his wife was required to attend on him when he rang the bell – no servants, his wife. If he didn't like a meal she'd prepared, he'd throw it out of the window. No wonder Lindsay wanted a fresh start.

If the Staintons didn't welcome a Jew into their midst, that was nothing compared with my grandparents who were appalled that I was to marry a shikseh. In their eyes 'marrying out' was about the worst thing a Jew could do. My grandfather told me, 'I don't mind you marrying a shikseh because you'll get divorced. The problem is no nice Jewish girl will have you after!' My parents coped manfully with the situation and they even held an engagement party for me. For a while all was well.

Professionally I had agreed to travel with the 69 Theatre Company to Edinburgh and oversee the productions as Artistic Director while the others rehearsed. A strange curve was thrown into that plan.

London Weekend Television was just coming into being. Joy Whitby, who had been the Head of Children's Television for the BBC, was to take that position with the new company. She asked to have lunch with me. She had an idea for a new series for the six o'clock slot on Sunday, the crossover between children and adults, and she wanted me to produce it, not only produce but also direct some episodes, appoint a script editor and generally be the major creative force. I had no experience whatsoever of television and never had the slightest yen to work in that medium. However, being me I accepted.

The idea that Joy had was *The Man Who Couldn't Die*, which seemed attractive. I was allowed to appoint my *Hang Down Your Head* colleague David Wright as Editor and we began work. It was an exciting time at LWT; the birth of a new company always is. Initially we were all crammed into a small building off Piccadilly – Frank Muir was heading Comedy; Jimmy Hill, Sport and we felt at an epicentre.

Whenever I was introduced to someone new in the company it sounded eerily reminiscent of my encounter with Marion Javits. Everyone was thrilled that such a 'talented' and 'brilliant' young man was working with them. They went on being thrilled and delighted until one night about three months later, when I was fired with more smiles, more handshakes and testimonies to my brilliance.

The problem was it became obvious to me that the idea of a man who couldn't die was a tragic one. He would get older and older but he would survive all his friends, wives, children etc. He might be subject to the most frightful diseases but he could never escape through death. He would probably go through a delusional period of being the Messiah and he would almost certainly spend some time in an asylum. I gathered together a formidable team of writers and encouraged them to examine the dark side of the story. As strange episodes – from, among others, Gerard McLarnon – about abortions, messianic crowd hysteria at Wembley and suchlike started to arrive, Joy began to panic. By now I was convinced that I was engaged in something brilliant. I bullshitted her and the Director-General of LWT, Cyril Bennett, to let me continue. Script meetings with Joy became farcical. The series started before the First World War and went up to the present day. At one meeting I was told that a rather good script set in the First World War should be transferred to the Second World War. I was furthermore told that it was to be ready by tomorrow. I insisted it would take a good week. She didn't see the problem. I was told just to change the word First to Second. I objected that they were very different wars. I was told, 'You're a purist.'

By now we had moved to Stonebridge Park on the North Circular Road near Wembley, cut off from the world, locked into this strange process. When they administered the *coup de grâce* it was frankly a release. It wasn't Joy's fault. I shouldn't have taken the job and, having taken it, I should have done it, not tried to change it into something different. Still, I had been rather better paid than I would have been with 69 and I had learnt at least that television would never be my thing.

CHAPTER 22

Edinburgh and Nuptials 1968

Had the television series been a success, I would not have been available to go to Edinburgh with the company. Now I was free but I wasn't exactly welcomed back with open arms. Casper was furious that I'd taken the LWT job, although he didn't say so at the time, and decided to punish me. I could come to Edinburgh, the company would pay me a per diem to cover expenses but I would not be on salary until we opened in Manchester. Father was disciplining a wayward son. I did not demur.

Lindsay came with me, and the directors and their wives – or in my case fiancée – all stayed together in a gloomy Victorian pile on the outskirts of the city. It was, to put it mildly, claustrophobic. Nevertheless the build-up to the opening of *Hamlet* was exciting. The festival is always at fever pitch and here we were, launching our new company as the centrepiece of the official programme at the famous Assembly Hall, headquarters of the Scottish Church, which Guthrie had made famous as a venue with his legendary production of *The Three Estates*. The press had given 69 terrific coverage, largely on the basis of Michael's fame, and we were probably exceedingly over-hyped; not that we cared as we were going to revolutionise British theatre.

Getting the shows physically ready was hard. The Assembly Hall is not a theatre and had none of the ordinary facilities, such as workshops, that are essential to productions. The staff worked in difficult conditions to produce the sets and costumes to grace the stage we constructed in the hall. We managed to make a stage not dissimilar to the thrust in Manchester. All obstacles were brushed aside because we were filled with excitement.

Hamlet opened to the national and international press, and we woke up the next day to find it had been slated by everyone. No one spoke in mitigation. It couldn't have been a worse birth; it threatened to finish off 69 before it had really begun. Poor Tom, as was the custom, had to face the press the next day and I had the job of being with him as the representative Artistic Director. It was a horrible experience but we were suitably defiant – not difficult for me, but Tom had to go on that night. He didn't flinch.

Harold Hobson's review in the *Sunday Times* probably saved the company's life. He castigated the daily critics for making the worst mistake since *The Birthday Party*. He had seen, in Tom's performance, the spiritual prince and he lauded him. This was the strength of Casper's production but in truth it wasn't a great evening. The concept had been that the play was the inner experience of Hamlet: like a dream. The stage was covered in black and the costumes were black from the feet to below the waist so that the actors would appear to be floating. It didn't work. The two blacks were clearly dissimilar and the cast merely looked as if they had been dipped in ink. The casting was uneven, although Dilys Hamlett as Gertrude, Anna Calder-Marshall as Ophelia and Russell Hunter as the Gravedigger were outstanding. The Players' scenes, choreographed by Litz Pisk and with music by George Hall, were quite brilliant. The rest was a little disappointing. Never mind, Hobson had saved us; we had changed from being a flop to a controversy.

By contrast *When We Dead Awaken* was a triumph. Michael's production, with Alexander Knox, Wendy Hiller and the very young Brian Cox, was universally praised. We had come through. Johanna had designed the mountainous naturalistic set and Michael had opted for an emotion-packed semi-operatic style for the actors. Casper felt it should have been the other way round: a symbolic abstract set and intensely naturalistic acting. I, who had been bowled over, began to consider production style in a much more sophisticated way than before.

During this period I started to experience, not for the first or last time, the difficulty of conducting a personal relationship at the same time as working. Lindsay had nothing to do in Edinburgh, we were engaged, presumably in love and she naturally wanted some of my time. I did what by now you would expect, broke off the engagement and sent her back to Suffolk. I didn't realise why this had happened, it just seemed to me that it couldn't work. The portcullis was down.

I expect her parents were delighted; the wedding was cancelled and the family dress studs, which were on the way from Rhodesia for me, were sent back. I, on the other hand, missed her immediately and bitterly regretted what I had done. The portcullis was up. I phoned her and asked her to forgive me. She did but her parents didn't. She would not be twenty-one until November and they withdrew their permission. Had they not done so perhaps we would not have gone on, but their opposition only goaded me further. I was doing my first production for the company, which was to open on 18 December, and we would get married immediately after that. In a bookshop I came across a book called *Linda Goodman's Love Signs*. It was about the compatibility or otherwise of the various signs and I dare say rather silly. I turned to Aquarius male–Scorpio female. It was a blank page with one word printed in the middle: DON'T. I laughed and put the book back on the shelf.

Marriage but to Whom or What?

My preoccupation now, as I write this, is to understand my relationship with Lindsay. My preoccupation then was with the three productions now coming up for me. That was presumably part of the problem. Theatre is a demanding taskmaster (mistress?). Lindsay had met me during an artistic lull and she must have been taken aback by the intensity of my commitment.

Two of the shows were premières. I had taught for a while at LAMDA and there had been struck by Anna Calder-Marshall. When Casper decided to do *Hamlet*, I took him to see her play Saint Joan at the old Birmingham Rep because I thought she would be the ideal Ophelia, which she was.

Shaw's *Saint Joan* is a very silly play, diluting the inspiring story with feeble jokes, sentimentality and an unplayable epilogue. Casper suggested that Gerard McLarnon be commissioned to write a new play. He began work immediately and I immersed myself in the trial documents and the history of the period.

Before that, David Wright and I decided to renew our partnership with a show about Manchester using the total theatre techniques of *Hang Down Your Head and Die*. The title *Have You Seen Manchester* came from Disraeli's novel *Conningsby*: 'You have seen the Seven Wonders of the World but have you seen Manchester?' The reference was to the time when Manchester, as the birthplace of the Industrial Revolution, was indeed the Eighth Wonder of the World. David Wood once again added new songs to traditional folk songs, the cast included Trevor Peacock, Julian Chagrin and Bridget Turner, and instead of a circus the show was presented as a cabaret. Among other things, it was an attack on the town planners and city architects who were tearing down the terraced houses, where communities had lived together for decades, and rehousing them in ghastly inward-looking crescent tower blocks and not even trying in the process to keep the communities together. The city was furious and heated debates took place in the theatre after the show. Time has shown that we were absolutely right. The tower blocks were hell-holes and have now been pulled down.

The third show I'll come to later.

Lindsay and I got married, after the opening of *Have You Seen Manchester*, in a register office in All Saints, Manchester, pursued by the press, with David Wright as best man and the only guest at the ensuing wedding lunch at the Midland Hotel.

It seemed to me that Lindsay underwent a complete character change that very night. Alongside the beautiful, intelligent, fun person I had married appeared a woman consumed by an almost insane jealousy. The jealousy was entirely without cause. Indeed, had I been guilty of the number of affairs I was accused of I would have to have been a sexual athlete to rival the prowess of Errol Flynn, let alone fitting them into the all-consuming timetable of rehearsals. I would return home to these accusations to which I could not or would not retaliate. I merely talked to the Lindsay I knew until the woman I married reappeared.

Of all the people I have contacted to talk to in the writing of this book, she alone has refused to meet, so I must puzzle it out myself. I am always amazed at anyone who can cope with being married to someone in the theatre. Theatre is a small world, peopled with human beings intensely preoccupied with themselves because they are the vessels of their art. It is an incestuous world with its own language or shorthand, and must seem impenetrable to an outsider. A director is a very powerful figure in this world. During the rehearsal period he, for better or for worse, is the only arbiter of the actors' work. He also has the power to hire and fire. He is, too, the overall creative eye of the production. He is constantly working with very attractive women who can easily fall under his spell. I believe that Lindsay was terrified of losing me. She loved me and I was her future. The theatre became a threat. Moreover, she was still at Oxford, so for months of the year we weren't properly together. This must have increased her insecurity.

Of course, I understood none of this; I was simply appalled and buried myself even deeper in productions. Until I sat down to write this, I had laboured for years under the delusion that the marriage lasted for only six months. I now find it lasted for two years. I suspect the reason is that we were so little together over that time and the pressure on those short times became progressively worse. It is difficult to keep switching from bachelor to married man, especially when the married man is the object of so much suspicion.

Before my next production, James Maxwell was to adapt George Eliot's novel *Daniel Deronda*, which Michael would direct with Vanessa Redgrave playing Gwendolen Harleth. I had never read the book, although I had read practically every other novel of Eliot's and when I did it moved me to the very root of my being. Deronda is an orphan, brought up in the grand style by an aristocrat, who discovers by chance, as an adult, that he is a Jew. During the book he goes in search of his roots, guided by a deeply spiritual old man, Mordecai, and a Jewish Miranda figure called Mirah, with whom he is finally united. This is set against his relationship with Gwendolen Harleth and her disastrous marriage to an English lord, Grandcourt, and her craving for spiritual succour from him. The clear message of the book that fascinated Max and Michael was that the English aristocracy had become so etiolated that the infusion of foreign blood was crucially needed for the country to be reborn.

It is hardly necessary to explain why I was so moved by the book. John Bennett was playing Mordecai and Michael asked me if I would take some responsibility for his performance, and indeed with Rosalind Knight who played the Alcharisi, Deronda's mother whom he finds in Venice. Michael felt that as a non-Jew he couldn't fully understand what drove Mordecai and the actual emotional quality of his passion. I was happy to do what he asked and as I worked with John I found that I had reconnected with what I can only call my Jewishness. I cannot believe that George Eliot did not have Jewish blood (just look at her nose) because she captures so well the melancholic, spiritual yearning which is one of the best sides of the race. Working on *Deronda* made me determined to embark on a course of self-instruction that would begin with reading the Old Testament, no less, not as a child but as an adult.

The actual production was somewhat clumsy and the adaptation very long but it combined some extraordinary scenes and performances. Vanessa was magnificent. The beautiful, wilful woman who was finally to be broken down and thereby gain the possibility of a spiritual future was, I think, the finest thing I have seen her do and her spiritual opposite John Bennett was mesmerising. I have watched two BBC costume drama museum-piece versions of the novel, which did not begin to approach this production at its best. *Daniel Deronda* is not George Eliot's most perfect novel, it is flawed, but I think it is her greatest. Lindsay was also deeply affected by it. She called me 'My Daniel Deronda'.

CHAPTER 23

She Stoops to Conquer: The Tug of War Starts

I went with Tom Courtenay and Casper to see a production of *She Stoops to Conquer* at the Oxford Playhouse, where Rodney Bewes, a friend of Tom's with whom I used to go to watch Chelsea (they played at home on alternate Saturdays to Spurs), was playing Tony Lumpkin. I thought it was an ideal play to do with Tom. He and Casper agreed and it was scheduled in the slot before *The Trial of Joan of Arc*, which Gerry had now completed.

Casper phoned: 'Casper here. It would be good if Trevor Peacock played, you know . . . em . . . Lumpkin.' I had thought that Tom was going to play Lumpkin but I shut up in order not to show my stupidity. Tom was to play Young Marlow, a part I had scarcely noticed in the Oxford production. Thank goodness I did shut up for it was a stupendous piece of casting that gave rise to the greatest comic performance I have been associated with, not to mention Trevor's wondrous Tony Lumpkin.

Although I was now well on the road to understanding properly the content of the serious plays I directed, I hadn't yet applied the same rules to comedies. They were either funny or they weren't. It all seemed like a jolly gig. Jimmy Cossins came back to play Hardcastle, Michael's wife, Rose, Mrs Hardcastle and Juliet Mills accepted the part of Kate. I'd always been good at making people laugh, good at comic timing and comic business, and rehearsals went with a swing. Only one scene proved intractable: the horse-pond scene. This is where Mrs Hardcastle instructs her son Lumpkin to drive her and her wretched ward Constance to her Aunt Pedigree, in order to prevent her marrying the man she loves. Tony fools her by driving the coach in circles round the house, finally depositing her in the horse pond at the bottom of the garden. The scene seemed resolutely unfunny and nothing I or the cast could do appeared to improve it in spite of repeated after-hours rehearsal, like being kept in after school. I admitted defeat, told the cast to do the best they could on opening night and we'd sort it out later. Opening night went wonderfully well and I gritted my teeth as the horse-pond scene started. To my astonishment the audience howled with laughter all the way through it. I learnt a lesson. The laughs came from plot and character. The audience loved to see the odious Mrs Hardcastle receive her come-uppance from her over-mothered son. In comedy, I learnt, the higher the stakes in human terms the funnier the scene.

As I write this thirty-seven years later, I have just done the play again and this time I took it very seriously. It is about a ghastly second marriage between the Hardcastles. Mrs Hardcastle has an unruly son rebelling against a smothering mother and she maltreats her ward out of sheer greed. The whole unhappy crew are locked up in the country miles away from anywhere. Into this mess comes Young Marlow, an almost schizophrenic young man who can only sleep with barmaids and the like, but who is frozen by the presence of what he takes to be a 'modest' lady. This is described as the 'Englishman's Malady' and indeed hasn't changed to this day. The scene where Kate Hardcastle disguises herself as a barmaid and he tries to seduce her is one of the funniest, sexiest ever written because it releases not only Young Marlow but Kate herself. I say all this to point out the difference of a director aged twenty-six from one aged sixty-three. I believe this second production to be more complete, because my interest now is not just about the young people, but the whole family including the parents.

The 1969 production, conceived as a nice short interlude, was an instant success and Theatre Projects run by Richard Pilbrow took it into London at the Garrick Theatre. The problem was that I couldn't oversee the transfer as I was about to rehearse *Joan*. This is where I first came across the other side of Michael. He offered to supervise the transfer for me, which seemed very generous. He also took the whole director's fee and a third of the director's royalties for the run. As with Casper, I was too overawed to argue. Worse was to come. A year later he reproduced the production for BBC TV without telling me. He replaced some of the cast but it was my production. That hurt.

On opening night in London, which I couldn't attend because of Manchester rehearsals, an overenthusiastic ASM polished the wooden floor without telling anyone. One after another, the actors came on stage and promptly fell down. Lindsay, who was there, told me that Laurence Harbottle, who was sitting in front of her, turned round and said, 'Don't worry, this will ensure good reviews.' He was right, it did. It played to full houses for six months and only closed because, understandably, Tom had had enough. His creation of Young Marlow was totally original brilliance. When I came to do it again, I could remember every inflection, every gesture he made, both as the shy young man and the lecherous rake. He understood the psyche to a T. Trevor Peacock as Lumpkin, his first West End role, was also quite marvellous. I dreaded overburdening the new cast with my recollections of those two performances. It is a testament to Milo Twomey (Young Marlow) and Celyn Jones (Lumpkin) that they created equally vivid creatures. I had not fully recognised the potential in Kate, so Juliet Mills in the role, although delightful, was not as well directed as Alison Pargeter in the present production. Des Barrit, the present Mr Hardcastle, could not be bettered in any cast. I'd love to have seen him, Tom, Alison and Trevor together.

The company had inevitably, as all companies do, got into severe financial difficulties. We were about £18,000 in the red, a great deal of money in 1969. Warner Brothers asked that Juliet Mills be released for a month to record the pilot for a new TV series called *The Nanny*. I refused. Their top brass flew over and asked me out to lunch. They plied me with drink until they thought I was beyond cogent thought and put pressure on me to release her. I named my price – £18,000. They were flabbergasted. There was no way they were going to pay out that kind of money. They offered all kinds of compromises. I held out. They collapsed. Juliet flew out, Bridget Turner took over for the month and the company's debt was wiped out. I said I was quite good at finance.

I was back in the West End and with a smash hit which, despite Michael's appropriation of some of the royalties, was making me money. At the same time I was rehearsing *The Trial of Joan of Arc* in Manchester. These two productions epitomised the tug of war within me that lasted for all of fifteen years. Did I want to be a famous West End director or did I want to put my heart and soul into the company I believed in, with the men I most admired? Was it to be fame and glory or fulfilment? The outcome was very much in doubt.

As far as fulfilment was concerned *The Trial of Joan of Arc* with, of course, Dilys Hamlett as Saint Joan, was the most fulfilling thing I had done to date. Gerry had based his play on the trial records and documents of the time. The true story was far more gripping than Dreyer's movie or Schiller's play. For weeks this slip of a girl was interrogated by a full court of sophisticated Catholic monks led by the Bishop of Beauvais. She held her own and outwitted them, fed by a purity of faith that was awesome. In Gerry's play her death was a triumph of the soul over venality. There are no superlatives that can describe Dilys's performance. We worked together as sympathetically and intuitively as I have ever worked with anyone.

The challenge was to stage the final burning. I remembered Michael telling me of an experience he had had in Crete at Easter, when a huge bonfire had been ignited in the village square where he was staying. It was so brilliant that he was blinded by it. This is precisely what I reproduced. At the moment of the conflagration we shone lights into the audience's eyes, then there was a blackout. At the curtain call on the first night the cast came forward to utter silence. The audience didn't want to applaud. Michael Meyer described it as 'better than a Cup Final'. The next night I cut the curtain call. The audience objected. They wanted the chance to applaud. The curtain call was reinstated. This was the first production of mine that seemed to approach the kind of effect that *Brand* had had on me in 1959.

Fame and glory or fulfilment?

CHAPTER 24
Armund Höhningstadt

It is relatively easy to write about one's outer life. The dates are all there to remind you of what you did when. It is hard to write about the growth of one's inner life. I was a voracious reader. I had been started on philosophy at school by a French master, Mr Carter, who was interested in Sartre and existentialism. I had always been interested in religions, especially the Eastern ones, though how and through whom I first met the wisdom of the I Ching I can't remember. In literature Dostoevsky had been my god. Who can read *Karamazov* or *The Idiot* and not be fascinated by man's relationship with the world that is not tangible, the other unseen world? All great artists in every art form have grappled with this huge mystery and to them I had always turned.

I used to haunt the second-hand bookshops of the Charing Cross Road. One day I discovered Cecil Court, a little alleyway that runs between St Martin's Lane and Charing Cross Road, near the Wyndham's and what is now the Noël Coward Theatres. This was a treasure trove of second-hand bookshops and I explored them one by one until I found myself in one that was unlike the others. It was called Watkin's. It was presided over by the gnome-like figure of Mr Watkin and it was a cornucopia of esoteric books, ranging from the wacky to the extraordinary.

The volume I bought on that first visit was by no means wacky. It was volume five of the Collected Works of C. G. Jung: *Symbols of Transformation*. The book opened my eyes to a whole new way of looking at the world. How the symbolism of myth, legend, folk tale, literature, fairy tale and religion was a sophisticated means by which humanity tried to understand the infinite, the other world, the godhead, the meaning of dreams, the access we all share to the common human experience whether we are supposedly civilised Europeans or from a primitive tribe in the rainforests of South America. This amazing book described how the same stories are told all over the world synchronistically, to make sense of our existence. It concentrated and focused my hitherto random reading and inevitably began to feed into my work. It also mirrored the preoccupations of Michael, Casper and Max (James Maxwell), who was swiftly becoming a fourth member of the group.

The phone rang. 'Casper here. Armund is coming to London tomorrow. You will meet him at Heathrow. Give him a drink at the Club (the Savile). He will see *She Stoops*. You will have dinner and take him back to Barnes where he will sleep; he has the keys. Bring him to Manchester where he will stay for a week and see the plays.'

'How will I recognise him?'

'He will know you.'

Armund had been to England several times recently, but I had never met him. I seemed always to be in the wrong city. I knew all about him. As Casper's mentor, he was the reason we were all here working together.

I set off for Heathrow. There was a thick fog over the airport. The place was heaving with people. It was chaos.

'You are Braham Murray,' in that Norwegian lilt.

'Yes.'

'You are an Arab.'

'No I am not.'

'Yes you are. I can tell from the way you wear your clothes.'

I was looking at a very tall scarecrow, dressed in a shabby beige mac and a battered brown trilby. His face was like a slice of banana, sallow and featureless except for the piercing blue eyes.

I took him to the car and drove him into London. I didn't know what to say. He wasn't the sort of person you would ask the polite questions of 'What was the flight like? How's the weather in Oslo?' I kept silent. London was in the grip of a dustmen's strike. Rubbish was piled up everywhere. Armund roared with laughter: 'Yes, yes, that's how it is, perfect!'

We arrived at the Savile and I offered him a drink. 'A quadruple whisky, please.' He drank it and another. 'Abraham was the first man, Braham is the second one. The letter B is two worlds like an eight continually interacting.' I took him to the play. He loved it. 'It's better than Jung.' He was referring to Young Marlow's split psyche.

I drove him back to Barnes. Casper and Dilys were in Manchester rehearsing Ronnie Harwood's new play. He produced a bottle of whisky. 'We will drink this very slowly and we will talk.' During the course of that night he told me all about myself, the sort of things you only surface in yourself at four o'clock in the morning. At some point after he had been telling me about Michael and Casper, he looked at me and said, 'You will be the one. You will be the future. You will be the bridge.' I did not know what he meant but Destiny had made itself very clear.

I drove him to Manchester where he saw the last night of Michael's magical production of *The Tempest* in which Max was an astonishing Prospero with Michael Feast as Ariel. The relationship between man and his creative spirit has never been better evoked. The spirits of the island, played by leavers from the Central School, were conjured up unforgettably by Litz Pisk to George Hall's music on Richard Negri's sand-strewn island. Armund was to stay up to see the opening of Ronnie's *Country Matters*, which starred John Wood and Graham Crowden, and spend the intervening time with me in my rented cottage in Bramhall.

In the first phase of that weekend Armund tested me. I think he tried to break me. How to explain? The weakness of Michael's production had been the Caliban. He had put John Bennett into a furry animal suit, so that 'this thing of darkness' was reduced to a pantomime creature. Armund demonstrated to me in my tiny sitting room what Caliban should be. When I say he danced and sang it, I mean he became like a shaman, a witch doctor, he seemed to incarnate savage bestiality. I understood him. It was terrifying, but it was properly terrifying. I was not terrified. I passed the test.

Thereafter he talked, prompted by me. Armund was like a computer of myth, religion and history. If you asked him what Ariel really was, his answer would take hours as he traced through centuries of spiritual connections. I could not follow it all, not least because he would go into a kind of trance as he travelled across space and time.

I had a phobia about spiders, was terrified of them. At night I would stand by the door, switch on the light and check the room before I entered it. I was frightened of going abroad where awful species might lurk in wild countries like France. They were a constant threat at the back of my mind. I asked Armund what this meant. 'You are afraid of your destiny. That is the spider's web.' I'll never love spiders but the phobia disappeared at that moment.

I was particularly fascinated, then, by the story of Beauty and the Beast. I had traced it back to its roots in the Cupid and Psyche myth, and read not only its Perrault form but also the Grimm version. How do you bless the Beast as Beauty does, rather than repress it as every religion seems to want to do? Anything that is repressed eventually will rise up against you. What else happened in Germany under Hitler? The Beast was rampant. I was interested in finding some way of putting the story on stage in adult form so I asked Armund, 'What is the Beast?'

We had once again been sipping whisky very slowly in order, as Armund put it, to heighten our consciousness. However, what happened next was not drunken imagination, it happened. We were sitting at a table which was against the wall of the kitchen. He was at one end, I was in the middle facing him, the chair at the end was empty. His reply to my question was, 'It's over there.' The empty chair was now occupied by a creature which was constantly metamorphosing between an ancient woman with Medusa-like snakes for hair and a wizened old man. The other world was in my kitchen, as real as anybody I have ever met.

This is an area of great danger, inhabited by many charlatans, fakes and manipulators. I am always highly suspicious and cynical of people who claim to have special powers, and I will invariably look for the ordinary, rational, scientific explanation for that which seems supernatural, but from that moment I have never doubted the existence of the other world and, as Casper had enjoined, I have tried to live with one foot in each world.

Armund was not a perfect human being. He did not understand and consequently completely underrated women. Indeed, this was one of the great lacunae in the group. No women were ever present at the big discussions; they were asked to leave the room. Armund's wife was fittingly called Agnes (shades of *Brand*) and his daughter became deranged. He became very ill. He told the doctors what they would find when they opened him up and what to cut out. He knew the symbiotic relationship between body and mind. On the day of his death he went to the barber's for a haircut and shave, visited various friends to say goodbye, shut himself up in his room and caused his heart to be attacked. I did not attend his funeral. It was said to be an extraordinary event. As the coffin was carried to the grave, thunder and lightning split the sky. The god Höhne was taken back.

CHAPTER 25

The First Two Musicals

Erb

My marriage was having a bad time of it. Lindsay was scornful and impatient of my interest in Jung and the areas to which that led me. This I found frustrating. It was an extension of the jealousy. She didn't want me going into another world. We took a belated honeymoon in Greece, motoring around it in my little Mini for a month. It was more of a bitter moon. I fell in love with Greece and especially the theatres. Every night as the sun set I felt the presence of the gods, a pretty commonplace feeling in Greece. I was especially eager to follow up anything about Dionysus and his cult. It seemed harmless enough – he was, after all, the god of the theatre and (equally important) of wine. Lindsay saw him as the god of licentiousness and found my interest offensive. It was not a happy time. I see now that I repeated the pattern I had followed with previous women. I did not try to find out what was really the matter, I was not sufficiently interested or caring to her. Would it have changed things? I don't know. Probably the chasm was too deep. I merely retreated into myself. I remember that we stayed with my parents the night we got back. Almost the moment we walked through the door the phone rang from Manchester and I was back on duty. I recollect the look on her face and her misery.

I was back to prepare my first musical. The idea had come from Ronnie Harwood. He had obtained the rights to an obscure Edwardian novel by William Pett Ridge called *Erb*. The story seems deterrent. It was about an early trade union official on the railways. In fact, it was a delightful romantic tale full of life and vigour, and evocative of the period. The brilliant idea was that Trevor Peacock should write it, because he was not only a playwright but also a composer of hit tunes.

Trevor, although a prolific songwriter, couldn't read or write music, nor could he play an instrument beyond laboriously picking out a tune with one finger on the piano. When he had a new number ready he would come round to me and, using his nose as a rhythm instrument resembling the

103

hi-hat on drums, his mouth as the brass section and his hand on the table to beat time, he would sing his creation. Fortunately Richard Pilbrow was interested in the project and supplied him with one of the top Arranger–MDs in London, Gareth Davies, to transpose into dots what Trevor had dreamt up. Gareth was a lovely long piece of spaghetti with a broad Welsh accent, and Trevor would sometimes drive him nuts. One of the most original numbers in the show was called 'Here's Ron, Here's Alf'. Trevor sang him the song.

'You can't do that, Trev.'

'Why not, Gareth?' Welsh versus Cockney.

'Because it doesn't work, Trev.'

'But I've just done it, Gareth.'

'But it's not allowed, it breaks all the rules of musical time, Trev.'

'But I've done it, Gareth.' Which goes to prove the rules don't exist if you don't know them.

Trevor himself was to play Erb, Bridget Turner his sister and a mouth-watering actress, Deborah Grant, his girlfriend. Lindsay was dreadfully jealous of her and was convinced that we were having an affair. Alas, we weren't.

I found that rehearsing a musical was very different from a play. Choreography takes the longest time, so has to be started from the word go. The music must be learnt before anything else can begin. The director really becomes the scheduler, the RSM. He doesn't get a look-in with the bits between the songs, i.e. the book, until well into the second week. On the other hand the choreographer and the MD are working to his brief because it will be his job to make the homogeneous whole at the end. The actors learn the songs, therefore, before they have explored their characters through the text. The director attends the learning sessions to help them characterise the singing. This means he sometimes has to demonstrate the songs. Unfortunately I am tone-deaf. I simply had to hurl myself at the tunes, hoping I'd get my point across, in spite of the gales of laughter coming back at me from the cast. I'm told I managed to sing in half-keys, which is an impossible feat.

It is very hard work, but when the final week comes and the different pieces of the jigsaw are put together it can be exhilarating. *Erb* opened to a rapturous reception in Manchester; the theatre was packed, Richard Pilbrow loved it and a London opening at the Strand Theatre, now the Novello, was planned.

There followed a difficult time between Richard and me. He wanted to replace Bridget Turner because she didn't have a good enough voice for the West End. As management he may well have been right, but I could no more replace Bridget than cut off my hand. Night after night at George's restaurant we shouted and screamed at each other. I refused to budge and eventually he conceded. The vexed question of what happens when a play transfers from Manchester to London, to satisfy different demands, cropped up endlessly in the years to come.

London rehearsals were not easy. A group of actors shut up in Manchester, away from their families, dentists, doctors, accountants and agents, is much easier to handle than the same actors in London, especially when they are in a West End musical expected to be a hit. The great Litz Pisk was not the ideal choreographer for a conventional musical behind the proscenium arch and Gareth, who had done wonderfully witty orchestrations for the small band in Manchester, got carried away by the full pit orchestra in London and overblew the sound of the show. The cast were dismayed that the golden circle we felt around us seemed to be slipping to the floor. The first preview was flat as a pancake, the management panicked, the theatre manager panicked and I panicked. However, with a Herculean effort we re-rehearsed every day until we got it right. The cavernous Strand Theatre needed a different energy from the intimate University Theatre.

The curtain went up on opening night in London and the audience were lukewarm. Ten minutes into the show Felix Barber, the *Evening News* critic, stumped up the aisle and slumped into the seat next to me. He promptly fell asleep until the interval. The reviews the next day were tepid. The reason was simple. What had seemed a fresh, original show in Manchester was to London just another Cockney knees-up musical; *Oliver!*, *Fings Ain't Wot They Used T'be*, *Sing a Rude Song* to name the most successful of them, and many, many more. To this day I believe the score that Trevor wrote for *Erb* was quite special. What a waste. Outside the theatre Richard had put Trevor's name in lights below the title. The idea was that after the anticipated glowing notices, pictures would be taken of his name being put above the title, the new West End star. It wasn't to be.

Jack (*Six Five Special*, *Ready Steady Go*, *Oh Boy!*) Good, who as I have said had brought rock 'n' roll to Britain, gone to America and produced TV specials for all the greats, most recently Andy Williams – Jack Good who was a great friend of Trevor's, had been at Oxford with Michael and had acted in *Hippolytus* for Casper – turned up to see the show and, brimming with ideas, was co-opted as another Artistic Director. I remember the feeling that with him on board we couldn't fail, we would be unstoppable. In the event, like Richard Pilbrow before him who had briefly been an Artistic Director, his highly individual and distinguished furrow made it impossible to give enough commitment to the enterprise. In his brief period with 69 Jack created probably its biggest public success.

Catch My Soul

Jack wanted to revive his rock *Othello*, *Catch My Soul*. He had staged it in
LA with Jerry Lee Lewis as Iago, but because of its racially sensitive theme
it had never made it to New York. As a fanatical Shakespearean purist and
a jazz fan who disliked any pop music on principle, I hated the idea. Jack
wanted Michael Elliott to direct it both because he was a brilliant director
and also because, having been Artistic Director of the Old Vic, he would
carry clout to raise money for a London future. I couldn't believe that the
extremely serious Michael would want to be associated with such a corrupt
project but he did. Jack would play Othello, a role he had been obsessed
with since he played it as an undergraduate at Oxford. My protests were
brushed aside. The project was scheduled.

Immediately before it I was to direct *A Midsummer Night's Dream* with
the young Brian Cox as Oberon/Theseus and the even younger Zoë
Wanamaker making her professional début as Hermia. I banished *Catch
My Soul* from my mind and started preparing the production.

About a fortnight before rehearsals were due to start Michael phoned and
invited me to lunch at the Savile Club. Such an invitation was a rare
occurrence as he had a strong Scottish side, so I accepted. When I arrived,
Jack was there as well. It appeared that Michael had been asked to develop
a screenplay of *Peer Gynt*, which he would then direct. It was an unmissable
opportunity, but it meant he couldn't do *Catch My Soul*. Jack would direct
instead – after all, he had done it in LA – but since he was also playing
Othello would I, as Resident Artistic Director, mind popping into rehearsal,
say, once a week and giving technical advice about the blocking etc.? 'But
you know I don't like the show?' That didn't matter, it seemed. I agreed.

I plunged into *Midsummer Night's Dream* and left Jack to get on with it.
Now my production of the *Dream* was heavily coloured by the fact that my
marriage was proving to be a disaster. Since my view of sexual relationships
was somewhat jaundiced, Shakespeare's comedy was turned into a humourless (for the lovers) bad dream. The Athenian wood was a Bosch–Brueghel
nightmare with hermaphroditic fairies endowed with an overabundance of
breasts and sporting an inordinate number of penises. The actors' bar was
right next to the public telephone in the University Theatre and on the first
night, as we gingerly celebrated, my wife could be heard yelling down the
phone at my mother that I was a degenerate fiend, that the production was
vile and that I disgusted her.

That weekend my marriage effectively ended. The following Monday,
emotionally drained and physically exceedingly hung-over, I crawled to the
rehearsal room of the Catholic Chaplaincy to attend the opening session of

Catch My Soul. As Resident Artistic Director my presence was required as a sort of mine host.

I had completely lost touch with *Catch My Soul*, the design, the casting, the music, everything. I knew that only the principals were starting this week, with the chorus (the Tribe of Hell) joining for week two.

They were a bizarre set of principals. P. P. Arnold (Bianca) was there with her entourage, P. J. Proby (Cassio) was already drunk (on apple wine if you please) and Elvis Presley's ex-drummer, Lance LeGault, all six foot three of him, seemed to be dressed to play Iago with two alarmingly real pistols round his waist. Matching them in eccentricity was Jeffrey Wickham, ex-head boy of Harrow, Oxford friend of Jack Good, classical actor (he had played Polonius to Tom Courtenay's Hamlet) engaged to play Roderigo, who sat there calmly knitting. Only our Emilia, Dorothy Vernon, maintained some connection to the normal theatrical world that I was used to. I slunk gratefully to the back of the room to join our nonpareil of company managers, Allisoune Browne.

Jack, at his most cherubically beguiling and most charmingly British, rose to his feet to give the director's opening inspirational speech to the company. It went something like this: 'Ladies and gentlemen, welcome to the first rehearsal of the greatest musical of the decade and probably of all time. We are going to dispense with the usual reading of the script and I am going to hand you straight over to our director Braham Murray to start the blocking.'

I went numb. I gaped at the sea of faces that now swivelled towards me. I could not move; I could not speak. Allisoune Browne gripped my arm. 'Get up,' she hissed and opened the script in front of me. I got up; I looked down at the text. It said 'Enter Othello'. I heard a voice I dimly recognised as my own say, 'Enter Othello up stage centre.' Where else should Othello enter? I began to block the show, which was predominantly the Shakespeare text dispensing with the first act – Venice – and starting in Cyprus, without any preparation whatsoever. The model of the set was in the corner of the room and I gathered that it was a psychedelic replica of the Globe Theatre. That was it. I reached lunchtime on automatic pilot. The actors broke. 'Stay here,' ordered Allisoune. 'I'll fetch you lunch, don't talk to anyone, look through the next portion of the script.' I did as I was told. I probably would have done anything I was told. Somehow I got through the rest of the day. I broke the actors.

I went over to Jack Good. Went over? I stormed over. 'What the hell do you think you're doing?'

'Ah well, I wanted you to direct the show. I knew you hated it, so this was the only way I could think of getting you to do it.' He had done it brilliantly.

He knew that if I hadn't responded as I did, the whole show would have collapsed. He also knew that I couldn't let it happen.

So began the weirdest rehearsal period I have ever been in charge of. I was smoking like a chimney, drinking like a fish, fuelled by a mixture of fear and excited fascination. What I began to realise was that Jack had dreamt up something rather brilliant. Like Verdi, he started the play with Act Two. He had edited the text and made it totally comprehensible but unadulterated. The lyrics of the songs were again lifted from the original with slight adjustments for the rhythm. The whole play had been transposed to Louisiana (the army were a kind of militia), so the social overtones were powerful. He had the text printed as prose, and the completely untrained performers had no difficulty with it. What the audience were going to get was a genuine Shakespearean experience, born out of Jack's great love and understanding of *Othello*, in a highly charged and accessible form.

Although there was already a score from the LA version, Jack wanted a lot of new numbers. He had a young composer, Emil Dean Zoghby, and he had the band from day one in rehearsal, so the numbers evolved organically with the performers. Week one went pretty smoothly with starting the musical process and with me tentatively starting on the scenes. The chorus arrived at the beginning of week two.

Where Jack had found the people I can't imagine. They were a mixture of the good, the bad and the downright horrible: the Tribe of Hell. This was before Equity had imposed control of entry into the profession and Jack had plucked them from some very strange places. Three of them were very large black males and they arrived with some very dubious white ladies in tow. 'Where could their girlfriends wait while they rehearsed?' they asked. Why had they brought them along? Oh, they were going to marry them that afternoon so that they could get work permits. To their bewilderment we dispensed with them immediately.

So there we had them all. Jack had liked the work the movement director Sue Lefton had done on *The Dream* so she was drafted in, poor lady, to work with the chorus. I ploughed on. P. J. Proby, who kept on announcing he wanted to play 'I Ego', got progressively drunker and had to leave rehearsals for two weeks to dry out. The revelation was Lance LeGault. He was a terrific acting-singing, guitar-playing talent, totally professional and committed. His scenes with Othello just about worked considering Jack was a white man blacked up, acting in the tradition of Donald Wolfit and with a very suspect voice (a member of the band had to sing one of the numbers, 'Put Out the Light' because he couldn't manage it).

Through some act of will on my part, spurred on by Jack, the show opened in Manchester and, such was its success, that a four-week tour was arranged to Birmingham and Oxford, then we would open at the Roundhouse in London.

Holding the show together was a huge task. The Desdemona had to be replaced; she couldn't sing. Marianne Faithfull came to see it hoping to take over, took too much of everything and collapsed in my hotel room. It's the only time I was a headline in a national newspaper; it didn't help my divorce. P. P. Arnold got bored with singing the same songs every night; she had to be replaced. One night I saw the show in Birmingham and it was like a Marx Brothers movie. A lot of people fell down a lot. Why? Someone had made a hash cake and everyone, innocently or not, even Jeffrey Wickham, had had some. On Thursday morning, in Oxford, I was woken early by a phone call from Pamela Hay from the Theatre Projects Office. What the hell was I doing arranging auditions for dwarfs, midgets and freaks? I opened my copy of *The Stage*. There was such an ad. I thought I was hallucinating, cracking up. I knew it had to be something to do with Jack. It was. He had decided it would be fun to cram the galleries of the Globe set with Bosch-type onlookers. I cancelled the auditions. One night I returned from London. The show began. The band played a riff I'd never heard before. Iago appeared and started a long monologue over the riff. The audience were invited to a bullfight. He was the matador and Othello was the bull. Enter Jack doing 'I am a bull' acting. The audience were asked to shout *Olé* at a given signal. Would they do a trial run, please. This went on for fifteen minutes. Jack's response when I charged into his dressing room afterwards was 'Oh I thought it was a jolly good idea. Don't you like it?' It was cut.

Almost needless to say, *Catch My Soul* opened at the Roundhouse, an inspired choice of venue, to sensational reviews. Harold Hobson said of the staging of Othello's epilepsy, 'It was one of the most inspired strokes of staging I have ever seen.' The truth is the sequence was such a mess that I said to the lighting designer, John B. Read, 'For goodness' sake put a strobe on it or something!'

The run was a sell-out, then we went to the Prince of Wales for another six months. I don't think there was a night when the whole company turned up. On one memorable occasion the show began with only a bass player in the bandstand. During the course of the evening the other players drifted in until they were at full strength. My eyes were dry when it finally closed.

To crown it all, Michael refused to take his name off the credits and insisted on taking half the royalties. What with him and Casper calling his own rehearsal of one of the Othello–Desdemona scenes, my new family was proving like all families: not so easy.

I did *Catch My Soul* once more in Paris at the Théâtre Marigny with a great, disciplined cast. It closed in a week. The critics were ultraconservative, Shakespeare was being profaned. Now who had said that before?

When I came to do *Othello* at the Royal Exchange with Paterson Joseph and Andy Serkis in 2002, I realised how indebted I was to Jack for the accuracy of his insights into the play. What a mixed bag of hell and enlightenment it was.

CHAPTER 26

The Beginning of a Long Run

When Lindsay had met Johanna at our engagement party she had been quite startled. Her comment was 'She's just like me'. They were both blonde, beautiful English roses and Catholics, at least on their mothers' side. There the similarities ended. If *A Midsummer Night's Dream* had finally parted Lindsay and me, it brought Johanna and me together. This was the seventh show we had done and we had had from the beginning an empathy and understanding that had deepened with each production.

We had perforce spent a great deal of time together but there had never been a hint of anything beyond the professional and a burgeoning friendship. With the same certainty that I knew I was going to marry Lindsay, I took Johanna to dinner at George's and asked her to live with me. She said yes. If my new compulsion came out of the blue to me, it did to her too. Later I wondered why she had agreed so quickly. She couched her reply in very odd terms: 'Well, you asked me to take up my bed and walk, so I did.' Now, my mother had always insisted that I was a virgin birth but even I didn't claim the powers of the miraculous and I didn't see Johanna as Lazarus, but that's what she said.

I was in the process of buying a house in Richmond with Lindsay; Johanna found the money to buy her part of it and we prepared to move in. Although the 69 was a great success, we appeared to be making no headway in our aim to have a permanent theatre built for us in Manchester. In spite of intense lobbying and municipal dinners, at which Michael made fantastic speeches that must have rivalled his father's, there seemed no prospect of any go-ahead. Therefore Johanna and I decided that Richmond was a good idea, since our futures professionally were likely to be in London. We were both very ambitious. We discussed our future one night in a restaurant in Bramhall and were in total agreement. Our careers were the priority, there would be no question of children for a long time. Almost immediately Johanna became pregnant.

The Tibetan Book of the Dead tells us that after death, when the soul has failed the tests that if passed would excuse it another incarnation, it visits a great valley full of thousands upon thousands of copulating couples. It then chooses its parents and prepares for reincarnation. This soul was evidently impatient to get going again.

I was delighted at the news but, like many other men before me, couldn't really imagine what it meant. I knew Johanna was going through something extraordinary but I felt completely detached from it, not in any unpleasant way, just detached.

Besides, we had a production to do. The 69 company was running out of steam, much to the delight of a bunch of radical students led by one David Edgar who regarded us as old-fashioned and conservative, and wanted us out of their theatre. I had been offered, but declined, to take over the Liverpool Playhouse, which had been pre-eminent in the region under David Scase but was in decline, and now Stuart Burge invited me to the Nottingham Playhouse to direct Sophocles' *Antigone* with Shirley Knight in the title role. Burge had asked Michael to do it but he couldn't and had suggested me instead. I jumped at it. I had seen Shirley Knight in the cult movie *Dutchman* and thought her marvellous. I also wanted a crack at Greek tragedy. The pregnant Johanna agreed to design it and I asked Flick Colby of Pan's People, who had done the West End version of *Catch My Soul*, to choreograph it. I read everything I could about how the Greeks would have done it and conceived as pure a production as I could based on music and dance. I had seen Anne Papathanassiou's *Electra* with the Piraikon Theatre Company and had loved their almost operatic style. That is what I set out to achieve.

Shirley Knight was now living in England with her husband, the television writer John Hopkins (she had briefly added the Hopkins to her name), so we were able to meet and prepare thoroughly. We got on very well. We were both devoted to the Method, though, as I was to find out, she was more of the American school of Lee Strasberg than Stanislavsky.

The play was to be given in repertoire with a Feydeau farce to be directed by Burge. He had cast it by then so most of my cast was already chosen. This was tricky because it meant that many of his excellent actors would have to be content with being in the chorus. I was allowed to augment the company with one or two of my own actors, Jeffrey Wickham, Michael Elphick (*Boon*) and Peter Childs, and rehearsals started.

It was a very intense and committed rehearsal period. *Antigone* is a great play not a million miles away from the St Joan story, though far more rooted in the ordinary reality of the family. I thought I was being duly inspirational.

On the first night two things happened. First, I became horribly aware that in spite of all the hard work, commitment and fidelity to the text, I had produced a well-meaning bore. It was a far more horrible realisation than with any of the other flops I had hitherto directed; *Fuenteovejuna* paled into insignificance; *Oom-Pah-Pah* was a mere blip. I had taken a great play and managed not to breathe a single spark of life into it.

The second thing was that Shirley gave a performance that bore no resemblance to what she had rehearsed. You could see the bemusement on the actors' faces as they were faced not with the indomitable, pure, fierce Antigone, but, not to put too fine a point on it, a fishwife.

On first nights, however it has gone, congratulations are the order of the day. Success or failure, everyone has worked hard, the reviews haven't come out and for a few hours it is possible to live in a dream world of success. On this occasion I couldn't contain myself. I stormed into her dressing room. 'What the hell did you think you were doing?' I demanded.

'Well, Braham, I got up this morning feeling angry. When I got to the theatre I thought that's it, Shirley, use your anger.' So much for the Strasberg Method, which has more than a tendency to make actors worship their own inner emotions rather than use them and refine them at the service of the play.

It was a painful experience. I have never attempted the Greeks since. I am gingerly flirting with the idea now. It is unfinished business. I know that to bring off Greek tragedy you somehow have to earth the play, something the Greeks didn't have to bother with. I do not know how you do this with the chorus but I'm getting there.

During the rehearsal period there was a phone call: 'Casper here.' This was not surprising. He had decided that Tom should do *Charley's Aunt* again, and Richard Pilbrow had agreed to tour it and take it to London. I readily agreed but my commitment to Nottingham meant that I couldn't spend the proper amount of time casting it so Casper and Michael were holding auditions for me. Not something I would contemplate now. He wasn't phoning about that; he was phoning to say that the breakthrough had occurred, that the Manchester City Council had agreed to build us a theatre on a green site. They would put up a third of the money, the Arts Council a third and the other third we would have to raise through public appeal. It was a heady moment. It meant that everything Michael and Casper had dreamt over and worked at with Richard Negri could be realised, for uniquely in Britain at that time we would be allowed to design the theatre ourselves. The usual pattern was for a local council to appoint architects to design a theatre and, when it was built, find someone to run it. That accounted for the endlessly boring, brown-box, erroneously conceived theatres that had been springing up all over England.

At this point starts the story of how the Royal Exchange Theatre came to be designed and how it came into being.

Although I was the initiating force behind the creation of the company in Manchester, in the designing of the theatre I was very junior; in fact, I did little more than listen and, as the various ideas reached model form, watch. The thesis was this. The two golden ages of theatre were the Greek and the Elizabethan. The design of their theatres expressed man's relationship to the gods.

In the Greek theatre the chorus who represented us, the audience, played in the orchestra, a thrust stage surrounded by the audience on three sides. Behind them the kings and queens acted out their drama on the raised skene, and behind them was the sky, the entrance of the gods and, in Epidaurus, the sea. The designers of these theatres, which were of course open air, had a secret knowledge of acoustics, so that in a 2,000-seat theatre literally a pin dropping could be heard by the entire audience.

In the Elizabethan theatre, the Renaissance theatre, the actors stood at the centre of the world, the globe, with the heavens above and hell beneath. The theatres themselves were the set, there was little or no scenery and the costumes were contemporary.

The Romans gradually destroyed the Greek form. The audience sat in the orchestra (stalls) and all the action took place on the skene. The proscenium was born. The skene was enclosed and the sky shut out. There was no longer a powerful entrance for the gods. The theatre became a place for spectacle, sometimes gladiatorial equivalents of video nasties.

As the Romans had done, so did the Jacobeans, led by Inigo Jones. The Jacobean playwrights mirrored the decadence of the time and the proscenium was reinstated.

Playwrights had written for and actors acted in theatres that had a cosmic force. What the group wanted to do was to re-continue the line of succession from the Greeks to the Elizabethans onwards into our time.

The process of designing and then building the theatre was going to take some years and it was clear that the University Theatre was outliving its usefulness. Sharing with the University meant that there was no continuity of work and the small seating capacity made it an uneconomical proposition. We conceived the idea of finding a space, maybe a disused warehouse or factory, as the Mermaid had done, and building a temporary theatre there. It had the added attraction that we could experiment with design while we were doing it. We all worked on the basic assumption that our new theatre would be some sort of thrust stage and this would be a great opportunity to perfect the concept. The hunt for suitable premises was on and we gave a year's notice to the University Theatre, which would shortly afterwards metamorphose into what is now Contact Theatre.

CHAPTER 27

The Last Show at the University Theatre

While Michael, Casper and Richard set to work, I turned to *Charley's Aunt* again. They had found the young actors for me. Joanna McCallum and Celia Bannerman played the girls, Gareth Forwood was a delightful Charley and David Horovitch, another ex-Central student who had returned to the company several times since playing Rosencrantz in *Hamlet*, played Jack. Jimmy Cossins played Sir Francis Chesney again, Dilys Hamlett the real aunt, and my Pozzo and Friar Lawrence, Wolfe Morris, made a rare comic appearance as Spettigue.

Once again Tom excelled, the tour was a sell-out success and we finally played the Christmas season at the Apollo Theatre. The critics were not kind, they found the production vulgar, but the audience didn't. It was an enjoyable time.

Peter Rawley was the agent for all of us at the time, including Tom, and he phoned to say that Mia Farrow was anxious to appear on the stage. Would I fly out to France to meet her and discuss possible projects? She was starring there in a Chabrol movie with Jean-Paul Belmondo. I arranged a date and began to wonder what to suggest.

Allisoune Browne, our Company Manager, came round to dinner in Richmond when Johanna was about a month away from giving birth. As we were sitting there having a drink she began to sing hauntingly 'Mary Rose, Mary Rose'. I asked what she was singing. 'Oh, it just came into my head,' she said. 'It's a play I did by J. M. Barrie. You should read it. It's rather wonderful.' She then told me the gist of it. A young girl, newly engaged, goes with her family and fiancé to visit a Hebridean island and while on it disappears. Years later she comes back but where everyone else has now grown old, she has remained at the same age. I read it. Barrie obviously wrote it for Mia Farrow. I flew out, met her, was duly enchanted, gave it to her, she agreed and we scheduled it for the spring of 1972.

You may have noticed that I have not used the word love hitherto. That is because I had no idea then, and little more now, what it meant. I had been in love with love, I had had obsessional relationships, I had been married and I cared for Johanna deeply and with great genuine affection. Were any of these love? If not, why not and would I ever know?

Johanna gave birth to Jacob on 27 September 1971 and when I saw him my heart danced. I was breached, I had no defences, not even the portcullis. Whether I liked it or not, the love was unconditional and total. It changed my life and I believe it made me a better director. There was a new warmth in my work rather than perhaps the overwrought intensity of emotion that had pleased some but alienated others in my productions up till now. We called him Jacob because Jacob came out of the womb grabbing hold of Esau's ankle trying to get out first. I liked that.

My delighted mother phoned to give me the number to ring to arrange the circumcision, the number of the Mohel as the circumciser is known in Hebrew. I rang the Mohel. He had a heavily accented squeaky voice. 'Certainly, certainly, not a problem.' I told him I didn't want a religious service. 'Certainly, certainly. I understand.' We arranged a date. 'Please have ready hot water and plenty bandages.' I asked why. 'To deal wis ze blood.' I cancelled the appointment and put down the phone. I phoned my mother and told her, and she put down the phone.

Ten minutes later it rang again. 'The royal family are all circumcised and he'll never be allowed to serve in the Merchant Navy.' I had to face the fact that I might be depriving him of the one profession he might set his heart on but I did not blanch. I took the risk. I did not want the mark of that despotic God on Jacob. The thought of that act of violence on an eight-day-old child sickened me.

My grandparents were reeling. They had been, no doubt, delighted that my marriage was over but here I was with another shikseh and I wasn't even married to her. Their grandson was a momser (Yiddish for bastard). My grandmother refused to have anything more to do with me and wouldn't see Jacob. My grandfather, thank goodness, did come and see him fairly regularly and they derived great joy from each other.

It was many years before I could understand and therefore forgive my grandparents. My grandfather was in fact a kind, soulful man but he was riddled with fear; a fear induced by the Holocaust. This made him in his actions a bigot and a tyrant, but not in his heart. My mother, who had been emotionally damaged by him, had saved me from the worst he could do. I resented him then; I feel a strange tenderness towards him now.

I was trying to be done with that despotic God for ever. Armund told me one morning, 'Last night I met the Devil about three miles above the earth. He asked me who wrote the Ten Commandments. I answered that God did. No, I did, how do you think I get so many souls down there in hell?'

It was the beginning of the Ten Commandments that was so riveting to me: 'Thou shalt have no other gods before me.' Not I'm the only one, but a tacit acknowledgement that there were others but he wanted them, the Jews, to obey him. Then the terrible warning: 'For I thy God am a jealous God, visiting the iniquity of the fathers upon the children unto the third and fourth generations of them that hate me.' The contract that the Old Testament was reporting was the offer of survival to the Jews in return for their total adherence. The Jews were, however, a stiff-necked people (hallelujah!) and, as the story wore on, more and more rules and laws are added until by the end of Leviticus and Numbers, Yaweh is attempting to control every waking moment of his recalcitrant people's lives.

There are prayers to be offered for every action you take from waking up to sleeping. On waking up the man says, 'Blessed art thou O Lord our God, King of the Universe who hast not made me a woman.' The woman says, 'Blessed art thou, O Lord our God, King of the Universe who hast made me as I am.' Have a good day! The last prayer at night is to protect us from impure thoughts while we sleep. What, no more delicious wet dreams? Look what happened to poor old Onan. He spilled his seed and was promptly boffed by a flash of lightning. Bit of an overreaction for a wank. The fear of sex and its subversive power is paramount. Lovemaking must only take place in the dark, there must be no conversation except over the technicalities of the act and both parties must decide on a verse of the Five Books of Moses to meditate on during the act.

The criminality of Yaweh reaches its climax in the Book of Job. Yaweh is talking to his sons and Satan (it is not clear whether Satan is one of the sons) up in heaven. Satan says that there is no such thing as a righteous man. God insists that there is and points to Job. Satan says, just let me test him and I'll make him deny you. God agrees and Satan devastates Job's life, taking away his livelihood, covers him in disease and kills his wife and children. Job remains true to Yaweh. So for a bet God allows Job to be put through the worst torment that Satan has devised. Job has done nothing wrong. Where is Yaweh's concept of justice? Well, Yaweh wins the bet but something in him must have stirred, for at the end of the Book of Job he appears before Job in a cloud and thunders his credentials as God before him, for over one hundred lines. Job's meek rejoinder is, 'You are the Lord my God.' In his book *An Answer to Job*, Jung argues that in that moment Job knows more about God than God does himself. Thereafter in the Bible there appears the figure of Sophia who sits on the right hand of God and intercedes between God and man. There shall be no more Jobs. You can see why I did not want Yaweh's mark on my son.

I talk about Yaweh as if he exists. If for centuries people believe in him, practise his edicts and follow and worship him, then to all intents and

117

purposes he does exist. The force of Yaweh exists in this world today, as does the force of Allah and the force of Christ. I am proud to be a Jew but I will have no truck with Yaweh and his religion.

All these great religions fail in one respect, even Christianity, which in its purest form seems to me the most evolved of them. They cannot deal with the lower half of the human body except by trying to repress it. Islam, Catholicism, Judaism have stored up years of repression that can only lead to disaster for them and for us. Whatever the new spiritual impulse is that will replace these great religions, it will have to bless and harness this mighty force in humanity. We are rightly called human animals. We are as much one as another and that is part of the wonder of our being. We cannot develop one at the expense of the other. That is the lesson of Euripides' masterpiece *The Bacchae*. Dionysus and Apollo are at the centre of our existence and always will be. This too is at the heart of all great theatre.

While all this was cannoning around in my mind, Eric Thompson, he of *The Magic Roundabout* who had acted with the group at the Piccolo Theatre and the Old Vic, was about to make his professional directorial début with an old play he'd found called *Journey's End*. This play has recently been revived to startling success in London. It made as great an impact then, transferring from Manchester first to the Mermaid and then the Cambridge Theatre. As it had launched Laurence Olivier's career when first produced, so it now launched Peter Egan's.

I was set to follow that with *Mary Rose*. I had heard a recording of John Tavener's *The Whale* and had been so struck with it that uncharacteristically I had written a fan letter asking to meet him. We did meet and I asked him to compose the music for *Mary Rose*, which he agreed to do. So started a friendship that was of great value to me. In his biography it is suggested that we drank a lot, womanised and generally painted the town red together. I really don't remember that, but I do remember his very special spiritual quality, which became more and more pronounced in his work. We have nearly worked together several times since, once on a project based on a modern retelling of the Holy Grail, once on his inexplicably unperformed opera *The Toll Houses*, but neither of these ambitious projects came to fruition. Anything may yet happen.

Mia Farrow was born to play Mary Rose. How many actresses do you know who can talk to a tree and be utterly convincing? Her sense of 'the other' was unnerving and powerful. Barrie's play was brought hypnotically alive by her inner radiance. Peter Saunders was due to bring it into London, but when he saw it he felt it was too special and would attract only a minority audience. How wrong he was. After a short tour the Shaw Theatre took the production and you couldn't get a seat for love or money.

The first night in London ended and the audience was leaving the auditorium. A tall lady jumped on to the stage and began to make for the wings. I interrupted her. 'Excuse me, you can't go there,' I said politely but sternly.

'I'm going to see Mia Farrow,' said Katharine Hepburn and strode on past me.

I'm not usually star-struck but, reduced to jelly by this glorious woman, I tottered backstage promptly to be introduced to an exceedingly tall man. 'Thank you for bringing magic back into the theatre,' pronounced the unmistakable tones of Noël Coward. Somehow the presence of those two gods made it a first night like no other.

Is there an actress who can play Mary Rose now? If so, let her come forward. The play should be revived. At any rate the production was my farewell to the University Theatre after seven excellent years. The company had one last show: George Hall's direction of *Guys and Dolls* with Zoë Wanamaker as Adelaide and Trevor Peacock playing Nathan Detroit, a part he reprised years later in Richard Eyre's production. A new phase was about to begin. We had found a temporary home, or so we thought.

CHAPTER 28

Higgledy-piggledy

Lots of things began to happen at once. The one with the most far-reaching consequences was our temporary home. I have read several accounts of what took place, none of them written by people who were directly involved. I was.

The search for a suitable building had been going on for some time. Nothing seemed right. Either it was in an inaccessible, run-down part of Manchester or it wasn't big enough. Then, it is said, in June Peter Henriques, in his bath, thought of the Royal Exchange. This was the old trading hall from the time when cotton was king and it had closed, with the demise of cotton, suitably enough in 1968 as the 69 Theatre Company started rehearsing *Hamlet*. Charles Clore had bought it and was making money out of the surrounding shops and offices but, being a listed building, all schemes to convert the great hall into a money-making enterprise had been rejected. The huge cavernous space had remained disused ever since. It lay right in the centre of Manchester and was the city's old heart.

It was an electric moment when the group of us – Michael, Casper, Bob Scott and I – first saw the space. It was filthy, it was cold, it was superb. Richard Negri saw it some time later with its three-quarters of an acre of parquet flooring under its three 120-foot-high glass domes: 'I knew what the previous few years and my unconscious thoughts of the relationship between the audience and the stage had been all about.' He wrote 'Rosebud' in the dust. He had been reminded of Xanadu in *Citizen Kane*. But this is to run on ahead. More immediately Laurie Dennett, presumably with help from Richard, was to design a 430-seat theatre to open in spring 1973. It would have a thrust stage. Unlike the University Theatre, it was to have a keyhole shape, the small part of the keyhole coming from backstage and the bulbous part to be surrounded by the audience.

Meanwhile Mia's husband, André Previn, whom I had got to know quite well and who had admired *Mary Rose*, asked me if I would be interested in directing a new musical that he had in mind. He had been to see a successful London musical, Arnold Bennett's *The Card* starring Jim Dale, and thought, 'I can do better than that.' This was more than flattering. André, one of the most entertaining and charming men I had met, was a god to me from his jazz interpretation of *My Fair Lady*, *Gigi* and so on. The material he chose was J. B. Priestley's picaresque novel *The Good Companions*. I went away to read it and spent three days in heaven doing so. It's about a touring pierrot company, end of the pier entertainers, who are joined variously by an uptight spinster, Miss Trant, a young schoolmaster, Inigo Jollifant, and a blunt working-class Yorkshireman, Jess Oakroyd. These three are all at crisis point in their lives and in the unaccustomed habitat of a theatrical troupe they find themselves again and finally leave, reinvigorated, to start new lives. It is a joyous novel with a serious undertone. Priestley was a Jungian and the book is really about the individuation process. Previn had secured the great Johnny Mercer as the lyricist and I suggested Ronnie Harwood as the book writer. What a line-up! We could pick and choose the producer and we chose Bernard Delfont with Richard Pilbrow's Theatre Projects as the Executive Management. I couldn't believe my luck. Work started then and there, and would continue over the next two years.

At the same time both Germany and France bought *Catch My Soul* for production and they both wanted me to direct. There was no competition. I chose Paris. France, or rather French, had already played a part in my life. From the moment I started to learn the language at Brockhurst I seemed to be able to speak it. At the age of ten I was sent on an exchange to a Parisian family, which cemented my fluency and then, as soon as I was old enough to go away on my own, I spent every summer holiday in Paris. Speaking French was like wearing a mask. I felt a different person, more relaxed, more confident and not so desperately introverted. Two months in Paris on expenses was not to be missed. Rehearsals were to begin in September, the moment the two-month French holiday was ended, and I was flown over to do the casting.

The theatre was to be the Marigny, Barrault's old home on the Champs-Élysées. It was run by Madame Elvira Popescu, *une monstre*, in other words one of the grandes dames of French theatre, and Hubert de Mallet, an aristocratic man of great sophistication. He had as his right-hand man Robert Manuel, himself a distinguished director. A great deal of money for the show was put up by Aaron Rothschild of the celebrated banking family.

Flick Colby agreed to do the choreography again and we had a wonderful time setting up the production, freed from the more lunatic aspects of Jack Good's tutelage. Working abroad on a show you have had a hit with is a heady experience. You are treated like royalty. This involved being wined and dined, and in Paris that meant something.

France had no tradition of putting on what they called *Comédies-Musicales* so it wasn't easy to cast, especially since the concept of the show was multicultural and based on a Shakespeare text. Several American expats were found. Gordon Heath, who owned a famous nightclub, was to play Othello, the totally sensational Nancy Holloway, who was and is a big star, Bianca, and an Algerian, Georges Blanes, Iago. Martine Clémenceau, who had sung for France in the Eurovision Song Contest, was to play Desdemona and a well-known actress, Jacqueline Danot, Emilia. The Tribe of Hell, Flick and I decided, would be all female and with the backing singers it was, from a male point of view, about as pulchritudinous a cast as you could imagine.

Something else had happened as a result of *The Good Companions*. It had jogged my memory of a play by Priestley called *Time and the Conways*, which I had read in the house play-reading group at Clifton. I read it again. It tells the tale of a typical family at the end of the First World War and takes its story to just before the outbreak of the Second. Its brilliant theatrical device is that the first and third acts are set in 1918, the second in 1939. You see the family in all its optimism, then what happened to them, mostly disastrously, in middle age, and finally return to where the first act had left off and watch them start to take the right or wrong turnings that lead to the second act. This is encompassed by the idea, expressed by two of the characters, that time is not, as in our Western conception, a continuum, but a simultaneous event so that by our actions at any given moment we can change our lives past and present. It chimed in perfectly with the ideals of our group and I wanted to do it in the temporary theatre. It had not been revived since its première in 1937. I applied for the rights. Priestley seemed reluctant to allow the production and eventually I was forced to change horses and begin work on Vanbrugh's *The Provok'd Wife* instead.

Finally I was also planning a production of *Endgame* for the about to be constructed theatre. *Godot* had been a great experience and in the Pozzo and Estragon, Wolfe Morris and Trevor Peacock, of that production I had the perfect Hamm and Clov. All these things were going around in my head in a great jumble and it was a relief to get on the train to Paris in early September.

A friend of my cousin Jacqueline had let me a flat on the rue de Buçi in the Latin Quarter, which I shared with Flick with whom I did not have an affair. The reasons why one does not have an affair are often as interesting as the reasons why one does. Flick was delicious, intelligent and talented. She also had the kind of outgoing temperament that I found highly attractive. Moreover, she seemed to like me. So why not? At various points in my life I think I have not had affairs as a sort of unconscious self-protection. Rather like people who always have deep relationships with people they haven't a hope of marrying, I seem to have not had affairs with women who might have been so absolutely right for me it would have pulled me away from, in this case, the right marriage and fatherhood. After we got back to London Flick asked half humorously, 'What was wrong with me?'

It took a while to get used to the French way of working. Before the day's rehearsal started, everyone had to shake hands with everyone else and exchange the ritual 'Comment ça va?' 'Ça va bien.' I persuaded them to substitute a little nod of the head like a bow, otherwise I threatened to start rehearsals a quarter of an hour earlier. On the first day I gave my introductory spiel, which is part of a director's armoury. Every time I touched on the deeper meaning of Othello there were audible murmurs of 'Ah, le philosophe'. It seemed that no actor could speak to the director before the leading actor had, after that the next in seniority, till little by little everyone was allowed to address 'Le Chef'. I abolished that. On the first rehearsal I asked Gordon Heath to move to such and such a place and he asked me if he could move somewhere else. De Mallet thundered down the aisle, 'Do you want me to sack him?' he hissed.

I was bemused. 'Why?'

'One does not question the director.' This indeed appeared to be the case. Apparently in the commercial theatre the director never received a fee, only a percentage of the box office. Thus if the show was a flop – and lots of them were – he didn't get paid. Directors therefore undertook too many productions, rehearsed them in a very short time (two weeks being the norm) and gave the moves and interpretation to the actors because there was no time to do anything else and certainly no time for argument. It took me a long time to relax the company enough so that they could join in the collaborative process I was now more and more enjoying. Not so long before, I might have been totally in sympathy with the French approach.

Worst of all, rehearsals started after lunch at 2 p.m. and went on until a quite late dinner-time. This meant that the actors turned up comatose after the traditional French midday meal: four courses, wine and a digestif. After a few days I changed the routine to the English hours of ten till one, an hour off, and two till six. They were thunderstruck. 'How can one eat lunch in one hour?' they asked. However, after the initial day when they appeared at ten, wonderingly saying 'I have seen the dawn!' they got used to it.

The Marigny was a beautiful theatre and it had a Green Room to end all Green Rooms. As you arrived at the stage door a bow-tied waiter took your lunch and dinner orders. The cooking was excellent. The food and wine were dirt cheap, subsidised by the management. After rehearsals you could linger there for as long as you liked, drinking, playing cards or chatting. I was now speaking French without having to think in English first. I was having a ball.

I was also, for the first time, unfaithful. Among all the beautiful women in the cast I was attracted to Clara Lesueur who hailed from Guadeloupe. Why? Some of the reasons were obvious. I was alone in Paris, as it were on a prolonged holiday, and she seemed willing and lovely. Why did I not keep it secret from Johanna? Some men always imbue their relationship with an importance that seems to justify it. I believed I was in love. When I got back to England I repeated the Virginia syndrome. I couldn't exist without her. I told Johanna. This is painful to write. She moved out of our home with one-year-old Jacob to a flat lent by Brian Block. I went to Paris, brought Clara back, arrived in London, realised my mistake, sent her back to Paris, begged Johanna to come back and forgive me, which she did, and we resumed our life together. At the time I felt little shame at what I had done. I felt I had to do it.

Two people meet, both on their individual paths. For a time their paths intertwine. They complement each other and they grow alongside each other. But no couple can be absolutely everything to each other; indeed, if they were there would be no further growth and like the lovers in Bo Widerberg's movie *Elvira Madigan* they might as well commit suicide. Therefore there is always something that stays outside the relationship which at some point has to be addressed. This is not an apology for infidelity – it is immensely hurtful and can be truly damaging – but it is an attempt to explain it, since it appears to be endemic in human nature. I'm not talking now about the seriously sexual incontinent; I am talking about people who genuinely want to make their relationship work. I believe that although I was almost frighteningly grown-up for a twenty-nine-year-old, in my emotional sexual life I was very immature. The relationship with Clara helped me to inch forward, for which I am immensely grateful to her. At the same time I am still ashamed of the hurt I caused Johanna, a hurt I would repeat twice more.

I have already said that the show was roasted by the critics. Gordon Heath was known to be gay and therefore, in their opinion, was unfit to play a Shakespeare lead. His use of a hand mike outraged them because to them he seemed to be giving a blow job. Georges Blanes, being Algerian, also was totally disqualified from playing Shakespeare. The show only lasted a few performances.

Still, I left Paris with a friend for life in Nancy Holloway and the best prescription to cure acute indigestion, from which I was suffering, that I have ever had.

'What do you drink at night?' asked the doctor.

'Pastis, some rosé, then over dinner red wine.'

'Pastis is not good for you, no pastis. There is no such thing as a great rosé and it is acidulated, so no rosé. There are great white wines but they are far too expensive also they too are acidulated, hence no white wines. This leaves us with Bordeaux and Burgundy for red wines. Obviously we must choose Bordeaux because those are truly great wines. I prescribe at least half a bottle of good Bordeaux with your dinner.'

This seems to me an excellent remedy, not just for indigestion but for all manner of illnesses. I recommend it and have forced myself to take it to this day.

I think that in many ways the production in Paris was better than the London one. The cast were far more disciplined and Blanes and Heath were fine actors with whom one could really explore the text. However, it probably lacked the electricity of the London version. It did not have that indefinable quality of excitement that a Lance LeGault or indeed a P. J. Proby brought to the stage. Its critical failure did not harm me much as they didn't know about it in England and there was plenty to occupy me there when I got back.

CHAPTER 29

The Tent

May 1973–January 1974

The Tent, as we called the temporary theatre, was a wonder in its own right. It cost well under £10,000 to build. It seemed that Michael Williams, our prodigious Production Manager, constructed it single-handedly. Seats miraculously appeared from a disused cinema and Tootal's supplied the material for the tent itself. When it opened with Max's production of *Arms and the Man* with Brian Cox, Jenny Agutter and Tom Courtenay (and indeed Jasmina who came back into my ken after an absence) the public took it to their hearts. Throughout the eight months that it stood there the theatre was packed; even in the winter when the audience was issued with army blankets, there being no heating, there was no seat to be had. Apart from the plays, the Ballet Rambert played there and late-night entertainments were given by, among others, Albert Finney, Edith Evans, Michael Flanders, Frank Muir and Geraldine McEwan. Its success was of course due to the quality of the productions, but also to the egalitarian nature of the venue. It wasn't like a theatre. It wasn't deterrently exclusive and Dennett's auditorium on one tier didn't have clearly defined superior or inferior seats; you simply sat as near or as far from the stage as suited you.

Preparing my first production of *Endgame* I had revisited the unconscious production of *Godot* I had done with Wolfe and Trevor. I realised that one thing Beckett was doing was dramatising the difficult interdependence of the mind and the body. In *Godot* Vladimir and Lucky are the minds and Estragon and Pozzo the bodies. They can't bear each other but they can't do without each other – the dilemma of the human animal again. In *Endgame* the stricken, blind Hamm, confined to a wheelchair, was the mind, dependent on Clov, the body. This concept, played out in Johanna's brilliantly designed room, which subtly suggested the inside of a skull, worked well. The clowning of Trevor's increasingly desperate Clov leavened the apparent bleakness of the text, the evening was a success and the play followed *Mary Rose* down to the Shaw Theatre.

Following this, Michael Elliott staged *The Family Reunion* with Edward Fox. This was one of his greatest productions. The appearance of the Eumenides in our tent was one of the most frightening things I have experienced in the theatre. Elliott and Eliot together made for an unforgettable night.

I was well into casting *The Provok'd Wife* when Priestley suddenly relented and we were told that we could after all present *Time and the Conways*. Without hesitation I switched at the eleventh hour. Dilys would play Mrs Conway and that virtuoso dancer and human being, Christopher Gable, made his acting stage début as the quiet but inspired Alan.

With two Priestley pieces on the cards, I at last met the great man at his home near Stratford, Kissing Tree House. He didn't give a lot of advice except rightly to advise me to cast young actors who would then age up for the middle act rather than the other way round. This made the middle act particularly heartbreaking. He also informed me that the first act wasn't very good so the best thing was to play it very fast. About *The Good Companions* his advice was to keep the cast list as small as possible, then 'you won't have to have so many bad actors'. His bluff Yorkshire exterior concealed a sensitive, wise man who knew a great deal about the theatre and, indeed, life. His output was prolific. Novels, plays, historical analysis, lectures, meditations, his was a first-rate mind that remains under-appreciated. Whenever one of his plays is revived, as with *Time and the Conways*, the critics are always surprised at how good they are and how timeless their message seems to be. Priestley wanted to reach a wide audience so he strove to find a popular means of expressing his deeper intent. The audience don't know they are being preached to because they are being swept along by the theatricality of the event. It is only afterwards that the play's effect works on them. That is what theatre should be, affecting the heart rather than the conscious mind, like music.

Time and the Conways was a wonderful play to rehearse and the first act was not as bad as he thought. Had it had a star in it, it would certainly have gone to London, for the reviews were excellent.

Priestley travelled to Manchester to see it. I was quaking with fear. I knew he would not mince his words. I met him in my office in the first interval. He downed his whisky and said not a word. In the second interval he announced, 'You know, that second act is one of the finest ever written!' At the end of the play he got up and made a speech to the audience. 'I think I might say a few words.' He loved the makeshift theatre and he had enjoyed the production. After that he met the cast. Rachel Herbert had been superb as Madge, the repressed spinster sister who had become a schoolmistress. He eyed her sternly: 'The trouble with you is you're too tall.' It was a devastatingly awful thing to say, short of arranging an amputation at the Manchester Royal Infirmary, inferring there was nothing I could do to help the hapless Rachel. Still, he approved of me and as I got to know him better and better over the next couple of years he spoke revealingly about his friendship with Jung and his particular liking for the works of Ouspensky. He wasn't actually a Yorkshire version of Armund but he was a fascinating and inspiring man.

CHAPTER 30

The Conception and Pregnancy of the Royal Exchange

I'm not sure when, but it must have been early on, Casper had his brilliant idea. Why go to a greenfield site away from the city centre when we could build our permanent theatre right here in the Exchange, just like our temporary one, for a fraction of the cost, saving millions? Everyone, including the funding bodies, leapt at that one and suddenly the whole process speeded up.

We had not yet decided what our theatre should be. The assumption was that the keyhole shape would be used again and the first model was based on that idea. Richard, however, kept on producing others. Time after time we would be summoned, usually to the Savile Club, to see the latest creation. Sometimes they were bizarrely incomprehensible. On one occasion we were confronted by a rubbish heap with two golden nails suspended above it. Was it a set for *Godot*? No, that was the theatre for all plays. Casper always seemed to understand what Richard was working through, but for someone like me it seemed that the final solution was a long way off. Then quite suddenly it all happened. At a meeting someone, I'm not sure who, asked, 'But if a god should come on to a stage in our time, how should he?' Someone answered, 'Into the same room as the audience of course.' After the Christian era, we were entering a time to discover the god in man. Again the acceptance of that was immediate and it could only mean one thing: a theatre in the round; everyone together, audience, actors and gods, using the same entrances and exits, united in a common cause, with no mysterious backstage, all the mysteries to be out there for all to see and share in. None of us had ever worked in the round before. So what!

Richard Negri was very small, with a face like a gnome. His button nose reminded you of one of Disney's dwarfs. He was a devout Catholic. He didn't as much speak to you as mutter at you; not only that but he would often start to walk away from you while he was muttering so that the end of what he was trying to say got lost in the ether. Since what he had to say was difficult to understand, even worse than Casper, it probably didn't matter much. He once tried to describe his vision of the opening scene of a

129

modern version of *Everyman*: 'The lights go up on a bare stage. A man is sitting on a chair. Don't take me literally!' He was also a genius.

We had been told that to be economically viable our theatre should hold 700–800 people. The other theatres in the round that we knew seated under half that. Richard had to solve this problem. How do you seat so many people without the auditorium being so vast as to lose intimacy? If you've tried sitting in the back rows at Chichester, which is only a thrust, you'll understand the problem.

Richard got his brainwave from the interior of a beehive. If you could somehow reproduce that structure so that in the holes of the combs you had people, you had your answer. His solution was, instead of building back, he built up in three tiers. On the top two tiers there were only two rows each. The ground floor has more but so near the stage as makes no difference. Most people in the theatre would be in a front row. No one would be more than thirty feet from the actors and there would be no bad seats.

I have said he was a devout Catholic. The theatre is seven-sided and each tier is articulated. There is a hole in the roof and at a certain time of day if the sun shines it shines directly on to the centre of the rose. It is a *pietà*.

Finally, Richard wanted the auditorium, as he put it, 'to hold the audience in space'. He conceived the walls to be entirely of glass. Then the audience would be suspended between the world of the gods in the outer hall and the stage where the actors who entered from that world would act out their drama. Like the Greek and Elizabethan theatres, the light in the auditorium would be directly affected by the time of day and the weather. The magician had his sleeves rolled up. Any magic would have to be created directly between actor and audience.

This was all breathtaking, but would we find architects capable of making this dream a reality? After exhaustive interviews we found the perfect firm, at that time pretty well unknown: Levitt Bernstein Associates. Axel Burrough was the technical expert and Malcolm Brown the one who had real understanding of Richard's vision. Our Project Manager was to be Michael Williams who, having built one theatre, was the obvious choice to build another. He held the balance between ourselves, the architects and the other consultants headed by Theatre Projects.

Their first problem was that the Exchange floor would not take the weight of the auditorium. The solution was to hang the building from the huge pillars in the hall in a contraption of the thinnest tubular steel that could be found. The steel cradles the theatre as though holding a baby.

All this came together so quickly that we were able to set a timetable for the building of the theatre, with an opening date in September 1976, by coincidence about the same time that the new National Theatre was aiming for. Evidently the temporary theatre would have to come down and we were faced with having to cease productions for over two years. How we decided to set up yet another temporary home in Manchester Cathedral of all places eludes me, but amazingly we did and used the opportunity to experiment with an auditorium in the round. By now James Maxwell and Richard Negri had become Artistic Directors, so we were five. In that season, for the first time, we called ourselves the Royal Exchange Theatre Company – 69 was no more. We had to obtain the royal patent to use 'Royal' in our title. We thought the title would give us status and I'm sure it did, but now I'm not so sure it was a good idea. It makes us sound a bit snobbish and exclusive, and may well deter sections of the public, especially young people, from coming to see us.

All five of us were involved in that season. Casper directed Max (and Bob Hoskins) in *A Man for All Seasons*. Michael and Richard co-directed Brian Cox in *The Cocktail Party* and I directed Kenneth Haigh in *Much Ado About Nothing*. None of the productions was particularly brilliant, the auditorium was gloomy and the energy of the company was across the road in the Exchange where the building was beginning to take shape. My mind had also turned back to the West End and musicals. The final act of the tug of war was about to take place.

CHAPTER 31

Not Such Good Companions

About twenty-five years after *The Good Companions* had been produced I came upon a biography of Judi Dench. As one does, I looked myself up in the index, turned to the relevant page and saw a, for her, vicious attack on my directorial performance. In her not noticeably humble opinion, I talked a good show but hadn't a clue how to deliver one. I must say I think she is a little harsh, but it is true that *The Good Companions* was not all that it could have been, although I'm constantly surprised how many people include it in their list of favourite musicals.

Although I had now directed a good many West End shows, including two musicals and two revues, they had all started elsewhere. I had not done a West End show from scratch. It did not occur to me that it might need a different approach. Musicals were still moving over from the old-fashioned Julian Slade type, via Andrew Lloyd Webber, to the big-concept shows we are used to today. *The Good Companions*, being in itself a period piece, needed a big-staging idea and it didn't get it because I thought it would be enough to tell the story as well as possible.

Unfortunately I also had to find another designer. Johanna had announced that she wanted another child. I was totally bemused. 'But we've got one,' I had objected. As an only child I couldn't imagine why we would want two children. Jacob seemed to be all that was needed. However, she had prevailed, thank goodness, and she was too pregnant to design the show. I chose Malcolm Pride, who also taught at Wimbledon and indeed had designed Casper's *Hamlet*. He was an excellent designer with great experience of West End musicals but of precisely the type that now seemed dated.

Recently there was talk of reviving the piece and I immediately thought of staging it as a pierrot show, so that it could be ingenious and original rather than the cumbersome event we created.

The next mistake I made was in the casting. I had assembled a curate's egg of a company. In those days there were mus.com.artists; people who went from one musical to another, hoping against hope for a long run to make their lives as peaceful as possible. I had a good smattering of those, mixed up with my actors like Malcolm Rennie, Roy Sampson and John Bardon with whom I had worked in Manchester. The two types operated in completely different ways and their styles never mixed well. This was simple ignorance on my part.

The principals were a different matter. Top of the pile was John Mills as Jess Oakroyd. He was a complete delight to work with, the only star that I can say had no idea that he was a star. There wasn't the slightest air or grace about him, just sheer hard work. Actually, he had been understudy to Fred Astaire when he appeared in London with Adele before the war, so he knew a bit about musicals and set about resuscitating his tap-dancing skills. Judi Dench played Miss Trant. She was already a distinguished actress, I had seen her Juliet about eight times and she too was a pleasure to rehearse with, whatever she thought about me. What is true is that although I had admired her work, I had reservations about certain performances, which seemed to me to rely too much on her natural charm and technique. This I told her about on one special drunken evening I'll come to later. It may have accounted for her harbouring an animus against me for so long. If so, I can't really blame her.

Chris Gable insisted on auditioning for Inigo Jollifant. He had found out that American directors made actors sing 'Somewhere over the Rainbow' because it was so hard. Try and you'll see why, especially the middle eight. Anyway, he passed triumphantly and of course his dancing was an asset to the show.

Casting Susie Dean, the ingénue in the Dinkie Doos and the love interest, was hard. Trying to find someone who was pretty but not wet, who could sing and play comedy, was taxing. Celia Bannerman, who had played Amy charmingly and wittily in my *Charley's Aunt*, captivated André Previn and indeed, with her perfect period looks and her freshness, she seemed ideal. Unfortunately, for one so versed in musicals, André was happy to let her audition a cappella; this had serious consequences.

Into this mix I introduced a choreographer from the Ballet Rambert whose work I admired, Jonathan Taylor. It was the wrong choice for such a showbiz event.

Previn, Harwood, Mercer, Mills, Dench, Gable, it seemed a must-win situation. Hal Prince has observed that the art of making a musical means getting the right team together. However starry the line-up, if they don't make a team you are not going to win. I hadn't assembled the right team.

The material was also not quite right. Ronnie had done a great job on the book but the score was a bit Broadway meets thirties England, especially the lyrics. Not only did the very, very great Johnny Mercer insert the sort of things that English audiences wince at (I particularly remember 'them's the breaks as William Shakespeare used to say') but he was locked in an old-fashioned era. At one meeting he suggested we do a song round a Christmas tree. But we didn't have a Christmas scene. Doesn't matter, put one in, he could write a good Christmas number. Previn's music was exceedingly tuneful and beguiling, but it still seemed to me that there was an obstacle between the Englishness, the period and the audience.

I am making this all sound awful but it wasn't that and although rehearsals were hard I don't remember them being as bad as Judi does.

We were due to open at the Palace Theatre in Manchester, of all places, for a fortnight prior to Her Majesty's Theatre in the West End. That is where Priestley's own play version of his novel had played years before. He was happy. 'Ay, it's a good take,' he pronounced, referring to the box-office capacity.

It was odd being in Manchester and having nothing to do with my company and staying in the swish surroundings of the Midland Hotel instead of digs.

It was not any easy opening. Malcolm Pride had misjudged the painting of the set so it looked as if the whole show was taking place in a swimming pool. He retired, with swollen ankles, to his hotel room from whence he refused to emerge, while I was left to try and rectify the matter. However, open it did, the local reviews were good, the houses were full and the audiences enthusiastic.

Bernard Delfont was not satisfied. In the time-honoured manner of West End musicals, I was summoned to a meeting in his room with the rest of the team at two in the morning after opening night. First there were to be changes to the script, the words naked and nude were to be expunged to avoid giving offence; the mind boggled. More seriously there were to be cast changes. Michael Balfour, who was playing the leader of the Dinkie Doos, was plainly too old to sustain the singing and dancing that was required. 'I know who we'll have,' said Delfont, 'we'll have that fellah, you know the one, very funny, in that TV show with the tall fellah, you know, the one in the double act, very funny, used to play in Variety, very funny sketches, you know who I mean!'

Even more seriously, it was clear that Celia Bannerman would have to be replaced. She was what is known as a Metre Freak, she couldn't keep time. A cappella was fine but a big orchestra and she were not on nodding acquaintance terms. I knew it had to happen. 'When will you do it?' I asked.

'I'm not going to do it, you are,' came the reply. I had to summon poor Celia to the Midland and deliver the *coup de grâce*.

She took it magnificently. 'If you'd fired me because of my acting,' she said, 'I'd probably slit my throat but I already knew I couldn't sing.'

After the two-week run, with a deal of cuts, rehearsals and putting the highly professional Marti Webb in the show, we finally opened in London, one of the most eagerly awaited shows of the season, alongside Michael Crawford in *Billy*, which was opening at Drury Lane.

The Dress Circle Bar at Her Majesty's is directly behind the Dress Circle. You push open the doors and you're there. At curtain up I stood with Priestley, Previn, Mercer and Harwood at the back of the Dress Circle. For the opening moment I had decided that there would be no conventional big overture. The curtain would rise on the Dinkie Doos and a corny piano would play a corny intro: 'da, da, dedadada—da'. Since there was no piano in the pit orchestra, a piano was installed backstage to be miked into the auditorium. The curtain rose. Absolute silence. No piano. The Dinkie Doos stood there frozen. The silence continued. As one the five of us shot through the door to the bar, downed double whiskies and went back into the auditorium, by which time the sound operator had remembered to switch on the sound.

The critics were lukewarm for the most part. They found it all too sentimental. However, it ran its initial allotted span of nine months and it didn't do me any harm.

Johanna was now heavily pregnant and, while holidaying in Florence, I proposed to her on the Bridge of Sighs. Neither of us had talked about getting married but it seemed perverse not to and I wanted to give her a sense of security.

Judi was my stag night and that was when I blurted out my reservations about her acting. In spite of all she was a jolly good stag night.

So the next day was my wedding day and a real Italian wedding it was, with Jacob running around the register office and Joe indicating he was well on his way. The Registrar seemed deeply embarrassed. The second marriage had begun.

It was clear to me that Johanna was going to have a daughter this time. It seemed pointless to have another son. The daughter would be called Sofia (wisdom). Just in case, a son would be called Joseph, the interpreter of dreams. In the event Sofia was not interested in these parents but Joseph was.

They had sent me out of the room at the moment of Jacob's birth but I was there for Joe's. Birth is commonplace; it is also miraculous. To witness a birth is to have your perspective on life altered for ever. It is simply unbelievable. Seeing that tiny head coming out of Johanna's body was almost unbearably moving. It is difficult to believe that anyone who has witnessed a birth can take a rationalist, materialist, reductionist, scientific view of the universe.

Joe had difficulty emerging; they would have to use forceps to turn him. I had to leave. The first time I saw Jacob after he was born he was serene and tanned (actually he had jaundice). Joe had a look of apprehensive fury on his face. It was so powerful that I heard myself saying out loud, 'Don't worry, we're delighted you're here.'

Now around this point of writing the book I asked Tuesday Spencer, who was typing it up from my illegible scrawl, for her comments. Her major reservation was that she still didn't know who the person was that was writing it. She said he appeared so obsessed with the theatre that life to him seemed incidental. I think this is perhaps no more or less than the truth. I was clearly locked off from my emotional centre. I was uncomfortably aware that I did not seem to have attachments like other people. The death of a father, marriage, these did not seem to breach the impenetrable wall. I could see from watching my own productions that there was a passionate, feeling person in there somewhere but he seemed scared of appearing in the real world for it would probably make him too vulnerable.

With the birth of my two sons came a change. They had made the breach. They were the centre of my emotional life.

What of Johanna? It is perfectly clear that she is the big story of my life. Our creative empathy was and is profound, and we had made two children. The problem was that we had no time to make a relationship with each other. It was either children or work and this was all-consuming. We were a great director–designer partnership and, I hope, good parents but we weren't husband and wife. Therefore there was always something that we were hoping for beyond our reach. I say 'we'. As is clear from my infidelities that was true for me but also, as I discovered much later, it was for her too. However, it was a satisfying and exciting time for both of us although we didn't have the wit to work on the man–woman relationship. I write, of course, with hindsight; at the time I was just bashing on. My suspicion is that had Jacob and Joe not arrived, I would have repeated the pattern with Johanna and broken off the relationship as I had with everyone else. Fear clearly still reigned inside me.

I can't believe this is unique. I was not given to self-analysis. I didn't know myself. Presumably that is what drove me outwards. Is this the make-up of others who presume to lead? If it is, it is a mixed blessing.

'Know thyself' are the two words above the oracle at Delphi. 'Love thy neighbour as thyself' said Christ. How do you know yourself? In no telling of the Grail legend does the hero find the Grail the second time and ask the right questions, because if you know what the question is you also know the answer. All I can believe is that one must continue on the quest. That at least is life-giving and, indeed, thrilling. As I write this towards the end of the eighth cycle of my life, it's as much as I can understand. At the very least, at the birth of my two sons life was no longer incidental and I was no longer the most important person in the world.

CHAPTER 32

The Black Mikado

– i –

Felix de Wolfe was now my agent. He was a gentleman of the old school but also very shrewd and witty. When Bernard Delfont had asked him if I would waive my royalties as *The Good Companions* was going through a bad patch he asked, 'At whom?' He phoned me to say that the producer James Verner had invited us to lunch at Rules in Maiden Lane to discuss a new project he had in mind. Felix explained that Verner had a dubious reputation. He had been the Executive Producer on the British production of *Hair* and there had been rumours of embezzlement. There had also been other Verner projects that had failed to get off the ground. In Felix's opinion, if Verner was surfacing again it was likely to be kosher as he couldn't afford to fail once more.

Rules is a reassuringly elegant Edwardian restaurant serving very English food, and has a fine wine list. This was Verner's preferred meeting place and very cleverly chosen.

Verner's idea was as follows. In the thirties in New York there had been no fewer than two hit versions of Gilbert and Sullivan's *The Mikado* running on Broadway at the same time: *The Hot Mikado* and *The Swing Mikado*. Verner wanted to produce an all-black reggae version called *The Bad Mikado*, bad being 'black' argot for 'good'. I killed off that title for obvious reasons.

I left the restaurant clutching the D'Oyle Carte record of the operetta, which I didn't know at all. It bowled me over. Every song seemed a winner, the witty book and lyrics were brilliant but I was worried that I was about to fall into another trap simply because I had been offered it and, with two children, needed the money.

I knew that Max would know the material well so I discussed it with him. He gave me the idea, the concept so lacking in *The Good Companions*, that I believe made it work. He suggested that I set it in a far-flung, last bastion of the British Empire, where the Pooh-Bah would be a white man. This chimed in perfectly with the satire of the piece, which lampooned Victorian society and, indeed, with Harold Macmillan's recent 'Wind of Change' speech.

Having listened carefully to the music, I felt that an evening of reggae would not match the eclectic mix of the score and would be very boring. It seemed to me to be better to use the whole gamut of modern music, jazz, blues, rock, reggae, pop, whatever suited best. Not a note need be changed, just the re-orchestrations were necessary.

At a second lunch at Rules, Verner agreed to all my proposals. In addition, having learnt from Jack Good, I asked that the band, who would be on stage as they had been in *Catch My Soul*, would be engaged from the first day of rehearsals so that we could grow the reinterpretation of the music together with the cast. Verner agreed to that too.

Felix negotiated an extremely good contract for me and for Johanna, who went straight from birth to designing, and rehearsals were due to start in late January 1975. There would be a six-week tour in Howard and Wyndham theatres, starting at the King's Edinburgh and proceeding via Newcastle and Leeds to the West End. It was all very exciting.

Since this was to be the first home-grown black show in London, casting was going to be tricky. There was not, as there is now, a large pool of trained, talented black performers; *The Black Mikado* was the trailblazer which led to that growth.

Verner knew the man for the main part of Ko-Ko. Derek Griffiths had become a star through BBC's *Playschool*. Generations had grown up watching him and loving him. I met him at Rules and he agreed to be in it even though he had reacted in horror at my over-the-top Diaghilev overcoat. 'Who is that prat?' he later told me he had asked Verner when I'd gone to the loo. Norman Beaton would play Nanki-Poo; Floella Benjamin, who was also making a name for herself in children's television, Pitti-Sing, and we found a beautiful young singer, then called Patricia Ebigwei now Patti Boulaye, who was quite literally Yum-Yum. We had to go abroad to find some of the Pretty Maidens. We discovered American expats in France, including an amazing large blues singer, Anita Tucker, to play Katisha. What with the lunches at Rules and the trips abroad I was enjoying myself.

The part that seemed impossible to cast was the Mikado himself. He, of course, among others had the famous song 'To make the punishment fit the crime'. He needed to have a deep bass voice and a considerable presence. Where were we going to find him?

I sat one afternoon chatting to Felix in his offices off the Strand when I heard this fantastic voice singing in the upstairs flat. It came from a six-foot-five black mountain of a man, Valentine Pringle, an American living right above Felix. It was unbelievable, you couldn't have dreamt it up. We were cast.

Johanna had designed an astonishing set of costumes, an amalgam of Victorian, Japanese and African, plus a beautiful set derived from the Japanese Kabuki theatre. It was all going so well that it seemed too good to be true.

– ii –

It was the first day of rehearsal. We were to be in Alford House in Vauxhall, where I had rehearsed *The Good Companions*. I arrived there very keyed up and very excited. The Company Manager was Verner's half-brother Chris. As I walked through the entrance he met me. 'You can't go into the rehearsal room,' he said, 'you have to go into the basement. The Equity officials want to see you.' I peeked into the rehearsal room, where I saw the exceedingly white Michael Denison who was to play Pooh-Bah, surrounded by the exceedingly black cast; the atmosphere was exceedingly expectant.

I went down to the basement. I knew the officials because I was co-Chairman of the newly formed Directors' Subcommittee of Equity. We were on friendly terms. The problem was that a West End producer who was not a member of the Society of West End Managers had to lodge two weeks' wages for the company with the Society before rehearsals began. Verner had not done so. 'What does Jimmy say?' I asked. Jimmy was not to be found. This was most peculiar. A producer naturally attends the first rehearsal of his new production. I phoned his secretary at his office at the Cambridge Theatre. She didn't know where he was. I explained the situation and asked her to get him to call me or, better still, come to Alford House as soon as possible.

Had they followed the letter of the law, Equity would have sent the cast away immediately. I pleaded with them for a stay of execution. This was a raw, inexperienced cast, if they were sent away now it might mean the collapse of the production and the production was important for the future of black performers in this country. They relented.

Eventually Verner rang in. It was all a mistake, an oversight; he thought he had done it last week, he would send the cheque round immediately by courier. He did, the cheque arrived, the Society confirmed it to the officials and we started.

I had never had such an electric, talented group of actors before; the energy was amazing. I had also never had a more difficult bunch to cope with. Some of the problem was the ill discipline of those who had never been in a show before, most of it was tribal. There were West Indians, Americans and Africans. Among the Africans there were Nigerians, Sierra Leonians, Ghanaians, you name it. Throw in the Hungarian pianist and my inspired Filipino choreographer Amadeo, whom I had found in Paris during *Othello Story*, and you had a combustible brew. But it was exciting. I knew we had something.

Verner finally made an appearance a couple of days into rehearsal with some Americans in tow to watch. I was incandescent. It made the cast self-conscious and it was far too early for there to be anything worth seeing. I was sulky and rude, and eventually they retired hurt. It was a long time before those two Americans reappeared in very different circumstances.

The next minor tremor came on Friday, pay day. No money appeared for the band and they prepared to walk out. I persuaded them to stay. I phoned the office. Another oversight because the band were being paid from another account; problem solved. I came back from lunch on the Wednesday of week two to find the Equity officials were back. 'What's the matter now?' I asked jocularly, 'have you come to close us down?' They had come for exactly that purpose. The cheque Verner had sent to the Society had bounced. We assembled the company, told them the news and sent them home. Equity told them to come back on Friday and if they were paid they could start again. We were shattered.

Michael Denison and I went round to the Cambridge Theatre to confront Verner. It was all a mistake, the money was going through Liechtenstein and had been delayed. Would it get through by Friday? There was no way of knowing. Did he realise that if it didn't it meant the end of the show? Yes, he did, but what could he do? How much money was needed? £3,000.

I was desperate for the rehearsals to continue. Not only did I feel in my gut we had a success in the making, but I had a Jewish empathy with the black cast. This would seem to them like another act of discrimination, just when they had their first big chance.

I had saved £1,500 against my sons' education. I went to my mother and asked her if she would match it. Verner came round to her house to be cross-examined. He was very plausible – he was always very plausible. The money would certainly be in the bank by Monday. In the meantime he would write an IOU. All this we secretly recorded.

Friday came, the cast and band were paid. One good thing happened: the company was united against a common enemy, Verner, and I was a hero. Order was established.

Sunday was my birthday. When I came downstairs in the morning I was surprised to find an envelope on the mat. I assumed it was a birthday card delivered by hand from a friend. It was a letter from James Verner announcing that he no longer considered me suitable as a director for *The Black Mikado* and that he was taking over forthwith. He had fired me.

First thing on Monday morning I went to Felix to discuss the crisis. I phoned the bank to make sure that the cheque had arrived from Verner. It had, they had presented it immediately and, guess what, it had bounced. I was penniless and sacked.

That afternoon Michael Denison came around to Felix's. Verner had announced his decision to the company and called a rehearsal, whereupon Derek Griffiths had headed for the door. When asked why he wasn't rehearsing, he announced he would return when I was reinstated. Michael asked if I would come to a meeting that night at his London flat to talk with him, Derek and Norman Beaton. Of course I would.

Over a meal created by Dulcie Gray, they said they would turn up to rehearsal the next morning and present Verner with an ultimatum: either I was to be reinstated or they would all walk out. They were as good as their word. The following afternoon Verner phoned me at Felix's office: he'd made a terrible mistake, would I please come back and rehearse. I walked up the road to the Adelphi Theatre where we were now installed for the rest of the rehearsal period. Verner was not there. It was the last time I saw him for rather a long time.

– iii –

Had rehearsals not been as wonderful as they were, I don't know that I could have held together. I had terrific back-up from Rosie Hoare, my DSM, but none from the management who owed me a great deal of money. We arrived at the final Friday before travelling to Edinburgh for the opening. The officials were there again. There was no money to pay the company. I went to the Theatre Manager of the Adelphi. He had been watching run-throughs of the show, knew it was terrific and was very sympathetic. The Adelphi was part of the Howard and Wyndham Group who were taking the show on tour and he agreed to advance the wages for the cast. I held a company meeting. I told them what was happening. I asked them if they were prepared to go to Edinburgh given the circumstances. They wanted to. They believed in what we were doing. Once again the show was saved. I wish I could remember the name of the Theatre Manager.

– iv –

The cast was due in Edinburgh on the Monday to start the technical rehearsal, the dress rehearsal was on the Tuesday and the opening night on the Wednesday. It was a tight schedule but we had a standing set with no changes and the band had been in all the rehearsals. We could do it.

Johanna and I went up on the Sunday to see the set come in and to light the show. Michael Williams, our 69 Production Manager, was the Lighting Designer. This seemed a bonus as having a production manager I knew on hand might be helpful.

We checked in at the Caledonian Hotel and went to the theatre. There was a full stage crew but no set. There was a full wardrobe staff but no costumes. All there was were a few stage props, samurai swords and so on, that apparently arrived in a huge pantechnicon to everyone's amazement. There certainly was no Jimmy Verner.

I got him on the phone. He was to the point. 'I haven't got the money to get the set and costumes released from the makers.' There was nothing to say. This was a nightmare.

Early on Monday morning Johanna and I went round to see Clive Perry, the Artistic Director of the Lyceum Theatre. Our idea was to beg him to let us raid his costume store, to put something on the cast. For the set we would go to the Parks Department and hire some large plants to create some kind of atmosphere. Perry was magnificent. 'If you do that,' he said, 'and the show goes well, Verner will never pay for the real set and costumes.' The Lyceum was a Howard and Wyndham Theatre. Perry phoned them and persuaded them, as the Adelphi Manager had done, to release tour money up front to get the stuff out of hock. The estimated time of arrival was some time on Tuesday (opening night on Wednesday).

The company was due to arrive at Waverley Station at lunchtime. I raced round and met them off the train, told them there had been some technical hitches and sent them off to a rehearsal room, which Perry had found for us, to rehearse the dances with Amadeo.

Set and costumes arrived at 2 a.m. on Tuesday morning. The costumes were fine, the set was just untreated wood. It would have to do. Michael and I were up all night lighting the show. The sound system couldn't go in until everything else was ready. The technical started on Tuesday afternoon. The set was ramped, which was a real hazard for the dancers. The technical was hard; adjusting to the set was hard; getting the sound right was hard. The technical was obviously going on into Wednesday. That night we relit the show and the next day we started again. By 4 p.m. it was clear that we hadn't a hope of finishing. I called the company together, admitted this was a ridiculous situation but asked them to take the risk and wing it. We couldn't give up after all this. They agreed.

That night was one of the most exciting I have ever had in my career. The cast exploded on stage, the audience went wild. We were right, it was a magnificent show. There were rave reviews the next day and sell-out business for two weeks in the 2,000-seater King's Theatre. James Verner wasn't there.

Prince Charles came to see the show. Anita Tucker bought a kilt, beret and tam-o'-shanter. When she met him she regaled him with 'Hi Prince. I guess I'm matching you in the clannage department.'

We were in high spirits. We knew we had pulled off a miracle . . . and I had my second affair. When she had walked into the audition room, I thought Glenna Forster-Jones was the most glorious woman I'd ever seen. She was Eartha Kittesque, a slinky, catlike woman who exuded life force. I was smitten. Johanna had gone back to London. I was alone in a pressure-cooker situation. I succumbed. Both my affairs came after the birth of a son. Again this is not an excuse, but the demotion of a husband in his wife's priorities when a child is born is a shock. I think I wanted reassurance. I also wanted to explore that side of my being that still seemed undernourished. Most of us were staying at the Caledonian Hotel with the bills going to Verner, who of course had no intention of paying them, although we didn't know that, so we had a riot of a time. The staid staff loved us. The corridors of the hotel at night were like Renoir's *La Règle du Jeu*.

— v —

Verner finally showed up in Newcastle, where we were repeating the success of Edinburgh at the Theatre Royal, who were finally being recompensed for the horrors of *Oom-Pah-Pah*. He asked me to come round to his hotel. His message was succinct. 'I know I owe you money. If you sue me I shall be declared bankrupt and the show will close and you will never be paid. Your only hope is to deliver a hit in London.' It was a horribly accurate assessment of my situation.

Every weekend of the tour was a cliffhanger. Either there wasn't enough money to pay the band or to pay for the get-out. Repeatedly, Michael Denison redistributed a large portion of his salary to bale us out. This sixty-year-old quintessential Englishman (actually he was born Yorkshire working class) was quite wonderful. I think he loved being surrounded by the Beautiful Maidens who, encouraged by Derek Griffiths, used to grope him during the dance routines. But his commitment was pure old school: the show must go on. His Macmillanesque performance was a joy and he was my main support system.

Among the company there was endless internecine warfare, which always exploded during the first act finale. In front of the audience it was covert but when the curtain came down it was anything but.

Somehow I held it together. I clung to Glenna obsessively and jealously. She was respite from the nerve-shredding tension of the daily fight for survival.

We arrived at the last date in Leeds, prior to London and the opening at the Cambridge Theatre. I was sitting in the bar of the Dress Circle having a quick whisky, before seeing the show for the umpteenth time, when I heard that utterance which I was so used to: 'There's that shit Braham Murray.' It was the two Americans who had gatecrashed the early rehearsal in Alford House. I burst into tears. It was the last straw. They were taken aback. I told them the whole story blow by blow. They were astounded. Verner had sold them an alternative version where everything was terrific had it not been for me.

Irwin and Paula Margulies, for so they were named, drove me back to London and at 2 a.m. summoned Verner to their flat in Eaton Square. As was his wont, he admitted everything. The truth was that he had floated the entire show on their initial £10,000. The rest was bluff. He hadn't the money to have the set finished, nor to put the posters up outside the Cambridge Theatre, which were still claiming to present the previous show, a disastrous musical about Jack the Ripper. He was in their hands. Although Irwin was the Vice President of Warner Bros, Paula wore the pants. Without her we would never have got the show on. With her there would be enough money to do it. With her, the help of Johanna, Michael Williams, Rosie Hoare and others would see us through.

Everything was last-minute. When we arrived at the Cambridge, we tried finally to have a proper technical. It was like one of those movies when someone says, 'Let's put this show on right here in the barn.' I was trying to rehearse amid scene painters, stage carpenter, ladders, electricians; everything happening simultaneously. It was chaos.

— vi —

An opening night anywhere is a night of unbearable tension for the director. He has done all he can, now he has to watch the company perform, powerless to help. The opening night of a West End musical is a huge occasion. Everyone is there. Half of them are willing the show to succeed, the other half willing it to fail. On this opening night I was also aware that if it didn't succeed I was in deep financial trouble. By now the bank had taken away my chequebook and I was living hand to mouth. I stood at the back of the auditorium, terrified almost beyond feeling.

The moment that Derek appeared to the chorus's 'Behold the Lord High Executioner' it was clear that this was going to be a memorable occasion. Everyone rose to it. Pringle was magnificent, Patricia Ebigwei captivated with 'The sun, whose rays' and Derek finally brought the house down with 'Titwillow'.

I never watch the first night curtain call. I like to be backstage to congratulate the cast as they come off. As I looked out into the house I saw a spontaneous, cheering, standing ovation. Nowadays standing ovations are commonplace, audiences seem to need to give them or they don't feel they've had a good evening. Then they were a rarity; I certainly had never seen one. We were home and dry; it only needed the unanimous accolades of the critics the next morning to put the official seal on things.

— vii —

From then on it should have been plain sailing, but it wasn't. Even though we were playing to packed houses, Verner didn't pay me back. Eventually Laurence Harbottle issued, on my behalf, a garnishee against the box office at the Cambridge Theatre, which meant the next £3,000 they took had to be paid to me and my mother. By an awful error the garnishee was served on the Cambridge Theatre Company of which Laurence was, embarrassingly, the Chairman. Eventually all was righted and we were paid.

Up and running in a West End hit, the company was every bit as bad as the *Catch My Soul* company had been. Actors calling sick were commonplace and many were the times I drove around London persuading people, especially Valentine Pringle, to appear that night. Also Johanna found out about Glenna in an unforgivable way. She had designed the Maidens to wear glitter on their bodies and one morning she found glitter in our bed. Astonishingly, she forgave me again. For my part I couldn't regret the relationship; it had moved me on again.

— viii —

The Margulies did everything to get their money back. Verner had managed things so that the show was never in the black week by week, which meant that the backers were not being repaid a penny, let alone partaking in any profit. They sent in accountants to look at the books. Verner had done a deal with Larry Parnes, the owner of the Cambridge, who had evidently been to the same finishing school as him. Parnes had the right to twenty seats each night and these were to be sold at the box office first, thus diminishing the official returns. The accountants found interesting bills presented by Parnes for payment. One, apparently, charged Verner £700 for the provision of stationery in one week. It was brilliant because nothing could be proved.

There were further frustrations. A hit like this should have been sold abroad, especially to Broadway, but Verner, through greed, messed up every contract. Instead of using his success to persuade angels to invest in new shows, as any sensible producer would, he seemed determined to swindle everyone in the pursuit of short-term gain. The mentality was quite shockingly self-destructive.

The Margulies asked me to dinner at Zen in Chelsea. They had wanted to know if, with another producer, *The Black Mikado* would make real money. I assured them it would. They had a solution. At a gesture from Irwin a smartly dressed navy-suited man rose from a nearby table to join us. They informed me that he would be the solution in dealing with Verner. 'I say,' I said in my best English manner, 'we don't do that sort of thing over here.' The man melted away.

Although, according to the books, vast amounts of money were being paid to the press representative, nothing appeared to be being done to promote the show, presumably because it was another scam. *The Black Mikado* ran for eighteen months; it should have run for a lot longer. How much Verner managed to salt away we shall never know. It must have been a considerable amount.

— ix —

How did he get away with it? First, he had a very good idea to sell. Second, he was always charming and plausible. He played to perfection the independent outsider, battling the established West End producers to put on important work. Third, as he himself explained to me while trying to get my backing for a production of *King Lear* with Ron Moody, he knew everyone's hook. For example, he guaranteed his half-brother's mortgage and the Production Manager's overdraft. With me, I suppose flatteringly, he said, 'Oh, I knew once you were committed to something you would never give up.'

With all that cleverness, he ended up on the Equity blacklist. Years later we had a production of *Moby Dick* running at the Exchange. I asked a black actor in the company, Leo Wringer, what he was doing next. 'I'm doing a new West End musical,' he told me. 'It's a rock version of Gilbert and Sullivan – *Utopia Unlimited*.'

'Who's the producer?' I asked quietly.

'He's called James Verner.'

'It won't happen, Leo.'

'Yes it will. We start rehearsals immediately after this closes.'

Guess what? It didn't happen.

CHAPTER 33

Two Lives

In a parallel universe, the Royal Exchange was being fully designed and an opening in September 1976 was forecast. Meetings were held in Michael's flat of a group of about twenty, comprising actors, directors, designers, administrators etc., whose job it was to make sure that the architects knew exactly how every part of the theatre functioned at its optimum. Since everything had to fit into the constricted space of the Royal Exchange, this planning was crucial.

Thus the actors said what they wanted in their dressing rooms; the designers what the wardrobe and workshops would need; it all amounted to the best-prepared theatre brief ever, although financial considerations meant nothing would be lavish. The first consideration was the stage and we worked outwards from there; the last consideration was the offices. That is as it should be. The money should go on the work.

As a West End director, I was now at a crucial point. *The Good Companions* had been by no means a failure, and *Catch My Soul* and *The Black Mikado* had put me right up there as a director of musicals. All I needed was one more hit and I could name my price.

The offers came rolling in. Perhaps because, in spite of Verner's erratic payments, the money was coming in from *The Black Mikado*, I narrowly avoided making disastrous decisions. Actually, narrowly was a euphemism; by the skin of my teeth is more accurate.

Spurred on by Amadeo, who had done such a fabulous choreographic job on *The Black Mikado*, I was approached by the mega French pop star-composer Eric Charden to direct his new musical *Mayflower* at the Théâtre des Champs-Élysées in Paris. It was about the first voyage to the New World. The book was frankly not up to much and the music was that awful French boring middle-of-the-road pop they thought of as 'now'. However, to be well paid in Paris seemed tempting. I flew over to meet the team, Charden and his lyricist Guy Bontempelli. We seemed to get on very well. They told me that the show album was already recorded and was soon to be released. I assumed there would then be a cast album after the show had opened as there would be bound to be changes during rehearsal. Charden looked blank. Changes? There wouldn't be any changes, the score was perfect. I kept my counsel.

'*Quelle sacrée équipe*,' they kept saying during the inevitably epicurean night. The next day I held auditions. Afterwards I sat with Eric and Guy to compare notes. After a short while Charden interrupted: 'The show is already cast.'

'With whom?'

'The singers on the album.' I flew back to England.

Next up was an offer to direct a new musical by no less than John *Star Wars*, *Jaws*, Williams. Unfortunately it was about Thomas à Becket, called *Thomas and the King*. The book was by the distinguished Hollywood screenplay writer Edward Anhalt, who had written the great Richard Widmark movie *Panic in the Streets*, and the lyrics by a well-known lyricist, James Harbet. With numbers like the medieval village maidens singing 'Bumpe and Grinde', it had the makings of a disaster.

Hollywood–Broadway meets *Henry II* didn't bode well. I was flown out to LA to work with the team. They seemed to understand what I was saying but when I flew back with the producer, the aptly named Sam Grossman, to find him casting a very good but totally unsuitable actor as Henry behind my back, I withdrew from that one too. Was I growing up? We'll see.

Sitting in Manchester Cathedral, watching my production of *Much Ado About Nothing* and experiencing the enthusiasm and liveliness of the audience, compared with the West End equivalent at the Cambridge Theatre watching *The Black Mikado*, I knew that this was preferable. It didn't mean the tug of war was over. I only needed one more hit.

Between these two parallel universes I was picking up my married life again. The affair with Glenna had ended. Both with Clara in Paris and here in London, I had experienced another culture and another life rhythm. It almost dragged me out of reality into a seductive night world, but not quite.

Johanna asked me what I would do if she were unfaithful. I remember my appalling answer quite clearly: 'I'd think you'd had a dreadful lack of taste.' That was it, I was the centre of the universe. Everything I did was justified.

Writing about being a parent is impossible. Suffice it to say it was totally absorbing, totally rewarding and it bound Johanna and me together.

My mother, too, was able to experience what she never could with me: a relaxed, cuddling relationship that I think opened her up. This was a woman brought up to fear anything physical. She was told she was too fat; she wasn't. She was warned off kissing because that was the way you caught germs. When she went to her mother, bewildered, at her first menstruation, her mother responded by slapping her face, to make the devil fly out of her. Poor lady, no wonder she was frightened of holding me. Here was a blessed release. My stepfather had obviously been waiting for this moment to be the perfect grandfather.

Indeed, this was the time when I could talk to them both about what had happened to me in my childhood. I could explain why I had behaved so horribly to them. It made a difference to me and I know it made a difference to Philip. I assume it made a difference to my mother but although she had heroically tried to lift the family curse, the Prevezer, from me, she hadn't lifted it sufficiently from herself to acknowledge it openly.

Life had got back to some semblance of normality. The new year 1976 dawned with a hit in the West End and a new theatre soon to open.

CHAPTER 34

1976 – Setting Things Up

– i –

A handful of us ran 69. We now had to contemplate running a full-time theatre, presenting nine productions a year and a full complement of concerts, classical and jazz, recitals, stand-up comics and anything else we could think of. We also had to run a large catering operation including a restaurant, cafeteria and bar.

Michael Elliott seemed to end my tug of war. He volunteered to move his family up to Manchester and run the company if I would join him. I agreed; I could scarcely do otherwise. Then, mysteriously, he seemed to forget about that; without any explanation I was left in no man's land. The key positions were quickly filled. Michael Williams obviously became the Production Manager and Allisoune Browne, who had run Michael's Old Vic company, the Company Manager. An exceptionally large person got off the plane at Manchester Airport from Australia, read an advertisement in the *Guardian* and was a heaven-sent Publicity Manager called Forbes Cameron. A mad sound nut called Ian Gibson walked into the offices and announced he intended to do our sound. He was brilliant. Slowly but surely the 150 permanent posts were filled with great care. We wanted only people who cared, both about the work and about other people. A tradition of true service was established, which remains to this day. A visiting American composer, Stanley Silverman, said with astonishment, 'There isn't a shit in the building.'

– ii –

The company has to date put on over 300 productions and I have done sixty-two of them. I have no intention of dealing with more than a handful, but the first season announced in June of that year is worth detailing.

We decided to open with two plays in repertoire, one night after the other.

Tom, of course, was to lead the company. Casper wanted to do Kleist's *The Prince of Homburg*, continuing the company's tradition of presenting virtually unknown European classics, and he suggested that Sheridan's *The Rivals* should be teamed with it. He suggested *The Rivals* because it was a true company piece with at least eight star parts, because it was so obviously written for the proscenium arch and because it was a great comic play. He suggested I should direct it. It was an honour as it would be the first play in the theatre and I was delighted.

Next we elected to produce a completely unknown play by the author of *Hobson's Choice*, Harold Brighouse, called *Zack*. The director Robert Cheesmond had brought it to our attention and I blush to say we pinched it from him. At Christmas we decided that there were quite enough pantomimes in the area already and I was allowed to do Orton's *What the Butler Saw*, which I had always craved to do. I thought it even better than *Loot* and it had failed twice in wrong-headed productions in London. At the same time, for matinées only, Derek Griffiths came to produce, star in and write his version of *Dick Whittington*.

After Christmas Max and Richard Negri came together to direct Thornton Wilder's *The Skin of Our Teeth*. Albert Finney, whom Michael had directed at the National in *Miss Julie*, agreed to do two plays: *Uncle Vanya*, which would also star Leo McKern, and *Present Laughter*, which Max would direct. Alec Guinness wanted to star in Ronnie Harwood's adaptation of *The Ordeal of Gilbert Pinfold* by Evelyn Waugh. He later withdrew and the production was postponed until another year when Michael Hordern stepped into his shoes to give a blissful performance. Finally, Trevor Peacock was commissioned to write a new musical called *Leaping Ginger*, which I would direct to close the year.

When you consider that later Patricia Routledge joined for both *The Rivals* and *Zack*, and that actors such as Trevor Peacock, Lee Montague, Alfie Burke, Freddie Jones, Cheryl Kennedy, Chris Gable, John Bardon, Lindsay Duncan, Marsha Hunt, Eleanor Bron, Joanna David, Michael Feast, Polly James, Gary Waldhorn and many others played once or more during the year it was quite a line-up.

An aim was declared at that press conference. We were presenting nine shows, which included one new musical and one new adaptation, but we stated that our real intention was one day to announce nine world premières in a season. To speak with the voice of today about the problems of today we declared to be the ideal. Nowadays the company is recognised as a powerhouse of new writing, but it was many years before we ever began to look like fulfilling that goal.

You might have thought that helping with the set-up of the company and preparing three productions, one of which meant working with Trevor on a new musical, was enough for me, but there was another of those telephone calls from my agent.

Ray Cooney had seen in Edinburgh, at a small fringe venue, a rock opera version of *The Merchant of Venice* called *Shylock*. He had bought it and persuaded its authors, Roger Haines and Paul Bentley, to expand it into a large West End show. The director of *Catch My Soul* was an obvious choice and *The Black Mikado* was still packing them in at the Cambridge.

I went to the Duke of York's to have the score played and sung to me by Roger (composer) and Paul (lyricist). I heard half a remarkable show and half a dud, but what the pair had created with the Shylock scenes was exceptional. They achieved the power of a genuine opera and were absolutely true to the material. The Portia and Antonio world had been amalgamated into a modern mafia milieu, Little Venice, NY. This was treated in a banal fashion, not quite as bad as the other was good, but very dubious.

I should have said 'no'. I didn't for two reasons. I was confident I could make it work. I still hadn't learnt. The other, bluntly, was money. I was resorting to the subterfuges that I know all young fathers supporting a family have to. I had four gold cards and four bank accounts. Cheques, with great skill, chased each other round from bank to bank. No bill was paid till the final demand and I played the old trick of putting in the wrong cheque with the wrong invoice. The evil hour was thus postponed but even then the debt collector's knock on the door was becoming routine. *The Black Mikado* was coming to an end and Michael had left me in limbo in Manchester. I had not yet learnt that doing something for money can be too expensive.

I accepted *Fire Angel*, as the show was unaccountably to be renamed, and arranged to fit it in between *What the Butler Saw* and *Leaping Ginger* at the beginning of 1977. It was going to be tight; in fact, I would only have one week between the two musicals. So I was to do four shows in well under a year and Johanna would design three of them. We shared the lunacy between us.

CHAPTER 35

The Theatre's Opening

Rehearsals would take eight weeks to open the two shows that were cross-cast and, with another three weeks for previews and openings, we decided to move the family up for the summer. Since Johanna and I were going to be needed in the theatre a lot, we took a nanny, Susan Peasely, with us to hold the fort. We rented a lovely house in Cheshire and, since this was the scorching summer of 1976, we had done well.

It was an exciting time. We were rehearsing in the Royal Exchange, but not in the theatre, since it was still being erected. We were therefore working blind because we didn't know the effect the theatre would have on the production. We didn't much care. It was a unique situation.

Wandering around Manchester looking for a new restaurant to eat in, I passed the Opera House. There was a poster up announcing the forthcoming production of the West End hit *The Black Mikado* directed by one Braham Murray.

Contractually I had to be offered any Number One tour of the show and naturally Verner had not been in touch. There followed a dispute worthy of Gilbert and Sullivan and Topsy-Turvey land. Yes, Verner knew he was obligated but had worked out that I wasn't available, so had decided to direct it himself. But I would have been available. Sorry, it's too late now. All right then, please remove my name from the posters. No, because it's the West End production you directed. In that case pay me my royalty. No, because you're not directing it.

We complained to the London Theatre Council, who found in my favour. I wasn't paid for about ten years, when Verner wanted to get off the blacklist to produce again. By then the amount I got was meaningless. So *The Black Mikado* haunted me to Manchester where it played in the autumn before the Opera House closed to become a bingo hall.

In the middle of August we were due to hold an acoustic test in the theatre in front of an initial audience. Rehearsals were interrupted so that everyone in the building could help put the seats into the auditorium. There it was, our theatre.

An acoustic test is a big moment. Theatre acoustics is a very inexact science. We prayed that if the theatre design was correct the acoustics would work, that somehow the secret the Greeks knew in their open-air theatres would be passed on to us.

The auditorium was full. Tom stepped forward on to the bare stage area and spoke the first words of Hamlet's soliloquy, 'O, what a rogue and peasant slave am I!' It was probably the single greatest moment of all. It was perfect. The relationship of the actor to the audience, the well-nigh faultless acoustic, the chamber theatre feel yet with 750 people present, it all conspired to make the spine shiver and the hair to stand on end.

Now we could rehearse on stage and the actors loved it as they have loved it ever since. It is the best space in the country and, as so many actors have said, it spoils you for everywhere else. It was a total triumph for Richard Negri and the team of architects.

I won't dwell on the productions. If you have James Maxwell as Sir Anthony, Pat Routledge as Mrs Malaprop, Chris Gable as Captain Absolute, Susan Tracy as Lydia Languish, Tom as Faulkland, Judi Bowker as Julia, Trevor Peacock as Bob Acres and people like John Bardon and Enn Reitel in the small parts, you shouldn't go far wrong and I don't think we did. Tom threatened to steal the show with his neurotic Faulkland, first cousin to Young Marlow, and would have done were it not for Miss Routledge's brilliant comic creation as Mrs Malaprop. Alongside Maureen Lipman, she is the most accomplished comic actress I have ever worked with and, despite stories to the contrary, as easy to direct as you like. Perhaps the staging was a little clumsy as the design had to be largely guesswork. It was our first go properly in the round but the preview audience loved it.

The first night was on 15 September. I woke so excited that I had to go into the theatre early. I arrived in at the unthinkable hour for theatre folk of nine o'clock to find that everyone else was there in the same state of excitement. It was as though we had been given a wondrous present and we wanted to experience it fully. We mingled with the crews from both television companies while the finishing touches were being put to everything.

Somehow we got through the day, the half came, the actors were called to their dressing rooms, the audience and critics began to arrive. The half, the quarter, the five, beginners please, the company came into the hall to stand outside the entrances. I stood with them next to John Bardon who, as Fagg, would speak the first lines.

Laurence Olivier, furious at his treatment by the National Theatre, who after he had handed over to Peter Hall had chosen to ignore him, had snubbed them and agreed to open our theatre. He stepped forward. He looked rather inconsequential, like a bank manager in a suburban branch.

He was to read an eighteenth-century poem written about the Royal Exchange, quite a nice poem, all about what exchanging should mean. He didn't read it very well; in fact, he seemed to mumble it. He finished. He looked up. He stepped into the centre of the stage. 'Ladies and Gentleman, I now declare this theatre [pause, and then a lion's roar] OPENNNNNN!' Poor John Bardon. 'Fuck me,' he said. 'How do I follow that?' I pushed him on.

Quite simply, it just couldn't have been better.

CHAPTER 36

Success

Although Miss Horniman had started the repertory movement in Manchester, there had been dire prognostications that there would be no audience to support a large theatre in the city centre. For their part the Library were scared that the newcomer would finish them off. Neither fears came true.

The success of the Royal Exchange was immediate. Within a couple of years the Palace, the Opera House and the Oldham Coliseum reopened their doors. Then the Green Room came into being, followed in time by the Lowry in Salford. When the Exchange opened there were only 500 theatre seats on sale each evening; today there are nearer 7,000. The Library still thrives. It didn't rest there.

As *The Times* acknowledged, the Exchange was the catalyst for the regeneration of the city centre. Manchester only became a city in the 1850s on the back of King Cotton. No one of any means lived in the city centre. The wealthy lived to the south or in opulent Cheshire; the less wealthy in the north. The centre was for factories and migrant workers.

When we started to build in 1975, the population of central Manchester was tiny and the city was deserted in the evenings. St Ann's Square where the theatre is had been the fashionable centre of the city; in 1976 its high spot was the Kardomah Coffee House. Now, as people either stayed in or came in at night, two shopping arcades opened in the square and with the reopening of the other theatres the place came to life again.

For several years the Exchange was the place to go. We could put on practically anything and fill the house. Even an obscure play like Hofmannsthal's *The Deep Man* would play to eighty per cent capacity. The theatre itself was a must-see object and with its exhibitions and restaurants was a meeting point throughout the day. It became the model for other regional theatres. We had achieved very quickly what the Arts Council had staked us to do. Thirty years later it is difficult to believe that we expected to run the theatre for five years and then hand it over to posterity, but that is what we intended.

I was soon back in rehearsal for *What the Butler Saw*. I felt a great empathy towards Orton, who was by now dead, of course, murdered by Halliwell. He wanted to let all the horrors out of the dark wardrobe into the light and to make us laugh while he did it. He wanted to surface his instinctual side as completely as he could and that to me was an act of great bravery.

That play never had a better cast. Lee Montague and Alfie Burke played the two doctors. Montague is a fine actor and a great – I use the word advisedly – farceur. He understood the genre better than anyone I have worked with. Rosalind Knight was Mrs Prentice with the sublime Michael Feast and Lindsay Duncan the two offspring. Capping it all was Trevor Peacock's Sergeant Match. One night he improvised an Ortonesque line: 'If you interfere with me, sir, I shall almost certainly have to blow my whistle.' I'm sure Orton loved it.

But now it was away from Manchester and back to London for the show that was to make my fortune.

CHAPTER 37

Fire Engine

I don't know why Ray Cooney called the show *Fire Angel*; everyone thought they had heard *Fire Engine*, which didn't help. For reasons he never explained, he changed all the names from the original so that Shylock was called Barach, for example. It was a difficult show to cast because it was vocally very demanding, but apart from the Barach role the parts weren't that good, rather like the Shakespeare. I did my best but I can't say that the result was very inspiring, with one or two exceptions, notably Julian Littman who played the Lorenzo role. The casting of Barach was, however, a triumph. We found Colm Wilkinson in Ireland and he was the great redeeming feature of the company. He, of course, went on to become a big star in *Les Misérables*.

I wish there were some funny stories to be told about the show. There aren't. I rehearsed with a will. The material remained very powerful to me and since the Jewish scenes were so well written and I had Colm to play them, I began to kid myself that things were going well. Actually, I wasn't the only one. Anthony Bowles, the doyen of MD/arrangers, was of the opinion that we were going to change the face of British musicals, setting new standards in the process. Ray Cooney was absolutely delighted. He told me he had never before produced a show where everything in rehearsal seemed right.

The crucial first band call with the cast was held in the bar at the Theatre Royal, Drury Lane. It was a thrilling three hours. Ant Bowles's orchestrations seemed wonderful, the cast was on song and everyone was in high spirits. Ray Cooney approached me afterwards. He was prepared to buy me out of my royalty for £20,000. I turned him down. He shrugged. He didn't think I'd say yes but it was worth a try.

Why didn't I see what was coming next week at the out-of-town opening in Wimbledon? Presumably I had kidded myself completely, because if I hadn't I would never have got through rehearsals. It's something that directors and actors do all the time. I knew I was behaving badly in rehearsals, reverting to the screaming and shouting director of yore, but I didn't click as to why. Somewhere, I must have known the truth of the situation.

The technical at Wimbledon was a nightmare. Johanna had designed a wonderful over-the-top set and magnificent Venice carnival costumes, some of which were impractical for the dancers. More than that, the carnival masks were superb but the singers couldn't be heard with them on. Arlene Phillips, the choreographer, and Ant Bowles were very unhappy. I was desperately trying to hold things together when the news came through that Jacob had injured himself by crashing through the glass kitchen door at home. Johanna had to go off to see to him. I imagine Jacob did it in sympathy.

By the time of the first night we just hoped for the best. We got the worst. The show didn't work, the audience were at most tepid. They weren't interested in the powerful part; it was too serious for a musical, and the other part wasn't good enough.

Ray demanded rewrites. In a rock opera this is a monumental task because any change means re-orchestration, more band calls, more technicals. The cast are rehearsing one show all day and performing another at night. You have to wait until everything is ready before substituting the new version, instead of bit by bit as in a normal show. The cast hated me, as they had every right to do for I was hateful, and I hated them. After a week of hell, the new version went in and it didn't make a jot of difference.

We were due to move to Her Majesty's in a week's time and we had a flop on our hands. The creative (!) team were summoned to Ray's house in Epping. He informed us that, since it was his money at stake, he was going to re-rehearse the show for a week. I was sacked. The wave of relief that rolled over me was quite marvellous. I was out of hell. I phoned Felix and he phoned Ray to make sure my name was removed from the production. Ray refused. He said it would only start the rumour that something was amiss; he would sue me if I tried. Further, he wanted me to come back when the technical started at Her Majesty's.

On Felix's advice I did what I was bid and began the technical. I watched what I thought were gratuitous or downright unhelpful changes that Ray had made, until we came to the finale of Act One. This took place in a synagogue after the Jessica character had eloped with the goy. There was a huge chorus of singing rabbis in prayer shawls and yarmulkes, wailing their grief at Christian perfidy. Roger had composed some wonderfully moving music for the purpose. Ray had decided that the vocal impact of the number was not sufficient. The singers were on general coverage mikes; sound was primitive compared with nowadays. To solve the problem, Ray decided to put the entire chorus on hand mikes. The lights went up on twenty rabbis singing into hand mikes, not radio mikes, with trailing cords. Well, I suppose that is funny looking back on it now, but at that moment it was so grotesque that I could take no more. I told Ray I couldn't continue and left.

I did go to the first night and I did try to make it up with the cast afterwards. It was a lost cause. I had no one to blame but myself. I think Ray behaved impeccably. I think everyone did their best. I think I behaved badly. That is what fear does to you. The critics roasted the show. *Fire Engine* was shunted away very quickly.

Even then it seemed to me that destiny was not going to allow me to be distracted from the Exchange. It's why I still have sympathy with actors and directors who became seduced by the money and glamour of London theatre. I'm afraid that I would have done, given the chance. I'm not sure the voice that had twice come from the depths inside me to say no would have spoken again if I had had the crowning hit I was expecting.

CHAPTER 38

Leaping Back

I had ten days to recover before rehearsals started for *Leaping Ginger*. I was pretty battered. I decided to go to a health farm, Grayshott Hall, to heal myself in anonymity. In addition to the fact that various actors were there as well, I had my nose rubbed in it again and again. On my first morning down at breakfast I was confronted by a picture of myself in the *Daily Mail* being read by someone at the same table. An apparently charming reporter had attached herself to the production to write about the making of a musical. She had been friendly and supportive; now she had written an article wondering how on earth we could have perpetrated such a fiasco, as she had always known that it would be a disaster. The show was discussed on Radio 4's *Start the Week*. Ned Sherrin, my absentee colleague from *Oom-pah-pah*, gave his opinion: 'It was always going to be a disaster. The producer was famous only for farces and it was directed by one of the two worst directors of musicals in the country.' And the presenter said, 'Sounds of writs falling through the letter box.' Had Ned been talking to Judi Dench?

I was so numb that by now all I wanted to know was who was the other director. It turned out to be Clifford Williams. Well, he was in good company . . . or I was.

When Trevor started writing *Leaping Ginger*, he asked me if there were any boundaries in the staging. I told him that whatever he wrote I could stage. *Leaping Ginger* was a life-force musical about a young criminal who is let out of jail and goes on a picaresque voyage of self-discovery. Trevor threw the lot at it: fairgrounds, greyhound racing, massage parlours, art auctions, even policemen who were porn addicts ('Of all the Boys in Blue, we are the bluest of the lot'). I rose to every one of these challenges well enough, with the help of Johanna, but there were two seemingly intractable puzzles.

The hero was called Leaping Ginger because he was famous for evading the police by leaping from the top of one building to another, and Trevor had intended a scene where the actor was required to do just that in full view of the audience.

The proscenium flying experts, Kirby's, came up. The paraphernalia of harnesses and fly-wires just wouldn't work in the round. What to do? Michael gave me the clue. If you can't move the actor, you'll have to move the theatre. He was spot on. Here's how we did it. We imagined a building site so the hook of a crane hung over the centre of the stage. There were two simple white right-angled barriers representing the skyscrapers. Ginger ran and leapt to swing from the hook while the stage crew moved the barrier across to where he was hanging. He jumped down. The audience erupted. The secret of the round is to use the audience's imagination. They love it.

The second problem was that Trevor had written a scene where Ginger visits an old ladies' home. This was impossible. Even if we could afford a dozen actresses for one scene, where would we get them from? I had only one pragmatic suggestion: the whole cast, male and female, would have to play the ladies. It's difficult to describe how powerfully moving this was. Richard Negri described it as 'a vision of eternity'. The sexes were reunited in one being.

The company had an outing. We realised that at Blackpool we could experience in one day a fair, a greyhound meeting and, surely, old ladies. We set out in a charabanc and arrived on the front. There on the esplanade was a small army of old ladies in their deckchairs. The cast had brought their costumes with them. They dressed up, exited the chara, hired some deckchairs and joined the old ladies. There was a slow dawning of recognition. Then suddenly that whooping, shrieking laughter of old ladies enjoying themselves rang out above the beach. It was sublime.

A week into rehearsal Chris Neil, who was playing Ginger, took me aside: 'I just wanted to say how much I'm enjoying working with you.' I detected a note of surprise. 'The cast of *Fire Angel* warned me that you were a complete shit,' he explained.

In addition to introducing Tilly Tremayne, who had been in *The Good Companions*, to Trevor Peacock, which started them off on a marriage lasting to this day, *Leaping Ginger* was a smash hit. So popular was it that we decided to bring it back the following year. It turned out to have a very important consequence for my artistic life, but that's to come.

The year was over, the company was well launched and on the advice of Alfie Burke I went with the family to a French seaside village called Cap Ferret on the coast near Bordeaux. We fell in love with it: 120 miles of beach, pine forests, oysters and the best wines in the world would for some years to come be the restorative that all of us needed.

CHAPTER 39

Between Two Worlds

All this time I had pursued my interest in matters Jewish and I had picked up an American paperback of five Yiddish plays. Three of them were of great interest, *God of Vengeance*, *The Golem* and most of all Anski's *The Dybbuk* or *Between Two Worlds*. The Dybbuk is the spirit of a man, who when he dies, enters into and possesses another human being. In the play Channon, a poor student, loves Leah. Leah's father Sender has already chosen a rich husband for Leah. On her wedding day Channon dies and invades Leah's body. She speaks with his voice. Eventually there is an exorcism, Channon leaves Leah's body but they are reunited. The dead Channon and the living Leah transcend the gap between two worlds. This was perfect for the Exchange; another little-known European classic of darkness and redemption.

Researching the play gave me some clues to the question: 'Who were the Jews before Yahweh chose them?' Channon was a student of Kabbalah and I did my best to find out what Kabbalah was. This is very difficult because it is an oral, esoteric tradition of great antiquity, which was not written down until medieval times in the Book of Splendour: *The Zohar*. Even then it is difficult to understand, which was deliberate on the part of the initiates. The rewards of study are to be hard won. Please forget the modern nonsense that Madonna is connected to.

My findings were revolutionary. The creator God, for example, Elohim, is plural, suggesting a male-female. Yahweh is Justice and is relatively minor on the left shoulder of cosmic man. Kabbalah deals with reincarnation, numerology and other arcane matters. It seems to share common cause with all the world's esoteric traditions.

What was clear was that the orthodox rabbis hated it. I visited the Head of Jews' College and asked him innocently his views of Kabbalah. 'There are some parched souls who are eager for drops from another world. There are enough problems in this world for the rest of us. Let it alone.' In Manchester, rabbis preached against the play and advised their congregations not to see it. Had their congregations obeyed, it would have been extremely bad for the box office; happily they did not.

What were they so scared of? The Yahweh religion is an enslaving religion and the rabbis are his gaolers. They were scared of Kabbalah, which strove to release the potential in all human beings. That meant no enslavement, no control and an adventure into the unknown that would take anyone beyond their reaches. For me the play was completely releasing. Sender and his orthodox family was Golders Green, Channon and the Kabbalah was a window to the other world which I had experienced and wanted to know more of.

The cast was huge, thirty-two in all. Perforce, most of them were non-Jews, goyim. There just weren't enough Jewish actors around. There were three massive performances at the centre from Jewish actors. Michael Poole played the father, Wolfe Morris played Meyer, the synagogue's functionary who, in one memorable scene, had to summon and escort a dead spirit from the cemetery to give evidence in the trial of the Dybbuk, and towering over them was John Bennett as the great Rabbi Azrael, an ageless wise man who presided over the exorcism. Most of the cast had to become Jewish for the play. For weeks the theatre resounded with Jewish jokes and the sound of actors going poi-poi-poi, spitting in the eye of the devil. We did have a lighter side. There were visits to synagogues and to the yeshiva (religious school) in north Manchester.

If *The Trial of Joan of Arc* in 1969 convinced me that one day I might aspire to direct something of the calibre of Michael's *Brand*, *The Dybbuk* nearly ten years later reinforced that belief. In Peter Bennion's wonderful design a lost middle-European world was conjured up that transported the audience out of themselves into a world where you knew it was good to be alive, because questions of the soul mattered. Ant Bowles's music, Michael Williams's transcendent lighting, Elizabeth Romilly's extraordinary Dybbuk-possessed bride, John Watts's Angel-Messenger all combined with my three Jews seamlessly. I was a happy man.

CHAPTER 40

The Group Evolves

It was exciting to start a new company, it was thrilling to create a new theatre, but sustaining that company year in and year out was a new reality that brought difficulties with it.

The first problem was the actual running of it. Michael had volunteered to be the Resident Artistic Director, but he was increasingly unwell as his kidney condition deteriorated. It is amazing that he ever managed to rehearse a play properly. He had to dialyse three times a week. In order to rehearse he dialysed at night, which meant he was recovering while he was rehearsing. He recovered in time to dialyse again so that only one day a week did he ever feel really well. Clearly he couldn't do the desk job.

We tried to rotate among ourselves, Max, Casper and I, but that drove Michael Williams, who was now the Administrator, and the rest of the organisation round the bend. We were all very different and just as they got used to one of us they had to cope with another.

Instead, we carved up the various responsibilities between us, I inevitably getting the political-financial side of the company, the other two the more artistic matters. Someone, however, had to be resident and that someone turned out to be me. For a year I was in the office Monday to Friday, driving back to see my family at weekends. It was a gruelling time. Determined to keep on the straight and narrow, I taught myself German during the evenings but I couldn't put up with the situation for ever. With Johanna's full backing I decided to sell up in London and move the whole family to Manchester.

Having taken the decision I was terrified. I used to have nightmares about it. I was going to leave the centre. I used to wake up in a cold sweat night after night. In the event, as I drove away from Beaumont Avenue in Richmond for the last time it couldn't have been easier. I didn't have one backward thought.

For the family it was an excellent decision. Because of the difference of London and Manchester house prices, we were able to buy a large corner house in Bramhall with a huge garden. It was perfect for bringing up children. In terms of education, too, the North certainly understood it better than the South. Nearby Ladybarn School was ideal at primary level and after a brief experiment with Jacob to attend Clifton, Manchester Grammar School gave them a fine education at a fraction of the cost of other public schools. The quality of life in the near countryside where we lived and the openness of Mancunians were priceless.

For the theatre it meant I could give more time and energy to the group. The main problem was the choosing of the seasons. This is the most important and the most difficult part of an Artistic Director's life. You are dependent on the availability of rights, of actors, constantly hectored by marketing and administration to come up with a season as early as possible and when you finally do, with a sigh of relief, you are faced immediately with the next one.

People ask how we decide the plays. The blunt answer, at that time, was horse-trading. We all had our pet projects, and rightly so, but had we produced nothing but them there would have been no comedies, farces or musicals in the repertoire. Most directors are attracted to tragedies first and foremost. The result was that I and Max, who was directing more and more, did the lighter shows, sometimes aided by Eric Thompson until his tragic stroke in 1981. Michael and Casper did the lion's share of the serious plays.

There were terrible undercurrents in these meetings. I have already spoken of the rivalry between Michael and Casper, but what I didn't realise was that it applied to me too. I asked Michael why he had suddenly dropped the idea of my joining him in Manchester. His reply was, 'Because I was frightened you would stab me in the back.' I was dumbfounded. This was the director I admired beyond all others, the man whose production had brought me into the theatre, whom I had fought to work with. What did he mean? Why did he think it? I believe, as it often is when someone accuses someone else totally unfoundedly, that he was projecting his own inner workings on to me.

Beyond this, the sieve through which they put all projects was a very narrow-meshed one. As I have said, their reaction against contemporary theatre was comprehensive. They were the keepers of the Grail and the flame had to burn pure. Projects of mine were sometimes turned down as if they were contaminated. Not just projects of mine either. I remember vetoing, with Casper and Max, a project Michael had with Alan Garner to do a stage version of *The Owl Service*. It was thought to be too corrupt.

The truth is that it pays to be as inclusive as possible; that which you exclude, threatens to rise up against you. As the company became more confident so it opened its arms wider. Max's criteria were right, I think: 'Is it for or against life?' Sometimes it is quite difficult to understand the answer. Where does *Oedipus Rex* fit?

These were hard meetings and often distressing, but I wouldn't have missed them for anything. They were the real makings of the group.

CHAPTER 41

Enter Robert Lindsay

The revival of *Ginger* gave us the chance to make improvements. Trevor, a master lyricist-composer, tended to be messy in the writing of the book, something I had found in *Collapse of Stout Party*. Here he refined the text and cut out extraneous plot lines. In the first version Ginger fell in love with a 'Beautiful, Wonderful Black Princess' which introduced a racial theme that had nothing to do with the show, although it did give rise to a captivating calypso, 'Me Daddy Play Cricket for de West Indies'. This meant replacing the excellent Alibe Parsons and I took the opportunity of bringing in John Bennett, out of his prayer shawl and into the role of the Kray-type character Jack Palace. I also wanted another Ginger. Chris Neil had been very good but I knew the part needed a more explosive type of animal and someone who could act as well as he could sing. This was asking for the moon but that's what I got.

I had never heard of Bob Lindsay but it was clear from the audition that here was the Ginger of our dreams. It was only when I had dinner with him during rehearsals and our table was surrounded by autograph hunters that I found out about his hit television series *Citizen Smith*. He was delighted because he thought that was why I had chosen him, rather than for his talent.

My artistic relationship with Bob, which lasted for the next five years, was one of the most rewarding creatively I have had with any actor. I recognised in him the actor I would have wanted to be if I had been an actor. That, of course, makes everything possible because you have no reservation about the person you are working with.

When I appeared on his *This Is Your Life* programme, I said he was *the* actor of his generation and that on him should fall the mantle of Olivier. He has only to walk out on stage and the audience fall in love with him. You can't learn that, it's God-given. He was also born with natural breathtaking comic timing. In addition he is fundamentally a lovely fellow and operates as an actor from a true-heart centre. He is a crucial part of the next section of my life.

He was a fabulous Ginger. The run was sold out before it opened. Ray Cooney came to see it and wanted to take it to London, but there was one proviso: there would have to be a star, he hoped Michael Crawford. I couldn't do it, nobody in the world could play the part better than Bob. If I replaced him why would anyone want to come and work for me? I refused. About a year later I was in Bob's house in Chiswick, listening to him on the phone being pleaded with by that same Ray Cooney to be in his next West End farce. It was ironic but it was also sad. *Leaping Ginger* was a great show, it should have been more widely seen. However, it brought year two to a cracking end.

CHAPTER 42

Behind the Iron Curtain

While Michael was reunited with Vanessa Redgrave for his much-praised production of *The Lady from the Sea*, my contribution to the autumn season of year three was to revisit *The Winter's Tale*, which was to tour in Western and Eastern Europe before coming in to the Exchange in November.

Michael Williams and I did a recce of the theatres first. We started in West Germany in Cologne and Ludwigshafen, then went behind the Iron Curtain to Hungary. Hungary wasn't too bad. The Hungarians had managed to hang on to some semblance of their former society. Although there were military everywhere and the streets were far from bustling, there were still coffee shops where good pastries could be had and the people seemed to have reached some equitable arrangement with the Russian authorities.

Romania was dreadful. It was my first brush with an atmosphere of pure evil, which I encountered again in South Africa before the end of apartheid. A whole population was in subjugation, the subjugation of fear and poverty. The sight of people setting up their stalls at the market to sell an egg, one bunch of carrots and a sausage was pathetic.

We, of course, stayed in a luxurious hotel for party members only. We had been warned by the British consulate not to talk to the Romanians for their own sake and that all the rooms would be bugged. This was a shock to the system for someone reared in moderate, liberal, democratic Britain.

We had a guide, Mrs Ionesco, who deposited us at the hotel, gave us our per diem and arranged to meet us the next morning to look at the theatre. Michael and I were the only diners in the excellent restaurant. The food and wine were splendid and there was a folk band playing just for us. At the end of the meal, we bought them a round of drinks, paid the bill and went to bed.

The next morning Mrs Ionesco asked us if all had been well. I said it had but the bill had been a little more expensive than we had expected and all our per diem had been spent. She asked to see the bill. She disappeared. She came back and off we went to the theatre. That night, when we returned to the hotel, the entire staff had been replaced. I had been researching the Holocaust more and more. This was the first moment that totalitarianism became real to me. It was a profound relief to fly back into Western Europe.

It had been fourteen years since I had done *The Tale* successfully at the Birmingham Rep but I made a terrible mistake. I did not go through a proper new creative process with my designer Peter Bennion or, more important, take into account how theatre had changed in that time.

I did understand the essence of the play very well and I gave an outstanding opening speech to the cast on the first day of rehearsal. The next morning I had come down with mumps. I realised I had terrified myself and mumps was a convenient way of not having to proceed with the production as my doctor assured me I could not. However, by now I was well aware of the psychosomatic root of actors' and directors' illnesses during rehearsal and to the doctor's astonishment I got rid of my swollen face in forty-eight hours and was back on the job. It was not a good job, although I managed to improve it by the time I had restaged it in the round for Manchester. It was a lesson hard learnt, not quite never go back but, if you do, find a good reason for doing so.

The rest of the season was pretty successful. Trevor wrote a proper non-pantomime version of *Cinderella* in which Gabrielle Drake appeared for the first of many times at the Exchange. Patricia Routledge triumphed in Max's revival of *The Schoolmistress*. Lee Montague was again movingly hilarious in the British première of Neil Simon's *Last of the Red Hot Lovers*, which went to the Criterion Theatre in London, but probably the most important thing was the first season we played at the Roundhouse in spring–summer 1979.

Thelma Holt, who was the Artistic Director of the Roundhouse, invited the company to play an annual season there and Richard Negri managed to design an auditorium which more or less replicated the Manchester configuration. The first season was all Michael's revivals: Vanessa Redgrave in *The Lady from the Sea*, Edward Fox in *The Family Reunion* and Michael Hordern in *The Ordeal of Gilbert Pinfold*. They were all mightily successful but it rankled with us. We felt we were being used as a platform for Michael's furtherance. This was not what a group was for. In hindsight he was a man who knew he would not live a full lifespan because of his condition and was cramming in what he could. He might have done it less ruthlessly.

CHAPTER 43

The Three Musketeers

Derek Griffiths and I decided we could write a show together. It would be a show with only one objective: to make people laugh. I had never written anything before and I was excited. One afternoon I watched on television an old black-and-white movie of *The Three Musketeers* with Don Ameche and the Ritz Brothers. It was great. The Ritz Brothers, whom I had never even heard of, were delightful and their sending up of the Dumas story inspired. I could see a Marx Brothers, *Hellzapoppin'* version with no holds barred. We set to work. Derek wrote all the music and lyrics, and I wrote most of the book. Johanna was the designer and together we cooked up more visual gags, bad puns, mangled French jokes, crazy disguises than you can imagine.

When he heard we were doing *The Three Musketeers*, Bob Lindsay volunteered to play D'Artagnan; Derek would play Athos; a lovely great fat actor who died tragically young, Terry Wood, Porthos; and Trevor, Aramis; with his wife Tilly as the Queen plus Gary Waldhorn as Richelieu.

The script I wrote was a director's script. That is to say I was imagining the production as I wrote it. On the page it didn't look very funny. For example, there was a scene that had to be played in the dark. Since it was summer in the Exchange, the theatre wasn't dark until about nine o'clock, so the joke was that the actors had to play in the dark when it wasn't. Very difficult to convey. My stars didn't react well to the first draft.

I invited them round to my mother's, who cooked them a Jewish banquet. I filled them with wine, then acted out the script in all its madness. They were won over.

Aided by Malcolm Ranson's fights, we concocted a pot-pourri which was so extreme that even we ourselves didn't know what we were doing. We continued in blind faith.

Finally we got to the dress rehearsal after a long complex technical. Afterwards I noticed that a lot of the staff had disappeared and Johanna was not to be found. When I got home she was asleep and waking up the next morning I found that she had gone. On arrival at the theatre for the preview, no one would look me in the eye. I realised that everyone was expecting a disaster.

My assistant on the show was one Sophie Marshall. This remarkable woman had joined the company as a Production Secretary in 1974, had worked her way up to become Company Manager and would then become the best Casting Director in the country. Her hard work, taste, discretion, purity of purpose and diplomacy were a mainstay of the company for thirty years. At this moment she had asked to be my assistant because she wanted to know in depth what a rehearsal process was like. What she made of it all I don't know but we made our way to the auditorium for that first audience with me in sheer terror.

The show opened with the ghost of Dumas addressing the audience in pompous French and slowly realising through the whispered promptings of the servant Planchet, played by another ex-Oxford actor, Doug Fisher, that the audience were English and therefore couldn't understand a word.

Second line, first laugh: the greatest sound I have ever heard. I grasped Sophie's arm and held it tight as the laughter grew and grew. Poor lady, she never uttered a sound but her bruises afterwards told their tale. The evening was a riot. The biggest laugh came when a large seagull shat on the Three Musketeers disguised as sailors. It was a shout of laughter so loud that I thought the theatre was going to break in two.

Afterwards Johanna had the decency to be abashed. It was a sell-out. A few years later Patrick Sandford revived it at Southampton. I had the unalloyed pleasure of seeing my script being directed by someone else. It was a heady experience because it was so different from directing.

CHAPTER 44

On Stage Again

I said I wouldn't detail every show I did and I won't, unless it meant something special to me; *The Lower Depths* in 1979 did. Casper suggested that we form a company to produce *The Cherry Orchard* and *The Lower Depths*; he to do the Chekhov, I the Gorky. The two great playwrights, who were effectively on either side of the Russian Revolution, had met in Yalta; there was a picture of them together.

I had never read *The Lower Depths*. I now think it is my favourite play. It is a hymn to humanity. This cross-section of our race, struggling to survive in the doss-house to which they have been reduced, some succeeding, some failing, is the most compassionate and profound picture of mankind I know. It can only be its appalling anti-box-office title that prevents it being done more often.

What a company we had. Max had Satin's great speech about the divinity of man, Peter Vaughan was the murderer Luka: 'Prison can't teach a man how to be good but a man can. One man can teach another how to be good.' Sorcha Cusack, Gabrielle Drake and Susan Penhaligon led the women; John Watts was the Baron and Peter Childs, Kleshch. Bob was back playing the thief Pepel and Trofimov in *The Cherry Orchard*. As Max said, plumbing the depth of this great play and trying to give it voice was like discovering the Grail.

But the production had another importance for me. I was down in London auditioning for the next show I was to direct, which was Gerard McLarnon's new play *Blood, Black and Gold*, when an urgent call came through. Dougie Fisher, who was playing the Actor, had fallen and sustained a hairline fracture of the skull. I had to go on that night.

I raced to Euston and got on the train. Then I realised that I didn't have a copy of the script with me. It was an agonising three-hour journey not being able to do anything practical except fret. I arrived in Manchester just before six o'clock. The play was in five acts and the stage management had divided the script up for me so I could easily study while they put me into the rags that were my costume. The Actor's part, although crucial, is actually quite small in terms of lines and I was able to go on without the book, learning each act in my times off stage. This wasn't as difficult as it sounds as I knew the play very well. I got the usual hero's reception afterwards, and went home a relieved and exhausted man.

The next morning the Company Manager phoned. Dougie wasn't going to be able to come back, I would have to play the part for the remaining month of the run. This was a different kettle of fish. Being a hero for a night was one thing, properly sustaining a role for a month another. I took out my script, carefully divided into beats and movements with the different objectives of the character. To hell with all that. Where did I come on from, where did I sit, where were my props, that's what mattered. It was the first time I understood that whatever else a director does, he must give the actor a secure footing.

Fortunately the Actor is an old ham, so I was type casting and therefore not too bad. After the actors had got over the shock of my first performance, when one after another they looked at me on stage and dried, we all relaxed and I enjoyed dropping my boss director persona, especially during the nightly gradual coming down from the high after the play.

I was working on stage with top-class actors and they began to give me notes about what I was achieving and what I was missing that were unlike a director's notes. Theirs were concerned with character and motivation but in a pragmatic way. This experience changed my whole approach to directing. Proper groundwork and sympathy, combined, I hoped, with insight and even sometimes inspiration, replaced shouting and screaming for ever. I now tried to put myself in the actors' shoes in every rehearsal.

I did like the rhythm of the actor's day. That two and a half hours on stage each night is a big task. You are allowed to get up late and do nothing although subconsciously you are being prepared for the evening. What actually happens in the theatre was a revelation to me. I imagined the cast getting into character, intensely preparing themselves for this immensely serious play, then during the performance quietly keeping themselves in character between entrances.

On the contrary, all I saw before the play was the most basic childish horseplay and during the show most of the company played games. Within days I was part of both. It was their way of keeping sane. They had their performances in them and they knew they could let them out when necessary. This didn't apply to everyone and the other thing I learnt was that there are no rules. Any system is there to help when needed. It is a guide, not a dogma, not a religion. Every actor has his or her own process and everyone's process, provided it is not an evasion, must be understood and respected. *The Lower Depths* was an education.

So, unexpectedly, was the play that followed it. Leo McKern, who had already played at the Exchange in Michael's production of *Crime and Punishment* with Tom as Raskolnikov, came back to do two plays. The big one was Ronnie Harwood's new play *The Dresser*, where he would be reunited with Tom, but he also wanted to take part in *Rollo* by Marcel Achard. None of us took to the play very much, so David Thompson, an old chum of Michael and Casper from Oxford, who had had considerable success at Stratford East, was engaged to direct.

One of my jobs as Resident Artistic Director was to make sure that visiting directors and their casts were happy. It became clear that this was not a happy company so I went to see a run-through. It wasn't very good but what was extraordinary was that Thompson spent the entire run-through pacing round the circumference of the stage. I had never seen anything like it. How did he expect the actors to concentrate?

Leo was deeply unhappy and wanted Thompson replaced. I did it with some pain, and agreed to take over for the last ten days. This is easier than it may sound. The actors are so desperate that all they need is a confident-sounding person who gives effectively the famous Tyrone Guthrie direction: 'Louder! Faster!' The education for me was working with Leo, or rather watching him working. You could give him an idea for a gag, which he would immediately execute a half-dozen different ways, all equally effective. I have worked with two other actors, Des Barrit and Espen Skjønberg, who seemed to have been born on a stage and could create their own stage rhythm. He taught me a great deal. Give the actors confidence and they will find talents they didn't know they possessed.

Having been sacked myself, I knew how Thompson must be feeling. His reaction was sad. He couldn't face going home and telling his wife what had happened. He stayed in Manchester and spent the days working in the City Library. On the first night he snuck in and watched the show from the back of the first gallery. The show was well received and we kept his name as director in the programme.

In the cast was Clare Higgins. I so enjoyed working with her that I persuaded her to stay on to do *Blood, Black and Gold*. That was a happy chance.

CHAPTER 45

International Success

The Dresser went into rehearsal and immediately hit a crisis. I went to watch a performance of *Rollo* and Leo asked to have dinner with me. He wanted to withdraw from *The Dresser*; the play was upsetting him so much he couldn't continue. He was prepared to go on doing *Rollo* and even do an extra week to give Michael time to recast, but he absolutely couldn't face another moment in the play. He was released and it was as if a great weight had been lifted off him.

The phenomenon of stage fright had hit Leo when he was on Broadway playing Cromwell in *A Man for All Seasons*, and he had walked, as had Lee Montague in the West End during Neil Simon's *Last of the Red Hot Lovers*, as have many other actors. It is a horrid reminder of the bravery of actors who expose themselves on a tightrope with no safety net in front of audiences night after night. I hadn't come across it before and it made me love actors. This long-lasting love affair improved me further as a director.

In this case playing an ageing leading actor who is soon to die was too close to home for Leo. Thereafter television audiences could revel in his Rumpole but to me it was tragic that the theatre was robbed of potentially the greatest Falstaff of all time. Leo never got his stage nerve back.

By coincidence, if such a thing exists, the extension of *Rollo* by a week enabled me to give Gary Waldhorn the chance to get his nerve back. Jack Hedley had a prior engagement and had to leave the company, and I asked Gary to take over. Gary too had lost his stage bottle after 'drying' on stage. To the public 'drying' means forgetting your lines, no big deal, but a true dry is much worse than that. Your mind goes blank and your mouth goes 'dry'. You can't hear a prompt, you are lost. Once this has happened you dread going on stage again, so you don't. I persuaded Gary that this was the ideal way back. It was only a week's run and a part that he could play standing on his head. Thank goodness he took the risk, otherwise we would have lost a fine stage actor.

Michael recast *The Dresser* with Freddie Jones and rehearsals began again. After the final dress rehearsal we all went out to dinner. Ronnie asked

Michael what he thought we had got. Michael said he thought we had a good play that would be of interest only to a minority audience. The public wasn't interested in a backstage play. It was a view nobody disputed. I had found it interesting as a practitioner, but felt it had little reverberation beyond its particular world.

It became the company's one international hit. Michael's production transferred to the West End, thence to Broadway, and then was eventually made into a film by Peter Yates with Tom joined by Albert Finney as Sir. What do we know about the ingredients for success?

CHAPTER 46

Another Surprise

Rollo had been one surprise, then there was another rather nice one. I was always going to do Gerry's new play, which had grown from our shared interest in alchemy, spurred by Jung and Silberer. It was a grand experience and put to rest the memory of empty houses and bad reviews from *The Saviour*. Clare Higgins had that unusual mix of sensuality and spirituality that makes her the potent actress she is and I immediately began talking to her about playing Isabella in *Measure for Measure* in the coming year. John Watts was also outstanding as her spiritual guide and Dilys added another string to her formidable bow, playing a terrifying old hag.

Michael was to have directed a French farce, which had fallen into our hands by a circuitous route. Actually the authors were Belgians, Maurice Hennequin and Pierre Veber. The play was called, not very subtly, *Come to the Point, Monsieur* and the version we were sent was an English translation of a German adaptation of the original called *Have You Anything to Declare?*.

It was very, very funny. The basis of the plot was that a young couple were in the process of consummating their marriage on their honeymoon. They were in a sleeping car about to cross the border. At the crucial moment a customs official banged on the door and demanded, 'Have you anything to declare?' The groom, de Trivelin, hadn't then or afterwards. On their return to Paris, with the marriage still unconsummated, the outraged father-in-law gives de Trivelin twenty-four hours to put the matter right. De Trivelin decides to visit a delightful cocotte, Zézé, to cure him but he has a jealous rival who hires a customs officer's uniform and stalks the hapless de Trivelin, so that every time that unfortunate young man seems to be about to be cured, he is confronted with the apparition of a customs official intoning, 'Have you anything to declare?'

Partly because of the West End transfer, partly because he was increasingly unwell, Michael had to withdraw and I took over. I got hold of the original French and found it infinitely superior to the version we had. Robert Cogo-Fawcett, now a producer, was the company's Finance

Director and I knew he spoke French, as did I. If he would do a literal translation, I would make it into an acting version. Other translations of French farce I found ponderous, lacking the vivacity of the original. The French speak very fast and they use more words than the English. The trick is to use as few words as possible in the English version so that the actors can speak as fast as the French. Anyway, with Brian Cox revealing unexpected (not by me) talents as a farceur, backed up by Dilys reverting to a more salubrious role, and John Phillips, it was a great success. We were planning the next Roundhouse season and Thelma Holt asked that this farce be included.

For me it was the beginning of an excellent sideline of translating with Robert. Once again it gave me particular pleasure because I could do something other than directing.

CHAPTER 47

Staying in the Group

The first four years had passed very quickly. The success of those years had been the result of the release of pent-up energy, especially in Michael and Casper, who were at last able to do the plays they had been storing up inside them. A change was now taking place; we were in for the long haul and the strains were beginning to tell.

There was increasing resentment against Michael. The outside world, who never believed in the group concept, saw us as Michael's company but Michael was less and less involved with the company, except when he had a project he wanted to do. In fact, it would be two years before his next production. Meanwhile he went on drawing a relatively high full-time salary. Richard, who had always felt that Michael's success as a director was in no small part due to his input as a designer, had insisted on directing his first solo production. I had fought against it. Richard had never directed a play by himself and I thought it inappropriate. Casper and Michael prevailed with the argument that we owed so much to Richard for the design of the theatre, and it would only be a one-off. The production of Shusaku Endo's *The Golden Country* was inert and lifeless, but not to Richard who felt he was being guided directly by God, and he was to direct a double bill of O'Neill's *The Emperor Jones* and Ionesco's *The Chairs* in the coming season. He, too, was on a salary, though not so large as Michael's, and did little to earn it.

The main burden of running the company was falling on me, although Casper and Max were very much there and for the most part good companions. The basic vision still glued us together. I was, however, becoming increasingly resentful of Casper's paternal hand. After he had seen *The Three Musketeers* he was very dismissive: 'You have . . . emem . . . for the first half-hour, the audience were not . . . emem . . . nourished.' If non-stop laughter wasn't nourishing, what was?

The other problem, which is difficult to explain, is that Casper's contributions as a director were not quite like everyone else's. There was no question that his insights into a text were at a deeper level than or as deep a level as anyone's, but he seemed contemptuous of the basic showbiz need 'to bring off a production' theatrically. Had he had a rehearsal period at least double the four weeks we had, it might have been all right but as it was he took his actors so deep into the experience of exploration that they weren't ready to emerge when the time came. Too many of the productions seemed just that bit underpowered.

One requisite of the group was that we endorsed each other's work. This began to be difficult and we started to retreat into ourselves, jealously hugging our productions to us. Quite often we didn't attend each other's press nights and this was significant.

I don't want to make it seem too bad but it was troubling. Again, it was an absolutely necessary part of the process. There was also another important player who was to join us for the fifth year.

Each year, as part of our search for new talent, we had an assistant director who helped us with our work and did his or her own late-night production. The hope was we would find someone who would grow with the company.

I did the initial interviews, and this year there came into the Spotlight Room a slightly owlish, rumpled, obviously Jewish young man called Greg Hersov. Within minutes we were at loggerheads. He was a Marxist-Freudian: anathema. We went at it hammer and tongs. It was quite clear to me this was a very considerable mind whom it was worth taking a risk on. Greg has been at the Exchange ever since.

CHAPTER 48

A Strange Year

The 1980–81 season was a curate's egg, perhaps reflecting the unease at the centre of the company. The first production was a notable success. Ant Bowles had persuaded me to go to Bristol to see Gabrielle Drake play Lavinia in *Titus Andronicus*, as a result of which she was now working at the Exchange happily, regularly. The production of *Titus* was strikingly good. It was by a young director, Adrian Noble, who was on the RSC's books as an assistant. I met him, we got on and he came to direct *The Duchess of Malfi*. None of us wanted to do Webster's play, the Jacobeans were too decadent; Adrian, the son of an undertaker, did. Helen Mirren and Bob Hoskins came back to lead the company and Pete Postlethwaite, who had played Adrian's Titus, came to play Antonio. If *Malfi* is a decadent play, Helen with her spirit and dignity kept the polarity alive, as did Pete. His was the only portrayal of sheer goodness I have seen that makes it seem as interesting as evil. With the next Roundhouse season beckoning this had to be there.

Richard's double bill was next and with it another crisis. *The Emperor Jones* was to be played by Errol John, who had been Casper's Othello at the Old Vic and was the author of the beautiful play *Moon on a Rainbow Shawl*. Something had happened to him since those days – he seemed a broken, unhappy man. Shortly after rehearsals started he was in my office. The production was demeaning to a black man and he was quitting. I think he just knew he couldn't hack it. I persuaded Pete Postlethwaite to stay on and take over. Against all the odds he brought off a coup of a performance, but overall the double bill did nothing to improve my view of Richard as a director.

That summer in Cap Ferret, Trevor had suggested we do *Godot* again. He had met Max Wall and liked the idea of doing it with him. Until I met Max I couldn't see why I would want to do the play again, but once I had I saw what Trevor meant. Wolfe Morris would repeat his Pozzo and Gary Waldhorn would play the hapless Lucky.

Rehearsals were tortuous. After lunch and his intake of Guinness, Max was unable to work. Before lunch we just about got through. A few days in, Max stopped in mid-rehearsal: 'That's it, I'm off, replace me!' I was stunned. What did he mean? 'You booked me, you knew what you were getting. Replace me.' It was the reaction of a music-hall artiste. 'You obviously hate what I'm doing. Replace me!' I protested, I loved what he was doing. 'There's nothing on your boat race!' So that was it. I explained that I laughed at new gags at first but as I got used to them I didn't. It didn't mean I didn't like them. 'That's another thing, you keep on stopping. I need rehearsals to learn my lines.' That was a stunner. We were going through a very difficult text for the first time and it needed discussing. The Braham Murray of recent years would have thrown a tantrum and kicked him out. The new, wiser version didn't. There was something so absolutely right about Max as Vladimir that it seemed worth fighting for.

We rehearsed, as Max wanted, in the mornings. Then, after he got drunk, I worked with the other three separately. Actually it was the other four. In *Malfi* my younger son, Joe, had made his début as the next ruler of the kingdom; in *Godot* Jacob played the Boy. We proceeded in this unsatisfactory way for about a week. Then I had an idea. I told Trevor that if I had to give a note to Max, I'd give it to Trevor instead. If Max wasn't picking up his cues, I'd berate Trevor. It worked; Max took all my notes by proxy.

I had wanted Max in the cast because Beckett wrote *Godot* to be played by two clowns; Max and Trevor were the ideal. The problem was to get Max to use his repertoire of gags. 'I can't do that. This is Beckett,' he intoned religiously. The famous routine where the tramps try on different hats cried out for Max's expertise. It was like pulling teeth. Eventually I got him to relax but he didn't trust me.

By now he had learnt his lines but I don't think he understood a quarter of them. I hated every minute of it, but something told me to keep on with it. We reached the production weekend and he was late for the technical, drinking in the bar. I was, justifiably, furious. He hated me. He nearly walked again. I grovelled; he stayed.

On the first night when Jacob as the Boy came on Max jumped to the end of Act Two; Jacob aged nine mercifully stuck to the right cues and rescued him. What a nightmare.

What bliss. The magic of Max and Trevor working together was bewitching. Together they captured the tragicomedy of the piece. That kind of magic cannot be summoned, it is either there or it is not. When the reviews came out and they were ecstatic, I turned in Max's eyes from a villain into a hero. This show, too, would go to the Roundhouse. There it would sometimes overrun for up to twenty minutes as Trev and Max elongated their clowning in inspired improvisation. You never get bored in this job. There's always a surprise on the way.

Trevor stayed on at Christmas to play, beautifully, *Harvey* and then Casper directed *Rosmersholm*. I had another visitation in my office on the day of the dress rehearsal. Chris Gable, who was playing Rosmer, wanted to walk out: Casper was browbeating him into playing Rosmer in a particular way and Chris didn't like it. Casper had a habit of doing this, especially when he identified closely with the part. Tom had suffered with him when they were rehearsing *Homburg*, until he had said, 'Go on then, Casper, you play the part if you want to but if I'm to play it don't make me do it as if you were.' It is a hook all directors are prone to get caught on, albeit unconsciously. I now always try to see before rehearsal which part I am likely to identify with. If you don't, it can seriously affect the show even to the casting of it. You may be casting a projection of yourself who is not really suitable.

I pleaded with Chris to stay because if he didn't the show couldn't open. I told him to go downstairs and tell Casper to fuck off. He did; the show went on. Casper knew what I had done. I was growing up.

Rosmersholm wasn't great but it did have Espen Skjønberg in it, I think the greatest actor I have seen. He was Norway's Olivier, a close friend of Casper and when I saw him in *Rosmersholm* I knew I had to work with him one day.

Now I was to return after five years to Shakespeare. My fingers had been badly burnt by *The Winter's Tale*, but Shakespeare is like a drug and I wanted another fix. I needed to put into practice what I hoped I had learnt from my previous failure. It was a big moment for me and it coincided with an earthquake in my private life.

CHAPTER 49

The Last Chance Saloon and Finally a Proper Director

My home life was on an even keel or rather better. The move to Manchester was a total success. We were both working ferociously hard, but we were doing it together and we were at home a great deal, so the children were not neglected. We seemed to have hit a good balance.

Earthquake is a dramatic word but that is how it seemed to me. I had read about this earthquake; I had watched Max, Michael and Casper, who were about fourteen years older than me, go through this earthquake more or less successfully and I was determined that I wouldn't let it happen to me. Some hope!

The forty-year-old crisis is as real as real can be. It is the moment when you either decide to go on with your life as it is, or break out completely to something new. At such a time the frustrated accountant becomes the actor he always wanted to be, the meek, quiet male becomes a criminal and the happily married man leaves his wife and family and runs off with the au pair. It is the last chance saloon.

It was as though the earth were constantly moving under my feet. There was no firm ground on which to stand. Did I really want to be a director for the rest of my life, did I want to be in Manchester, why on earth was I married, even what was I doing with children? Every corner of my life was being questioned. I felt permanently not quite right, not exactly dizzy but not standing firmly, shaky on my feet.

This coincided, I'm sure not coincidentally, with my last infidelity, with our new Assistant Finance Director to Robert Cogo-Fawcett, Maggie Saxon. She has since become one of our leading administrators, holding the post of Executive Director at Stoke, West Yorkshire and Chichester. This was her first step on the ladder.

I danced with her one night at a do at George's and an electric shock hit my body. The affair started soon afterwards. I think it saved me from cracking up. Maggie provided me with a haven, a place to escape to where I was exclusively looked after, fed with special foods, plied with wine and taken care of physically. She was warm and she cared for me and I clung to her.

The affair lasted longer than the others and, unlike the others, I was riddled with guilt throughout it. Johanna had done nothing to deserve this. She was bringing up two children and designing three shows a year at least, besides running the house etc. etc. I continually broke off the relationship with Maggie, then went back. It must have been intolerable for her.

It was one of those risk-taking relationships, the only one I've really had. Moments in offices, in corridors, nights snatched away, a relationship that was about asking to be found out. Denise Wood, our General Manager and a friend, had said to me that if you really didn't want to be caught you could conduct an affair in absolute secrecy. She's probably right. I think I always wanted to be found out; I wanted Johanna to know what I was going through because I always thought of it as growth that she should know about.

She did find out. Uncharacteristically, she opened my briefcase to look for someone's address and found a bill from the Priory Hotel in Horton-cum-Studley near Oxford.

She was terribly, terribly hurt. I was having an affair with someone in the place where she worked. How was she ever to go into the theatre again? What was the future to be?

Still in the middle of my personal limbo, I had to decide what to do. Make a break or hang in? The critical decision finally led me to a firm piece of ground. I had been entrusted with two precious sons whom I loved dearly. The one clear thing was that that trust could not be broken. That meant my marriage with Johanna had to be saved. I recommitted to Johanna and made a secret vow to myself that I would never be unfaithful again. I kept my vow but my mistake was not to tell Johanna I had taken it. She must have spent the next ten years or more wondering what further betrayal lay just around the corner.

The effect on Maggie was bad. She became ill and eventually left the company. She seems to bear no rancour and my gratitude to her remains total.

At the beginning of this phase Johanna and I were working on *Measure for Measure*, the production with which I think I finally grew up as a director. I had always been good on text and I was now pretty good at working with actors, but my failure with *The Winter's Tale* made me determined to go further. I realised that to make Shakespeare really come alive, like any other period piece I had to build a bridge across the centuries to the present day.

Measure was the ideal play to do it with because it can be set at any time and in any place. I was determined to do it now and, with Johanna, I worked hard to bring every nook and cranny of the play alive. The key that really unlocked it came in an amazing way.

The Duke, reconciling Isabella to her brother's execution, has an extraordinary speech, 'Be absolute for death', in which he makes death seem a relief and release after the horrors of life. I was reading, for my own interest, *The Tibetan Book of the Dead*, when I came upon a passage that was almost identical to the Duke's speech. It was as if Shakespeare had read it and taken it lock, stock and barrel into the play.

It gave me an idea. Why not have the Duke disguise himself as a Buddhist monk rather than a Christian one? In all the productions I had seen, to have your leading actor constantly cowled seemed a disadvantage. Alfie Burke, who was playing the Duke, thought this wonderful. He played him in a wig and apparently shaved his head to become the monk. This made him a very modern questing figure and allowed him to connect directly with his audience.

The end of the play always seems to pose a problem. How do you make the audience accept the marriage of the Duke to Isabella? I took the Coghill rule: if that was what Shakespeare wrote, that was what he meant. Here it worked. You knew that the journeys of the Duke and Isabella were complementary. Because of Clare's sensuality, you knew she had been in denial, as the Duke had been. Now they were both ready for each other.

Michael had said, in an uncharacteristic burst of praise, that he had found the evening, as a director, inspiring. I'm not sure really how good it was finally, but it was the first time I felt I was a proper grown-up director. I was thirty-eight, the age when most directors are beginning their mature period. I had already done more productions than most directors do in a lifetime, seventeen years of them; now at last I felt in control.

Godot and *Declare* went to the Roundhouse, together with *Malfi* and Casper's production of *The Misanthrope* with Tom. It was a triumphant season and Spurs beat Manchester City in the Cup with Ricky Villa's unforgettable goal. The company was riding high.

Alas, it was to be the last Roundhouse season, as Camden withdrew their support for Thelma and established a Black Theatre Centre which scandalously ran through £3 million in a very short time and closed the building until it opened again in 2006 due to the philanthropy of Torquil Norman. We have been trying to find a London showcase venue ever since. The Roundhouse seasons had a dynamic effect on our national profile, bringing us better and better actors, and making us more attractive to sponsors. We are one hundred per cent a Manchester company but we want to present our alternative view of theatre in our extraordinary space, at the heart of the nation from time to time.

CHAPTER 50

Andy Capp

Alan Price was a member of the Savile too and he had played concerts at the Exchange; in fact, the very first one in 1976. He wanted to do a musical of *Andy Capp*. It seemed a good idea. I asked Trevor to write the book and perhaps be involved with the lyrics, and he agreed. Tom phoned from New York, where he was playing *The Dresser*, to say he would like to play Andy. You bet! Ray Cooney, a glutton for punishment, paid good money to secure the rights for a West End transfer. Alan would actually be in it too with his band. It was looking good.

It proved impossible to get the show written. Trevor was working non-stop and without the book being created how could we put the show together?

Trevor was appearing at the Haymarket as Willie Mossop in *Hobson's Choice*. I rented a flat nearby with a piano, and locked him and Alan up in it for a week. I let Trevor out, just before the half every evening, to play Mossop and picked him up afterwards. It was the only way.

A rehearsal script of sorts emerged but it wasn't terrific, nor were rehearsals. Patsy Rowlands, she of *Chaganog*, who was to play Andy's wife Flo, left the cast. Val McLane was promoted. Tom and she didn't get on. David Firman, the excellent MD-Arranger, had Alan's band replaced at the last moment because they couldn't read the dots. It was all a mess. However, it had an excellent score, a warm heart, and trained pigeons that every now and again did what they were required to do – and Manchester loved it. It sold out.

There then followed an endless wrangle between Tom, me and Ray. In a nutshell Tom didn't want to go in to London. He didn't like the script and he didn't like Val, especially after she'd got rather good notices.

I promised him that we would rewrite every word of the book if necessary and eventually he agreed. We did just that, rehearsing constantly during the run, and the show got better and better.

We opened at the Aldwych Theatre and had wonderful notices. I remember thinking that my school fees problem would finally be solved. Ray was delighted and called the company together on the second night. He congratulated them and told them to make their dressing rooms cosy as they would be there for a long time. But . . . no one came. Why?

In those days it was the Jewish audience who, if they liked it, ensured the first three months of the run would be full. My mother explained: 'What do they want with an unemployed Geordie with a cloth cap who drinks beer?' I suppose she was right. Andy Capp was as Jewish as Rugby League and camping holidays. At any rate, much to Tom's pleasure the show didn't last. I was bewildered. To have a show of such quality with two big stars and a terrific critical reception and for the audiences to stay away was heartbreaking.

The good thing that came out of it was my relationship with Alan Price. I asked him why he looked so dour all the time. 'Cos if He looks down and sees me smiling, He'll clobber me.' The tough, abrasive, Geordie exterior masked a romantic softy, which accounts for his success as a songwriter: he mixes cynicism with romanticism in a most beguiling way. He's also a vastly entertaining companion because he sees conspiracies everywhere. Actually, judging from the calamities that have happened to him the only conspiracy seems to be against him.

I arrived back in Manchester to find that one very good thing had happened. Greg had done his first main house production and he had done it triumphantly. It was *One Flew over the Cuckoo's Nest* with Jonathan Hackett in the lead and it was quite marvellous. I was delighted. We had a new director and he was obviously in love with the space. I took him out to dinner, congratulated him and also told him the general despair I felt about the direction the company was taking. It had completely lost that first impetus and was ricocheting between good and bad work.

There was a way of getting to my office, without going through the stage door, by cutting through the bar and going up the back stairs. The next three productions were so awful and I was so ashamed that for a long time no one saw me in the theatre apart from my secretary.

They included Michael's production of Ronnie Harwood's next play about Sarah Bernhardt, *After the Lions*, with Dorothy Tutin. We all knew it wasn't a good play, Michael certainly knew it. It was thought that he went through with it because he wanted to direct the movie of *The Dresser*. If so, that objective failed. Our unwritten law was, and remains, that if after hearing the objections of the group an Artistic Director insists on doing a production he must be allowed to. The reasoning is simple. In a normally run company the Artistic Director has carte blanche and the same, after all the checks and balances, was to apply to us. We needed to have the final say in our own artistic development.

At all events, all three productions failed and the gloom was deep. I wondered if I wanted to go on and began to make tentative enquiries of schools in London in case I felt the time had come honourably to withdraw.

CHAPTER 51

The Child Grows Up a Bit

Now Casper was to direct his own adaptation of Nadezhda Mandelstam's account of her husband Osip's persecution under Stalin's regime *Hope Against Hope*. He augmented her account with extracts and reminiscences of Anna Akhmatova, the poet. This was for him a deeply felt personal account of his relationship with Communism. The Russians had taken away his childhood and he wanted to express his love of their soul and his hatred of totalitarianism. Avril Elgar was to play Nadezhda; Dilys, Anna; and David Horovitch, Osip.

This was so important to Casper that we all steered clear of him. No one went near him, not even to see a late run-through. His absorption in the rehearsals and his concentration were quite terrifying.

On the production weekend I received a phone call from the Company Manager. Casper had been taken seriously ill with bronchial pneumonia, would I please go and see him. I drove into Manchester and went to his flat. He looked dreadful, racked with coughing and scarcely able to speak. He was never going to recover in time to see the production through so he asked me to do it for him. That meant overseeing four crucial days until opening night.

I knew there was no question of refusing but the prospect was frightening. I was still Casper's child. A rather more mature side of myself made the crucial proviso. Yes, I would do as he asked but on the understanding that I would do what I thought right without consulting him or seeking his permission. This clearly displeased him but he had no choice. His demand was that I would come and see him every night and tell him what I had done. He promised not to protest.

I didn't know the show so the technical, which took the whole of Monday, was done by the Company Manager, Carrie Rodd. Technicals take for ever and are about technical matters: light, sound, props, entrances, exits etc. It was impossible to have any sense of what state the show was in.

Finally, there was a dress rehearsal on the Tuesday afternoon. There were two obvious problems. It was far too long, well over three and a half hours.

Casper had been frightened to leave anything out, so there was far too much obscuring the main drive of the script. I had to cut it down to, at most, three hours. That is a lot of material to cut.

The other problem was the acting style. The production was as cold as ice. The actors confirmed that they had been instructed to repress all emotions. Presumably this was to ensure that nothing would intrude between the audience and their understanding of the text. For a director like Casper who detested Brecht this was a bit odd. It was also anathema to me.

I gathered my courage and let the actors off the leash. For this they were profoundly grateful. The play came alive. I took myself over to Casper's and told him what I had done. He was as good as his word and said nothing.

We rehearsed in the same vein on the Wednesday and had a successful preview. On the Thursday the actors assembled in my office for my final notes. Suddenly the door opened and there was an emaciated Casper leaning on a walking stick. He said nothing but walked, or rather limped, to the centre of the room and pointed at each actor in turn, nodded to them and left. They knew nothing of what had passed between him and me, and I think it gave them heart. I simply prayed that I hadn't betrayed him utterly.

The piece was very well received but it was at least ten days before Casper was able to see it. I lurked backstage afterwards to find out what he thought. He went straight to David Horovitch's dressing room and I heard his raised voice through the door: 'My dear, anyone can have a success!' and then the dressing down, the sense of betrayal. He was very angry. It was a long time before he would so much as look at me and it was nearly two years before he took me aside and said, 'You made my play possible. You saved me from myself. Thank you.'

I'm sure his illness was the part of him that knew another hand would have to prevent his work from failing, taking him out of play. I like to think I was true to the centre of what he wanted. It certainly made me grow up a little more.

CHAPTER 52

At Last – And Big Changes

I suppose every director hopes to do *Hamlet* one day because every director has a Hamlet in him. Because you identify with Hamlet so much, you have to wait until you meet the actor who is your Hamlet. The one who will speak the words and will speak for you as well as for himself. Bob Lindsay was that actor for me. I asked him to do it, he agreed and do it we did in the late autumn of 1983.

No one thought this was a good idea. Max, a confessed bardolator who had lapsed, could no longer see any merit in the play. Casper thought Bob was the wrong casting and Michael was pretty uninvolved. He was preparing his own version of *Moby-Dick* and, being Michael, that was all that mattered. This time I stuck to my guns and, according to our rules, I was allowed to go ahead. It was the first time I had insisted on this right for myself.

Emboldened by *Measure for Measure*, I set about finding a means of doing *Hamlet*. Bob and I spent a lot of time together discussing it. At an early meeting he told me the line that meant everything to him: 'How weary, stale, flat, and unprofitable / Seem to me all the uses of this world!' He spoke them with such passion that I knew I had to plug the play into now. But how?

A modern-dress production seemed wrong. It foundered on the question what is a king today? There was no modern equivalent. To do it in the Elizabethan period seemed simply to turn it into a museum piece. To do it in any other century seemed daft. Why do a play written in the seventeenth century in nineteenth-century clothes in the twentieth century? I was stumped. There was no period that was right.

That was the answer. Don't do it in any period. Do it in rehearsal clothes, artfully designed rehearsal clothes to suit the characters, but don't attempt to lumber the production with any period detail. The idea would extend to the set. Don't have one, just a neutral wooden floor. Same with the lights, four great north lights would suffice. The actors, as in a rehearsal, would sit round the stage sharing the banquettes with the audience and if there was

196

any sound that was necessary they could conjure that up themselves. The only exception to this austerity would be when the Players entered. They would bring with them all the paraphernalia of the theatre: costumes, lights, sound, music, movement – a mini-RSC production.

It worked. Here is the example that pleased me most. The scene where Hamlet meets his father's ghost had never worked for me. It was always a director's scene with spooky music, spectral effects, ingenious prestidigitation, nothing to do with the content of the scene. In Shakespeare's day it would have been played in daylight with no effects whatsoever. This was the equivalent. Bob went on stage and Philip Madoc, who was playing the Ghost (and Claudius), got up in front of him. It was Hamlet's reaction that told you everything you needed to know. The scene became what it should be: a confrontation between father and son, the father laying a cursed burden on the son's head. It used the audience's imagination and they were electrified.

Preparing a text for *Hamlet* is like doing detective work. There are at least three extant versions and you choose between them, effectively making up your own play. Bob and I agreed that our version would strip away all the politics, to reveal the family story at the centre. A young man at the moment in his life when the scales fall from his eyes and he sees his parents as they really are. His father dies, his mother remarries. He discovers the awful truth, 'The time is out of joint; O cursèd spite, / that ever I was born to set it right!' Then this special young man, riddled with conscience and guilt, becomes a killer and finally a victim as he wrestles, as all young people do, with the world.

Bob was beyond description superb. The theatre was packed every night. There were *Hamlet* groupies; people queued from four o'clock in the morning to get the seats that were available on the day. Teachers wrote their thanks, young people hung on every word. What did Bob do? He spoke for a whole generation. Here in the great soliloquies he did what I have seen Ken Dodd do. He made every member of the audience feel as if he were talking to him or her personally. He shared his misery, his bewilderment and his rage. Emotionally he spared himself nothing.

Richard Negri had designed an extraordinary mobile theatre which was a 400-seat replica of the Exchange, and which could be erected or dismantled in eight hours. After eight weeks in Manchester the production toured for another six weeks in the mobile theatre, visiting small towns that didn't have one.

The reaction in the venues was even more extraordinary. Rather as with Century Theatre, here were audiences who had never been to the theatre before and didn't know *Hamlet*. They would interrupt the last scene

197

imploring Gertrude not to drink the poisoned chalice; you could hear them audibly gasp as the play unfolded. The reception they gave the actors at the end was heartfelt gratitude. This was a reminder to us all of what theatre could be and once was.

Finally, the mobile theatre arrived on the roof of the Barbican in London and for three weeks was packed out again. I was forty years old; probably this was my farewell to youth. What it certainly was, was the first time I had achieved a production that I was totally proud of, a *Brand* production.

It couldn't have happened but for Robert Lindsay. Casper warned me, 'You know he won't work with you again for a very long time.' I didn't know what he meant. 'You made him behave himself.' Casper was right. To this day, although we have met and discussed projects, he has never worked with me again. What Casper meant, I suppose, was that I made him give of himself in such a pure and unsparing way that consciously or unconsciously it would take a lot to make him go through such a process again.

Bob has not taken up the mantle of Olivier as I predicted. He has chosen the way that most do of easy television with good money. I don't blame him but I think it tragic. If theatre can be a power for good, there are many great roles he should play. There is still time.

On the first public performance of *Hamlet*, probably a public dress rehearsal, Casper had intercepted me on my way backstage after the show: 'You're not going to let him play it like that, are you?' I asked what he meant. Casper was horrified that Bob was playing Hamlet without, as he saw it, any spiritual dimension, which, of course, had been the great strength of Tom's performance. I went straight to Bob's dressing room, raised my hand to knock on the door and stopped. What was I doing? What was I going to say to Bob? This was our *Hamlet*, not Casper's. I didn't agree with him. When I did finally go in to see him it was to congratulate him, nothing more. It was a crucial moment of freedom. I never lost my love and respect for Casper, his wisdom was immense, but I never again obeyed him without question. Whether he liked it or not our relationship was at another, I think more mature, stage.

Hamlet was a great success but the discontent that had been rumbling between us now came to a head. I stood accused, particularly by Michael and Casper, of abusing my position in the company. I was making it my company, my production manager, my company manager and so on. I was deeply upset. To my mind I was carrying the main burden of running the place and inevitably my relationships with the staff were closer than theirs. There was no abuse. On a pettier level Michael Williams had queried a small item on my expenses claim. I was furious with him and he brought it up with the others. This was humiliating.

The row lasted for a very long time. It was acrimonious and quite, quite horrid. None of us was going to budge. It reached a terrible point where either Michael or Casper said that it was quite clear that we had reached a moment when we could no longer work together. Our only course of action was to resign with a year's notice, so that we could hand over the company in good working order.

I broke down in tears. The idea that I would be the cause of the company, the group, breaking up was completely shattering. I begged them not to do it. I would resign and leave the way to go forward. This was the turning point. I had abandoned my position, they abandoned theirs. We had forgotten what we had in common, now we remembered again.

We talked through the last couple of years and traced what had gone wrong, how we had lost touch with each other and retreated into our own little directing worlds. We admitted how little we were interested in each other's work, how little we trusted each other, that we never shared our ideas or asked for advice on our own projects. We were no longer a group. We were little islands.

What we resolved, there and then, was to plan a season for the following year that we would co-direct. We'd choose the plays and casts, work with the designers and even attend rehearsals together, although one of us would be designated the rehearser of each production. This would bring us back together and re-establish our common sense of purpose.

We had been talking for hours. Everyone in the building knew that something was going on. When we finally emerged in the evening people were anxiously waiting in groups to find out what on earth was happening. Thank goodness we had avoided catastrophe and could reassure them in good heart. It was a rebirth at exactly the right time.

At this moment of rebirth Laurence Harbottle resigned as Chairman. He had done us proud for fifteen years but he felt we needed a chairman with genuine Manchester connections. Alex, now Lord, Bernstein had been on our Board for a while now, and Michael and Casper approached him to succeed Laurence. It was an inspired choice. The world was changing. During Thatcher's premiership the arts were under constant threat, an era of raising money through private sponsorship and donation was starting and the company had finally to become a professional outfit. Today the turnover is around £5.5 million and it was pretty near the equivalent then, and we had to throw off the easygoing slightly amateur approach. Alex was perfect. He really cared for the work and had true aesthetic sensibilities, and he was at the same time as Chairman of Granada an astute businessman. Kindly but firmly he led us into a new era.

Finally, among all these changes we had a new director in our midst. Tom wanted to do *Jumpers*, none of us wanted to direct it and Max suggested a young director whose work he had seen called Nick Hytner. Nick came, did a great job and stayed for nearly four years. It was just the right moment to let another impulse into our midst. It was rejuvenation.

Preparation for our collaborative season, which would comprise the autumn–winter of 1984–85, got under way. It was clear that of the five Artistic Directors, two were less than enamoured. Richard wanted to direct on his own and Michael was essentially a one-man band. From this point Richard had less and less to do with the company, until 1986 when his position became honorary.

The first three plays of the four were quickly chosen. Casper's idea was that it should be a themed season called 'England Now'. We would do *Cymbeline*, Shakespeare's birth-of-a-modern-nation play, an adaptation of *Great Expectations* led by Max, which is about the end of an old England and the arrival of a new breed, and Trevor Peacock was to be commissioned to write another musical, *Class K*, about the stream in schools of children who were deemed impossible to teach. All three projects were about the emergence of the underdog to become the future, Posthumus in *Cymbeline*, Pip in *Great Expectations* and the children in *Class K*.

One afternoon, when the Test Match was rained off, I watched on television an old film of J. M. Barrie's *The Admirable Crichton*. It had exactly the same theme. Shipwrecked on a desert island the social order is reversed, Crichton becomes the master, Lord Loam and his daughter the dependants. It became the fourth play.

It was agreed that Michael would be the rehearser of *Cymbeline*, I would do the Dickens, Max the Barrie and the musical would be directed by Greg with me as a hands-on producer. Casper, by choice, wanted no direct connection with any of the projects but would look after the whole enterprise as the co-ordinator.

It was a huge communal undertaking; we had to agree artistic teams for each show, adapt *Great Expectations* and cast all the plays together. Then, on 31 May as I was watching Liverpool winning the European Cup, Michael Williams phoned to tell me that Michael Elliott had died. He had undergone a second kidney transplant and his heart had given out. I phoned Michael Meyer, who was his great friend. As Michael said, 'Thank the fuck Liverpool won!'

Michael Elliott

Michael's last production had been *Moby-Dick*, which followed my *Hamlet*. He had made his own adaptation and you could say it was a vivid way of expressing the demons of his life at the last. Michael was a blood brother of Captain Ahab relentlessly pursuing his nemesis and *Moby-Dick* was Michael's story.

He very nearly had Patrick McGoohan to play Ahab. Brand and Ahab united, that would have been something. McGoohan withdrew after watching himself on screen in some awful film he had made. He knew he wasn't up to it any longer. Brian Cox gave a mighty performance in his stead.

The production was the polar opposite of my *Hamlet*. It had everything in it, including the whole stage inflating to become the White Whale at the end. At the time I thought it was all too much; now I think he was trying to put everything into this last statement.

As you can see from previous chapters, Michael was not an easy man, but I think he was a heroic one. His birth inheritance was difficult and complex, and I believe he did the very best he could. Some of his closest friends and colleagues became alienated by his unpalatable ruthlessness on behalf of his naked ambition, but my answer to that was and is, 'Michael was on the side of the angels.' He was admired and respected for his genius as a director, but whatever happened he stuck with the group and used his influence and power to establish the Royal Exchange Theatre. I believe he knew that it was vital for his own survival that he did so. He needed to keep alive that pure flame inside himself.

After the second transplant operation, when he probably knew he was dying, he said to Rohan McCullough, with whom he was now living, 'I think I'd better get out of their way.' I think he meant that we were going into an area of collaboration that held little interest for him but that he recognised as essential for our survival. He had played his part.

Straight On

The outside view was that the group was finished, that Michael had been the leader and that, as one newspaper put it, the rest of us were 'clinging on to a rudderless ship'. But the outside world never really believed in the group. In their view there has to be a leader, there is no other way of running things. They are simply wrong and what happened next proved them so.

The group met on the morning of Michael's funeral to finalise the new season. This was not callousness, on the contrary it was the whole point of what we had all subscribed to. We knew that Michael's hold on life was always at risk and we had adjusted accordingly. We had already been running the company without him for a fair time. Now it was our job to carry on. We reallocated the tasks: I would rehearse *Cymbeline* and Greg would be asked to rehearse *Great Expectations*. We went to the funeral and returned with the mourners for the wake in the auditorium.

The question came up again and again: 'What are you going to do now?' The answer was the same: 'Carry on.' In a very short time the press decided it was Braham Murray's company. This was equally ludicrous, especially considering Casper's presence, but they were not to be dissuaded.

We came to cast the season. Max and Avril volunteered to play the King and Queen in *Cymbeline*, and we set up general auditions to see who was around. The auditions were extraordinary; through the door came Janet McTeer, Amanda Donohoe (Casper's comment: 'She's going to be you know . . . so we'd better you know while we can'), Hugh Quarshie, Art Malik, Aiden Gillett and many others. It inspired us to form a basic company to go through at least the first three shows; the musical would require special skills.

The preparation of *Cymbeline* was the purest form this experiment took. It is a huge multifaceted play, fuller of experimentation than *The Winter's Tale*. Between us, led by Casper, we cut and rearranged the text. I was very attuned to the Iachimo side of the play and Max to the Roman. Casper was interested in the spiritual side and the Europeanism of the text. I went into rehearsal more completely prepared than ever before with such a huge project. The pooling of our various insights meant that the whole play could be brought more vividly to life than if I had prepared the production alone.

It is an extraordinary play. At the end, Imogen marries a commoner and together they will rule over England with the two sons of Belarius who have been brought up far away from the seat of power in the wilderness. It indeed presaged a new way of looking at ruling, through a rich and varied group.

I think Janet McTeer one of the most remarkable actresses I have worked with, her recent *Mary Stuart* was one of the very few truly great performances I have seen. Directing her as Imogen was a great experience – well, rehearsing her anyway.

Working out how to conduct rehearsals as a group was tricky. Max was in it so that was easy and Greg was too junior to dare to say too much, but Casper, of course, had a lot to say. The positive thing was that the actors were released from the burden of having to please just one person. The negative was that constant interruptions drove me round the bend. I couldn't bear having my concentration broken. Eventually we reached a compromise. Casper would wait for a break in rehearsal before raising his often excellent points and then I would have a chance to digest what he was saying before handing it on to the cast, or not as the case might be. This was eventually how all the plays were rehearsed. It seemed to work.

It became clear that there was a limit to our energies. The plays were not in repertoire so we were rehearsing the next play, *Great Expectations*, during the day while playing *Cymbeline* at night. This was going to go on for more than six months.

Max was the King in *Cymbeline*, effectively the adapter of *Great Expectations* and the rehearser of *Crichton*. I, exhausted from *Cymbeline*, didn't have the will to sit in on rehearsals of the Dickens, especially since I was helping to prepare the musical. As the season wore on, the rehearser became more and more the director, working closely with the designer, not as part of a group. By the time Max did *Crichton* it was more like a conventional production and the musical, which was another Peacock success, was completely different terrain.

Despite all this the experiment worked. It produced four cracking shows on the trot, which proved we could survive and, more important, it broke down the barriers between us and this affected our working relationships on all future productions. We took an interest in each other's work and opening nights became once again a celebration of our togetherness as a group. In the process we unleashed a terrific bunch of actors on to the British theatre.

As a result of all this the company was back on track artistically. There was no more creeping up the back staircase for me. I reprised *Long Day's Journey* with Dilys, but this time with Max as Tyrone and Michael Mueller a remarkable Edmund. Casper did a superb *Three Sisters* with Janet McTeer, Emma Piper and Niamh Cusack, plus Espen Skjønberg's extraordinary Chebutykin. Adam Ant came to do *Entertaining Mr Sloane* for Greg and I rounded off the year with Alan Price's new musical *Who's a Lucky Boy?*: another great score from him. Trevor Peacock was soon to be a memorable Willy Loman for Greg and Janet returned to triumph as Rosalind in Nick Hytner's memorable *As You Like It*. Confidence was resoundingly restored and the atmosphere was probably more relaxed and friendly than ever before. This was because the Casper–Michael rivalry was no more.

CHAPTER 53

Enter David Threlfall

Michael Fox, our Literary Manager, suggested to me a stage version of Russell Hoban's novel *Riddley Walker*. I'd never heard of the author or the book. I read it and fell in love with it. I don't intend to go into its intricacies in detail – you should buy it and read it yourselves. In brief, it is set several thousand years in the future after the world has all but been obliterated by a nuclear war. Society is in a very primitive state, and man is slowly but surely finding the means to create weapons again that are more deadly than bows, arrows and spears; they are searching for 'the one big one'. Riddley is a storyteller, a puppeteer, who travels between the settlements telling the Eusa story, their creation myth. He keeps hope and culture alive. The book recounts his adventures, chiefly his battles with those who find his storytelling subversive, and he travels with a pack of dogs that would need to be incarnated on stage. The book is written in a strange form of near English which is quickly intelligible and, when spoken on stage, no problem at all.

A poor attempt at dramatisation had been made and I reckoned only Hoban himself could do it. Hoban, an expat American Jew, lives near Fulham Broadway in a wonderful house, chock-a-block with the bric-a-brac of his imaginative life: paintings, puppets, what have you. He is a remarkable man, I think our most original novelist and one who does not lower his art in the interest of best-sellers but goes into the dark corners of the human soul where few dare enter and re-emerges holding a light. It is a privilege to know him.

Rus agreed to do the adaptation with slight misgivings, since he didn't know theatre, and I reassured him that I would help the shaping of the piece. In the event he worked tirelessly through eight drafts until we were satisfied.

The obvious man to play Riddley was Bob. We had been looking for something to do that could possibly rival *Hamlet* and he and I thought this was it. Then Bob opened in the West End in the musical *Me and My Girl*, scored a fantastic success, went to Broadway with it and withdrew from *Riddley*.

Michael had directed Olivier's *Lear* for television with Bob playing Edmund and David Threlfall as Edgar. David was my next choice and we met at Mon Plaisir in Monmouth Street, which had replaced the Savile Club as our London office. He agreed to do it. So started the next important creative relationship with an actor. This one lasted nearly fifteen years.

David was a different kettle of fish from Bob. If you could put them together, you would have the greatest actor the world has ever known. Whereas Bob traded on his natural empathy with an audience, David insisted on his specialness. He is an actor who is capable of complete physical and vocal transformation. It is impossible to know who the real David actor is, his escape into a part is so complete. He doesn't come to meet his audience like Bob, he insists that they come to meet him.

Bob and he were like brothers, they lived round the corner from each other, they worked together on television in a series called *There's Nobody Here but Us Chickens*, they envied each other the talent or success the other had and they were rivals, sometimes quite bitter ones. We tried to get them to lead the company together for a season; it never happened.

Riddley Walker was the next show after *Hamlet* that meant to me that I was measuring up. It's also the only show that wasn't a classic that has meant that to me. The design was Johanna at her brilliant best. She simply blew up the Royal Exchange – not literally, of course, the IRA did that later. She created the illusion that a bomb had exploded in the auditorium and bits of it were everywhere, and that was the set. Fergus Early was the inspirational choreographer; the cast became the dogs, the untamed animality in us all. Chris Monks, so long my composer, excelled himself, together with Phil Clifford, the sound designer, and Bob Bryan conjured up the magical lighting in and outside the auditorium. I name them all because it was for me a total creative triumph, an amalgamation of talent, which is how theatre should be.

Rus had also agreed to progress the book further. In the original, Riddley merely survives to continue his storytelling. Now Rus decided to include a new puppet in the story. Riddley had met on his journeys an Anima figure, who appeared in many guises, but finally as Mother Nite. The character, played by Pam Ferris, awakened the feminine, redemptive impulse in Riddley and now she featured in his puppet show. There was progress.

Manchester had a magazine, rather like London's *Time Out*, called *City Life*. That year *Riddley Walker* topped two of their readers' polls. It won Best Production and it won Worst Production. That's how controversial it was. I have never before or since received so many extraordinary letters of thanks from members of the public. One letter said that the Black Dogs had helped her face her cancer. Russell Hoban had written a masterpiece and we had brought it to life and given it a further dimension.

At the centre of it, of course, was David. He revealed an uneducated but totally charged human being, striving to make sense of a hostile, terrifying world. You could see inside his head. It was the first of many stupendous performances with me and Casper that he would give at the Exchange.

CHAPTER 54

The Tenth Anniversary Season

I managed to break my ankle during the run of *Riddley Walker* on a country walk on an icy hill. While I was recuperating, Ian McDiarmid came to see me. Casper had formed a close relationship with him during his production of *The Wild Duck* and was suggesting he join the company as an Associate Artistic Director. Ian decided he liked the idea. He's a hugely intelligent man and clearly felt the time had come to spread his wings.

I was very suspicious, not of his talent, which was and is undoubted, but because of our differing tastes. You will note from the repertoire I have sketched in an absence of, say, Brecht and several contemporary playwrights such as Bond, Brenton and Barker. I knew that Ian favoured such artists and I wanted to be clear about my opposition to them. We had a frank discussion and he accepted my position. Except he didn't and the next couple of years became very difficult as he tried to force his agenda on to the company. I was greatly upset. I was still carrying the burden of running the company and I didn't want to support work that seemed to me the opposite of its ideals. The relationship ended acrimoniously after Ian published an open attack on us in the *Manchester Evening News*, which was grist to the mill of our enemies, especially the critic Alan Hulme who led in his feeble way the opposition to us for twenty-five years, happily to little effect. Ian and I have long since made it up. We were two equally passionate men who came together in the wrong place at the wrong time. His huge success with Jonathan Kent at the Almeida bears witness to his gifts.

Looking back now, I can see the beneficial effect he had on our work, especially in collaboration with Nick Hytner who was going from strength to strength. Their first work together was their famous production of *Edward II* with Ian as Edward and Michael Grandage as Gaveston. It was an enormous hit with critics and public alike, but Casper and Max hated it and I duly went along with them.

Casper and I had a horrendous – in retrospect – lunch with Nick when Casper told him how much his production had desecrated the play. I now squirm with embarrassment when I think of it. God knows what Nick thought. He had directed a supremely successful show and he was being treated like a pariah.

Casper had, many years ago, directed the play with Max as Edward at the Edinburgh Festival. Their concept of true kingship, the divine right of kings and the spiritual side of Marlowe's play was a million miles from Nick's radical modern reading, which centred on the homosexuality and the tragedy of a king who could not be allowed to follow his nature. We should have seen *Edward* as it was, an entirely successful attempt to bring the play into our time. Nick also did a terrific *Country Wife* with Cheryl Campbell, Gary Oldham and Alex Jennings joining Ian. Mix in with that two further excellent Mobil winners, Geoff Noon's *Woundings* and Ian Heggie's *A Wholly Healthy Glasgow* and Greg's successful *Alchemist*, and the company could be happy with the way things were going.

And I got to work with Espen Skjønberg at last. The only problem with Espen is that he has a marked Norwegian accent, which makes it difficult when it comes to big speeches; you can easily lose the sense of what he is saying, although not the inner purpose. My idea was that he would play Shylock. It's a great part but a small one, he only has three scenes before the trial scene and he doesn't appear in Act Five; moreover, a foreign accent wouldn't matter a jot.

We spent hours together talking about the play and, of course, in particular what it was to be a Jew. Espen asked me to record the part with a Jewish accent, which I did. Ostensibly he wanted me to do it so that he could practise his English, but I think he also wanted to see if unconsciously I would give him any keys to the playing of it. What he found in the part was Jewish humour. 'Hath not a Jew eyes . . .' was done with irony, almost gently comedic until of course after reasonably taking us through 'If you prick us do we not bleed . . .' he arrived at a quietly ferocious 'Shall we not revenge?'. It was a truly great performance: the depth of grief at the loss of his daughter, the implacable avenger and finally the transforming acceptance of 'I am content' can surely never have been bettered.

I was lucky enough to find a Portia who could match him in the trial scene, and make that one of the most riveting I have been connected with. Harriet Walter walked into it looking like a young tyro Italian lawyer, exchanged blows with Shylock, man to man, then finally led the court to its resolution. She also played the last act of the possibility of love but the difficulty of its survival in such an unhappy world with unrivalled heart-rending simplicity.

The production was by no means perfect. Having created a minimalist style for *Hamlet*, I saw this as a solution for all Shakespeare: a group of actors, acting out a play. To this day the green dressing gowns I made them wear as they entered and took their places on the front row evoke mirth. Once the dressing gowns were off, I had done a perfectly serviceable modern-dress production set in the financial quarter of Venice.

Since the first production in the sixties, my feelings about Judaism and anti-Semitism had broadened and deepened. I was now increasingly researching and pondering the Holocaust; it was a topic I found reduced me to tears with alarming frequency. I wanted to understand and this play, which had quick-started my consciousness of my Jewishness, allowed me to go much further, as well as expunging the horrors of *Fire Angel*.

Casper then twinned *Oedipus Rex* and *Oedipus at Colonus*, with David playing the two ages, for our hundredth production, and I finished the year with a show that it is worth briefly mentioning.

John Lahr approached me with a revue he had written, culled from the monologues and playlets of Woody Allen, to be called *The Bluebird of Unhappiness*. I thought it very funny; Michael White, the West End producer, put money into it in the hope that if it worked he could take it to the West End and off-Broadway. This enabled me to fly over the New York composer Stanley Silverman to write songs to John's lyrics, also taken from Woody's work.

Trevor Peacock, John Bennett, Derek Griffiths, Pam Ferris, Haydn Gwynne, Teddy Kempner and one of the company's stalwarts, Ian Hastings, now Artistic Director at the Dukes, Lancaster, were an ideal cast. We had a ball rehearsing and duly opened successfully.

Michael White was very delighted and plans were put in train for its future life. Because none of the material had been performed before, there were things in the text that didn't quite work. Particularly the right punchlines for a stage performance were understandably not there, but there were other gags that needed adjusting too.

It was arranged that I would fly to New York and with John and Stanley talk to the great man about possible tweaking. Woody was in the middle of cutting his latest movie but we were assured that he would see us, although we might have to hang around for a day or two for a suitable moment to occur.

I had what I thought was a brilliant idea. To back up my notes I would make an audio recording of the show so that Woody could hear where the laughs were coming and where they weren't.

We met this intense, serious, apparently humourless and more than slightly neurotic comic genius and had a constructive conversation. I gave him the notes and the tape and returned to England. A couple of weeks later a vitriolic letter arrived from him. He had listened to the tape, found it unbelievably crude, thought the actors hammy (why couldn't we have

Gielgud?), his work was desecrated and there was no way the production was coming to New York. I wrote back suggesting that if he wanted me to be interested in a film he had directed, he wouldn't expect me to judge it by the soundtrack, which at least would be properly pitched, unlike a theatre performance which by its nature sounds crude, because it is being projected to reach hundreds of people. No good. I spoke to his manager who simply said, 'He's a megalomaniac. I'm amazed he even gave you permission in the first place. You haven't got a chance.' We were dead in the water, Michael White was furious with me and I haven't been able to watch a Woody Allen film since.

CHAPTER 55

The Scottish Play

Macbeth is famously the unlucky play. When I had done it at Century Theatre the production was beset by disasters. The reason is that so much of it is an invocation to evil spirits. It is the play Shakespeare must have written at his darkest moment. If you rehearse it properly, you are endlessly contacting the darkness in yourself. The spirit of the play pervades the rehearsals. There is no avoiding it.

David Threlfall wanted to play Macbeth. I was very wary of going back into that darkness and, after *The Winter's Tale*, I knew that one shouldn't go back unless there was more to say. The *Macbeth*s I had seen in the interim all seemed to be productions of a play for two leading actors and an otherwise largely anonymous company. What seemed to me the greatest play about evil ever written never came across like that. I told him, a bit as I had with Bob in *Hamlet*, that I'd do it when we had found a way of making it work.

David recommended Frances Barber to play the Lady. I went with him to Leicester to see her in *Summer and Smoke*, we had dinner together and she agreed. In fact, she had just been offered the same part down in Bristol but she preferred to do it with David, whom she had been friendly with, in various ways, for some time.

I have said that I was becoming more and more obsessed with the Holocaust. I wanted to understand how such a thing could come about. The Stalin-type genocide to preserve power, or the Rwandan-type genocide to control territory are two familiar recurring themes in the history of the world, but to want to wipe a whole people off the face of the earth for no apparent gain, this I craved to comprehend. If that could be understood, perhaps it could be avoided in the future; if not how could it be? What was it in human nature that could connive at such atrocity?

Johanna became worried about my obsession. She even said it was counter-productive for Jews to go on about it. My response was to point out that had our family been alive in Hitler's Germany, she would have been all right and she might not mind me being carried off to the gas chambers, but

Jacob and Joe would have been slaughtered too. She realised that was a cogent point.

The best book about the Holocaust is Primo Levi's *If This Is a Man*. I was reading it and its sequel, *The Truce*. In the latter the prisoners, released from the concentration camps, are sent back by the Allies to their homeland. The journey is endless and, although they are now free, tortuous. To preserve their sanity, each time they stop off at a village or town they put on a satirical show featuring the main players in their plight.

The greatest play about evil and the greatest evil of our time – if I could marry them I would have a production. My idea was simple: after lights out in a concentration camp, the prisoners rehearse a production of *Macbeth* to try to understand how the evil that enveloped them had come about. Their production would have only the props and so forth that they could scavenge: barbed wire crowns, primitive weapons made out of shards of wood and so on.

Macbeth vividly describes how the warped love between two people projects itself outwards to those they rule over. Scotland becomes a nuclear winter area where 'Each new morn, new widows howl, new orphans cry'. The last act is pure Hitler in the bunker.

I had dinner with David and Frances at Le Chef, Michael Meyer's favourite restaurant near Connaught Square where he lived, and put it to them. It would mean concentration camp costumes only and bald heads – men and women. They enthusiastically agreed. Preparation began in earnest.

It was an unusually strong cast that assembled to support Frances and David. Old chums like Tilly Tremayne, Ian Hastings, Max's son Dan, James Clyde and indeed John Watts, my first Macbeth, who came to play, among other parts, Duncan. There were powerful newcomers too like Sandy McDade, John Hannah (Malcolm) and, pretty fresh out of drama school, Andy Serkis.

Mixing two infernal worlds created a tense, volatile atmosphere. We watched the harrowing footage of the camps, we tried to imagine ourselves into the prisoners' shoes, you could feel the electricity. Some members of the cast were overawed by the task; I tried to drive them forward.

At the beginning of the second week Frances came back in a dreadful mood; something had clearly happened. She took me aside: her mother was dying of cancer and she wanted her to sit in on rehearsals. I blanched. Anyone sitting in on rehearsals is distracting to the actors; to have the dying mother of Lady Macbeth there seemed to me to be a bad idea, not only for the production but also for Frances. Nevertheless, during the day I consulted the other members of the cast and the consensus was that since we were doing this play out of our feeling for humanity, we should accede to her wish. I sought her out and told her. Her response? 'Too fucking late.'

Rehearsals became exceedingly tense. After a few days I told David I was going to have to talk to her. I asked her to come to my office. I told her it seemed to me that she had taken against me and could we discuss it. Her reply, uttered with a venom that made my blood run cold, 'I'd like to cut your fucking head off.' She added that she wasn't going to leave the cast either.

She certainly didn't. On the contrary, her aim, it seemed, was to turn the cast against me. She worked on them all out of rehearsal, in corners, even my friends. She suddenly refused to shave her head and tried to persuade the other women that it was my assault on their femininity. They stuck out against her. She came up with her big idea that she should play Lady Macbeth as one of the camp whores, which meant make-up, proper clothes and of course a full head of hair.

Company note sessions were horrible, the verbal onslaught was constant: this company hated actors, no wonder Ian McDiarmid had left, it was the worst company she had ever worked for and so on and so on. David had eventually to cut off from her because she was making him ill, but the rest of the company, while not exactly on her side, was to an extent under her spell.

What kept me going was that she was giving a dynamite performance; in fact, everyone was. For all the hell we were going through, I had no doubt the concept was working.

The final tirade came on the last note session before the production weekend. She announced that we were trivialising what those prisoners had gone through and so the audience should see that they were actors, and this would be achieved by the cast getting changed into the prison garb on stage. I can't remember what I said but I overruled the suggestion and we went into the final lap, a group pretty well on edge.

The actors were sitting round the acting area that they had created from the camp beds, and at the dress rehearsal Frances appeared in the costume she had demanded, looking like a Jewish whore outside King's Cross Station, applying her lipstick and make-up during other people's scenes.

I went to her dressing room afterwards. I told her that I knew she hated my guts but that if she went on like that on the first night, the critics would laugh her out of town and her magnificent performance – for such I thought it – would go for nought. It had its effect. She submitted to a bald wig and a scarf, and we arrived at opening night.

The audience was stunned. At the end of the play, as John Hannah as Malcolm made his speech about a new future, the doors opened, search-lights played on the prisoners and they left to go to their deaths. The run was a sell-out and for many distinguished people it was the best Shakespeare they had seen. It wasn't, however, for everyone. It only really worked if you knew the play. If you didn't, the whole concept was a bit of a mystery and, with all the prisoners looking similar, who was doubling each part was difficult to work out. I cannot therefore say that it was a total success, but in terms of providing a context in which the play could come alive in every scene, I don't think I have done better.

Frances, who continued to treat me like a particularly repulsive cockroach, had to endure a stream of friends coming up from London who loved the production and thought her wonderful. She presumably didn't mind the latter but the former must have been hard for her.

I was away for a week during the run visiting South Africa to research Dolores Walshe's Mobil play *In the Talking Dark*, which I was to do with another Frances, this time Tomelty. Frances Barber had a sort of fit on stage during one performance and refused to go on. The management did what they always do on such an occasion and asked one of the other ladies to go on for her. Apparently this provoked a ferocious response from Frances, that the Exchange was taking advantage of the vulnerability of the actors and they should do no such thing. The performance was cancelled.

I don't think I have ever been so relieved when a production closed. The fallout went on for about two years as members of the cast, especially my friends, needed to talk through what had happened.

I tried to make a bridge to Frances on the last day but it was of course blown up. I imagine what happened was that playing that part, 'Come, you spirits / That tend on mortal thoughts, unsex me here, / And fill me from the crown to the toe top full / Of direst cruelty!' took her over. It's how that play works. At any rate she gave one of the best performances that I have been associated with.

CHAPTER 56

1989–90

I try to rush on, but every time I do there seems to be something more that needs to be said. Another Mobil prizewinner was due to be produced: Michael Wall's *Amongst Barbarians*. All of us detested the play except James Maxwell. We tried to talk him out of it but he would not be dissuaded and invoked the Artistic Director's carte blanche. We disliked it because it seemed totally negative, cashing in on the easy drama of capital punishment and portraying the family of one of the condemned men as, well, unregenerate barbarians. Casper went so far as to say that if the company did this sort of play he didn't want to be connected to it.

Max was right and we were wrong. He had perceived a real desire to battle through in the play and invested it with a heart none of us had seen. However, there was now a strain among us four. This is where the next drama probably started.

It was also round about now that the long-running saga of *The Count of Monte Cristo* began. Jonathan Hackett had recommended to us that this was a novel worth adapting for the stage. None of us knew it except through the various fairly entertaining but pretty straightforward movies. The complexity of the book took us by surprise, the intricacies of Edmond Dantès's revenge, involving many disguises and psychological brilliance, was obvious dramatic material and Max undertook to adapt it. The problem was it was going to have to be two plays over two nights in the manner of the RSC's *Nicholas Nickleby*.

Bob Lindsay was the obvious casting and Bob accepted. Duncan Weldon wanted to take it on, which was fine because Bob wanted London. The production was going to be very expensive and it was agreed that rather than start it at the Exchange and then convert it at great cost for the West End, we would open the play at the Palace Theatre in Manchester.

Michael Yeargan, the American designer, was appointed after I trawled the world for a proscenium arch designer who I thought could bring off this spectacular show with its Château d'If, its sea scenes, its opera houses, *Arabian Nights*-type caves and a host of other locations. We worked intensively and began casting. The press launch took place on the Manchester Ship Canal, as befitted a seafaring story. Duncan thought the two-part idea was terrific, the perfect answer to a Michael Billington article that had accused West End managements of being too timid.

Then it all went wrong. The American impresario, Jimmy Nederlander, was going to be a big investor. After *Me and My Girl*, Bob was very bankable and he saw a big future for the show in New York. Jimmy was going to present a second visit of the RSC with the two-parter of *Nicholas Nickleby*. Alas, it didn't work, the audiences stayed away and Jimmy lost faith in the two-night idea. Duncan asked me to conflate the show into one night. I knew this would be a disaster. It would eviscerate it into a shallow potboiler and decimate Bob's part. Bob agreed with me. I refused to do it.

The discussions became increasingly unpleasant. Nederlander flew over and we had a big battle in his hotel. I was not aggressive, I was pleading. I was sure that the conflated show would be a flop and I couldn't bear all the wasted effort it had taken to get it to its present state. I asked him how he thought it could be condensed. It turned out he hadn't even read it. Bob and I left in despair.

Eventually I was lying in bed in Bramhall a couple of weeks later, exhausted by it all, when Duncan rang from New York. He was sitting in Nederlander's office with a cheque for £1 million in his hand. If I would agree to a one-evening version we had the money, if not the whole thing was off. It was an awful moment. I could not agree. I put the phone back on its hook. It was off. I was numb with misery.

In 1989 I had been to Bristol and been very taken with Phyllida Lloyd's production of *A Streetcar Named Desire*. She agreed to join the company as an Associate Artistic Director and in early 1990 *The Winter's Tale* was her first production. It was better than mine. She followed it with *The School for Scandal* in a sparky modern-dress version designed by Mark Thompson.

Also in 1990 I directed *The Tempest*. I felt this would be my farewell to Shakespeare. I conceived it as an inner journey. The storms hit Prospero's study, shattering his life as an ivory tower scientist. The island was his breakdown introversion where he confronted all the sides of himself, the cowardly side with Stephano and Trinculo, the power side with the Lords but, of course, most importantly his feminine side through Miranda, his creativity through Ariel and his animal side through Caliban. He released all the creatures he had locked up inside him so that they could be integrated in him, except Caliban. He managed 'This thing of darkness I acknowledge mine', but he left it on the island. It was as far as he could get in his lifetime. I now wanted to go further. It was a special production for me. David Horovitch played Prospero, with Emil Wolk as Ariel and Dan Hildebrand his 'thing of darkness'. I knew my view of the play was very much to do with me, although I hope I didn't have the disastrous impact I had had on *A Midsummer Night's Dream*. The design process with Johanna was particularly difficult. To create those archetypal images is hard and, as I would find out, our inner journeys were taking very different paths.

In 1990 as well, we came within a half an hour of having a London home. Spitalfields was to be developed into a banking centre. The architect, Richard MacCormac, fought for an anti-philistine device: a theatre. Richard Pilbrow was the marriage-broker. MacCormac was a wonderful man to work with as he created his version of our building, which he admired. Indeed, there was to be a whole culture square with cinemas, galleries and restaurants, and we would run the whole lot. It was a done deal. In the summer of 1990, while I was on holiday in St Cyprien in France, Tower Hamlets were going to sign the contract. I knew the day, I knew the hour, I asked the theatre to phone me, I had the champagne on ice. Half an hour before the signing ceremony Chris Patten, prompted by his ex-boss Norman St John-Stevas, called in the plans. St John-Stevas was anti-American and the overall firm was American. The plan was shelved. It was scarcely believable.

Finally, in 1990 Phyllida did her best production for the company, the British première of Wole Soyinka's *Death and the King's Horseman*, a play that Casper had pooh-poohed me doing as being not good enough. He was very wrong.

CHAPTER 57

All Change

The other major event of 1990 was that Casper resigned, giving the company a year's notice, as his contract required. I remember his letter started with the mysteriously banal statement, 'All good things must come to an end.' There had been threatened resignations before, particularly from Max, but this was real. A letter had also gone to our Chairman, Alex Bernstein.

The reason Casper gave to me was that at the age of sixty-one he needed to turn his mind more and more to matters of the spirit, and theatre was keeping him too firmly anchored to the earth. He wanted now to lead a more personal life.

For me this resignation was serious. It meant an even heavier burden at the theatre, but it also meant that my father was going. It was liberation, but liberation brings its own demands. I would now have to become an adult. I believe Casper knew that was necessary, both for my own good and for the company's. It was also the beginning of a transition that has lasted to this day. Now we were three and three wouldn't do.

If Casper's resignation was the first herald of a change in my professional life, there was also a herald of a similarly huge change in my private life, which had been running on a smooth track since my affair with Maggie. That summer Jacob, who was nineteen and going to Oxford to my old college, Univ, to read English, announced he wouldn't be coming on our annual family summer holiday. It didn't mean much to me. He was at that age where your parents are not necessarily the people you want to spend your holidays with, but to Johanna it was as if someone had kicked her in the stomach. She had seen the end of motherhood, which had been so fulfilling for her. Joe was sixteen; it wouldn't be long before he did the same. The birds were about to fly the coop.

I only dimly realised this then. I was forty-seven, Johanna forty-six, life was going to be different and we would have to negotiate a new contract. I saw no urgency in either of these upheavals. Casper would be around for another year and Joe didn't seem to be on the point of following Jacob yet.

CHAPTER 58

Rough Weather

The Calm Before the Storm

– i –

The year 1991 was artistically a very busy and successful one for me in which I did four productions. The first was the best new play I have ever directed and, I believe, one of the best new plays of contemporary theatre.

The author, Rod Wooden, had been a social worker in Newcastle. He wanted to be a writer. His marriage broke up and he decided to use the money from his share of the matrimonial home to leave his job and write. He holed up in a flat above the Nationwide Building Society and wrote, determined to stick at it till the money ran out. He saw an advertisement for the Mobil competition, entered a play for it and, just as his money ran out, won it. The play was called *Your Home in the West* and I wanted to direct it.

As you started to read *Your Home in the West*, it seemed as if it was going to be just a slice-of-life play, a BBC 'Play for Today'. The 'West' is the West End of Newcastle, the slum area of that city. The play is about a family battling for survival: the mother a part-time whore; the husband a hard man, a brute; there's a daughter, a lodger who falls for the mum and there's an idiot son, and the grandmother. Doesn't sound promising, does it? What Wooden had done was to give it the dimensions of a Greek tragedy. The hard man, terrifyingly played by David Threlfall, self-destructs at the end of the third act, leaving the mum and the lodger to have a chance of breaking the curse. Lorraine Ashbourne, who played the mum, and Andy Serkis, who played the lodger, had been in Max's production of *She Stoops to Conquer* as Kate and Tony Lumpkin and, although I didn't know it, had cordially hated each other. Lorraine was like a reincarnation of Dilys, who played her mother in the Wooden play, fearless, passionate and able to do that rare thing for English actresses, play sex. Andy had driven me mad doing *Macbeth* where he had every night invented outrageous business as the

Porter, once even appearing to urinate on stage. I knew he was a very unusual, original talent, with a big heart.

During rehearsals for *Your Home*, they decided one night to dress up in character and spend a night in Manchester, the tart and the punter. That night they fell in love and have been together ever since, now with three beautiful children.

Lorraine nearly walked out of the show after a week of rehearsal. She is an explosive, extrovert person and she was playing an abused, battered woman who finds her voice only in the last act. I spent the whole of the first week making her repress her emotions. It drove her round the bend. What it led to was a volcanic performance. You could feel the pressure building within; when the explosion came so late in the play it was tremendous.

It was also a work that required all of us to dig deep into our emotional memories to mine the profundity of Wooden's perceptions. Rehearsals often ground to a halt because the memories triggered by the play were so overwhelming. Both for David and me the theme of maternal abandonment – he because his mother had died tragically young, me from my apparent banishment to boarding school – was especially traumatic, but as ever in theatre it proved therapeutic. This was a play of immense power.

We opened on a Thursday and by Saturday night the whole run was sold out. It was one of those phenomena, as if there is for certain plays a bush telegraph that operates. It united people of all classes who recognised themselves in the characters. At the after-show discussion there were battered wives who had gained comfort from it, although one had to be restrained from going up on to the stage to give the Threlfall character one in the eye. *Your Home* never went to London, partly because Rod insisted I had to produce it, partly because it is so difficult to get the second production of a new play. Rod, however, was instantly recognised as an important new talent, a recognition he either took full advantage of or squandered, whichever way you look at it.

– ii –

Summer brought a huge musical, the last one I ever did. It was called *Dr Heart* and was a long-running hit in Budapest. I flew Trevor Peacock out to see it, and he agreed to do the book and the English lyrics. Peter Mueller was the creator of the show and he was very much a man with a foot in each world, as was the show itself. Dr Heart, Andy Serkis again, made a machine that could bring back the dead. In Budapest its message of transcending this world, set as it was during the Russian occupation of Hungary, struck an obvious chord; here it was dismissed in some quarters as too 'New Age'. Nevertheless there were many who loved it. Johanna's designs were spectacular and the lyrics powerful, but perhaps the music didn't quite match the ambition, so not enough people came and it cost a lot of money. New musicals were becoming too risky, so we stopped doing them for a long time.

– iii –

I had taught Maureen Lipman at LAMDA in younger days. She launched her latest book one lunchtime at the Exchange and told her audience that 'Bra', as she called me, had never asked to work with her since. I was told this, phoned her and the result was that, after much reading of plays, we agreed to do *The Cabinet Minister* for Duncan Weldon in the West End, arriving there for a Christmas season after a tour. All well and good.

Tom phoned me and said that he wanted to do Molière's *The Miser* at the Exchange and would I direct it. I read it and couldn't see for the life of me that it was either funny or interesting, but Tom was asking and I felt I couldn't say no. He had done so much for the company over the years. We met for lunch at the Savile. I explained my reservations but said I'd do it, and do a new translation with Cogo-Fawcett. The problem was when. It was an ideal Christmas show but I was doing *The Cabinet Minister*. I worked out a tortuous schedule whereby I would rehearse the Pinero, open it on tour in Plymouth, rehearse *The Miser*, spend the weekends on tour keeping an eye on *The Cabinet Minister*, take a break from *The Miser* to see *The Cabinet Minister* into London, and finally open *The Miser* at the Exchange, and that is what happened.

The Cabinet Minister did a triumphant tour but had a horrid opening night at the Albery; the atmosphere was tepid. The critics accused the play of being anti-Semitic. It is a play about insider dealing, and one of the characters called, unfortunately in today's climate, Joseph Lebanon is obviously Jewish, as was Pinero. He is an outsider in a very English society. For Maureen and me to be labelled anti-Semitic was as funny as anything in the play. However, we survived the critics and had a successful three months. Maureen, the delightful Derek Nimmo and the splendid Gwen Watford were all from slightly different worlds and I couldn't meld them well enough. This was upsetting as I liked them all, especially Maureen, and I longed to work with her again. Still, it was making me money.

So was *The Miser*, which Duncan took on a national tour but didn't, I think wrongly, bring to London. It was for me an odd success. I rehearsed it as best I could, and because I didn't think it was funny I just determined to tell the story as clearly as I could. We updated it to the thirties. Simon Higlett, who had also done the Pinero, did a brilliantly witty set of a crumbling old house and the cast included the inventive, full-hearted Polly James, another Exchange stalwart, Colin Prockter, and the alarmingly funny William Armstrong. I rehearsed away in faith but not much hope until, after a run-through one of the cast, Andrew Callaway, told me how funny it was. My mind boggled. I asked Marketing to arrange a hundred or so people to see the final run-through on the Saturday of the production weekend. A hundred people turned up and fell about. I was totally stunned.

The show was a storming success. Tom was at his best, grotesquely, appallingly funny, a master comic actor on top form. You think you are progressing as a director and then something happens that breaks every rule. That too was making me money as it toured England after Manchester.

The icing on the cake was that Southampton was presenting *The Three Musketeers* as its Christmas show. I didn't have to do anything to earn those royalties.

I had hardly seen my family for months. Johanna had come to the London first night – I remember thinking that she looked especially beautiful – and she came with me to see the Dumas at Southampton; otherwise I was nose to the grindstone. Still, with all those royalties I could take her and Joe for a fabulous holiday at the Grand Hotel in St-Jean-de-Luz and back to our favourite villa near Cordes. I wasn't due to direct another play until the summer. There was time to rest and reconnect with real life.

The Storm

Casper had set the ball rolling when he resigned; now Johanna followed – she resigned from me. She told me she wanted to separate. It came as a bolt from the blue. I had had no inkling that this was coming. There were two reasons. First, she had for the last twenty years been my wife, the mother of my children and my designer. Now in her late forties, she didn't know who she was and she wanted to find out. Second, I had been unfaithful and gone on my journey but she had not. I had not given her the love she needed and she believed she was now in love with someone else and that it was recipro-cated. In fact, it wasn't, because the person was gay but that was irrelevant. 'I don't want to go to my grave a nun.'

I was deeply shocked. She was prepared to throw away twenty years together without even trying to find a way forward. My anchor was being removed. When you are about to lose someone, you realise just how much they have meant to you. She was adamant. I had no recourse but to agree but I begged her to wait eighteen months until Joe had got into university. I felt strongly that to spring this on him now would be destructive. She agreed and we embarked on a weird eighteen months of secrecy.

Reeling though I was, there was a tiny part of me that felt a certain relief. Like anyone who has been married for a long time there had been moments when I longed to break free, and I don't just mean the affairs. They probably kept me sane. There was one other crucial thing. Our sons meant everything to Johanna and this would greatly upset them. We were a very close-knit family. If she was prepared to upset them, she must indeed be desperate. If I could not dissuade her – and I tried often to do so – then the best I could do for all of us was to acquiesce in the process so that when the moment came there would be no acrimony for the boys to witness. The last twenty years must not be poisoned.

It was hard, the person she was attached to treated her shabbily and I had to witness her distress and remain positive. On top of all that, we were already committed to working together on *The Recruiting Officer*, which was opening in the summer. Trying not to let our relationship cloud the frequently tense director–designer process was a huge difficulty.

Eventually we settled into this new routine. Sometimes we almost forgot what was happening and those times seemed to increase, but there was no changing her. In the midst of all this she began to train as a Chinese physician and I even became her guinea pig as she learnt reflexology; much later I did it again as she learnt acupuncture. This was weird. As well as the I Ching, I myself had always favoured any alternative to Western medicine; indeed, I had a volume or two on Chinese medicine on my bookshelves. As we prepared to part, we became closer in other ways.

Suddenly and increasingly, as the decade evolved, it was things other than productions that became primary. We did *The Recruiting Officer*, more or less, and the three of us went on the holiday I had booked. Joe had no idea what was going on. It was hard in the hotel in St-Jean-de-Luz and we found means of going our separate ways, but easier when we went to the house near Cordes in Tonnac, a benign place and large enough to have one's own space. In the autumn we collaborated again on Michael Meyer's adaptation of Gissing's novel *The Odd Women*. Whatever the personal stresses, our umbilical creative cord would not be broken.

All this time I was still running the company and trying to find new Artistic Directors to strengthen the group. I was acutely aware that we had been exclusively male and I invited Harriet Walter to join us. Her career was in a transition and she liked the idea, believing that acting work would be increasingly difficult to come by as she got older. Joining us was for her like a magic wand: her career sprang into life once more and the experiment came to nothing. Nevertheless, for a very short time we had the experience of quite another impulse in artistic director meetings.

As 1992 gave way to 1993 and our last six months together, we still kept the secret. Early in 1993 I did a production I was once again proud of. Gerry McLarnon proposed he should adapt *The Brothers Karamazov*. This was my favourite novel. In my youth I had been Alyosha and later Dmitri, subsiding in bad times into Ivan. Gerry had done a version of *The Idiot* for four people that Greg had directed; I wanted this to be an adaptation of the whole novel. Gerry agreed and we scheduled it sight unseen. We only gave it a three-and-a-half-week run because we imagined it would be one of those special events that not many people would want to see.

Gerry phoned to say that he had finished his adaptation and was sending it to us. I anticipated it arriving in a large post office van, it being a vast novel. It came through the normal post, a mere sixty pages long. It was an extraordinary achievement: he had condensed the whole novel into sixty pages and seemed to have left nothing out.

It was a vintage cast, Tom Mannion as Dmitri; Michael Mueller, Ivan; Ian Shaw, Alyosha; Philip Madoc, Karamazov; Johnny Moore, Smerdyakov; Graham Crowden, no less, as Father Zossima; and Lorraine Ashbourne, again sexily outstanding, as the whore Grushenka. Johanna didn't do this one; Simon Higlett did and marvellously too. He set it in a mud pit with a giant thurible hissing in the air above it. It was a perfect symbol.

Three and a half weeks . . . we could have run it for double that. It was an electric event and a much-needed one for me. I know it is to be published soon; it is surely worthy of revival.

Johanna and I were to work on one other play before the split was to become public. I had gone to see Vanessa Redgrave in *Heartbreak House* at the Haymarket. I had dinner with her afterwards and asked her to come back to the Exchange. She was very pleased; she had felt rejected after Michael's death. I explained I had thought that she was Michael's actress and assumed she wouldn't be interested.

We discussed various ideas and then she made a proposition. She admired the Russian playwright Mikhail Shatrov, who was now leaving Russia in the new political climate, and she wanted the Exchange to commission him to write a play about the McCarthy era. There would have to be another playwright attached to translate and to make the play accessible to the British audience. If we would do this she would commit to being in the play in the summer of 1993. I jumped at it, commissioned Shatrov and the American playwright Keith Reddin, and set the project in motion.

It turned out to be a nightmare. The play was written in dribs and drabs, and wasn't awfully encouraging. I got a phone call from Vanessa who was filming in Charleston. Instead of presenting the play conventionally, each night we could show it as work in progress, invite the audience's reaction after every show, rewrite overnight, re-rehearse during the day, present the result in the evening and so on. I had to fly out to South Carolina and dissuade her. Max bet me the show would never get into rehearsal. Fortunately, or perhaps unfortunately, he lost the bet.

The warning flares went off on day one. I gave my opening spiel and Johanna presented her set and costumes. After the session, Vanessa asked to see me. She explained that the set was all wrong and that it would have to be redesigned. I asked her what was wrong with it and she produced a notebook where she had written down everything about her character's past, and this character wouldn't live in such a house.

Vanessa is one of the greatest actresses in the world but her process as an actress is completely secret. She constructs the internals of her character with infinite care, and she will not or cannot commit herself externally until she is ready. This places a great strain on her fellow actors and her director. Fortunately for her, her charisma and talent are such that they are prepared to support this process. Anyway, on this occasion I simply gave her our equally valid rationale for the set and explained that it was already being built.

The other problem was that the play, the details of which I now forget, dealt with matters on which Vanessa was an expert, not only that but she felt passionate about them. As each scene came up she demanded rewrites, especially for the Trotskyite character (whom, bizarrely, she wasn't playing). Thus progress was painfully slow.

In the rehearsal room were Keith Reddin, Shatrov and an interpreter for Shatrov, so that everything I or anyone else said was being simultaneously translated in a Russian growl. Shatrov was in his sixties, a white-haired roly-poly Russian uncle; Keith, although in his late thirties, looked like an earnest student out of high school; they didn't seem to communicate. I relied entirely on Keith to produce a script that was remotely viable. He was tireless and extraordinarily balanced about it. He was a hero.

Midway through the second week we were nowhere near through the play for the first time. The other actors were very supportive; fortunately I had John Bennett, Melanie Thaw and, a splendid actress, Margaret Robertson whom I hadn't worked with before, but I was getting worried for them. We came to a scene that I reckoned was well written. Two minutes in Vanessa stopped to complain about it and I lost it. I knew I had a fearsome temper and I thought I had it under control. I hadn't lost my temper for years, but I did then. I shouted, I screamed and I swore. As I did so I heard the calm voice of the interpreter translating into Russian and I heard and saw Shatrov nodding '*Da, da*'. At the end of it Vanessa was as good as gold. For at least three days we rehearsed normally. I stored up the incident in my memory bank for further use. Loss of temper could be useful.

We got to the technical, which should have been a simple affair; it was a single-standing set. For Vanessa everything was wrong. The chairs were the wrong height, other furniture didn't look right and so on. The technical churned on and on. In any technical there are probably about fifty members of staff from wardrobe, wigs, workshop etc. sitting in the auditorium watching their handiwork and being ready to make adjustments; this marathon technical had an audience. We reached the last scene where the incriminating papers, don't ask me to remember what, were to be burnt. It was a climactic moment and I arranged for them to be burnt in a metal waste-paper bin on top of the table. This had been part of the production for a month.

Vanessa objected. There was a fireplace on stage, the papers would have to be burnt there. The fireplace was small, non-functioning and in a weak position. It was there to give the room character and, being in the round, it had no back to it. Logically Vanessa was right; dramatically I was right. She wouldn't give in. I sensed the restlessness in the auditorium. This was the moment. I faked a temper, rather well as it happened, and Vanessa subsided. The company burst into applause.

It was after the first public performance that I understood how Vanessa worked. The play switched through flashback between the present day and the McCarthy era, and these flashbacks were done with sound and light. When we were in front of an audience, I realised that once they had experienced the first flashback, I couldn't merely repeat them, I had to cut down each subsequent one. Vanessa came to me practically in tears; I was going to ruin her performance. She had constructed her inner life to coincide exactly with the timings we had arranged during rehearsal. Once again I knew I was right and rather more gently I told her I wouldn't budge. Fortunately her brother Corin came to see her that night and backed me up.

On the first night Vanessa was frequently inaudible. I was in despair. I collared her agent Jimmy Sharkey in the interval. 'What can I do?' I asked. He explained that if she didn't feel it inside, she wouldn't bother to be heard. He was right. When Vanessa played the part at full throttle she was extraordinary, incandescent, she made the play seem tolerable; when she was off form she was like any other competent actress.

She had phenomenal energy. She'd dash up and down between London and Manchester to berate the Foreign Office or belabour some other politician; she even got me to accompany her. She arranged an extraordinary

International Day at the Exchange on a Sunday. She bussed up Yugoslavian refugees from London, concentration camp survivors, Daniel Day Lewis, Bono, Robbie Coltrane and God knows who else. All this she arranged while rehearsing the play. She even got me to host the day.

She is an irresistible force, a wonderful woman and a great actress, but cor blimey!

All this was taking place as Johanna and I faced telling our sons about the separation. On the first evening of the technical Vanessa had come to me in the Green Room and announced, 'I can't work on that set.' I called Johanna over and we sat there wrangling for hours. Johanna is as combustible as designers come, we often had flaming public rows and our personal relationship was at a low, but we had to unite to contend with this crisis. At three o'clock in the morning it seemed to boil down to the fact that Vanessa's character would not have a copy of *Doctor Zhivago* on her bookshelves. I turned to Johanna and in measured terms I asked, 'Johanna, might you see your way to replacing the Pasternak novel with something else?' Johanna appeared to think carefully and then with great apparent effort said, 'Yes, I will.' Vanessa was overjoyed; she couldn't thank us enough. It shows that under fire we just hung on to our professional relationship. The moment of crisis for the family was coming and we were both dreading it, but something happened that made it somewhat easier for me.

CHAPTER 59

Coup de Foudre

I went to an Equity meeting to be attended by all the subsidised theatres, to complain about the Arts Council's funding policy. It was at the National Theatre. I sat down in my seat, looked across the table where the Equity officials were sitting and fell in love.

When it was over I went and introduced myself to her and told her that if she wanted any help I'd be happy to give it. The next day I phoned and asked her to dinner. She accepted.

This was extraordinary. It was the first time it had ever happened to me. I try to understand now why it did. I think when I looked at her for the first time I saw the part of myself that had been locked away. I saw two big, brown, beautiful eyes in a lovely warm face. It is that moment when you think 'If only I can have that I'll be happy for the rest of my life.'

We dined at Vasco and Piero's restaurant in Poland Street and I found out about her. Katherine Sand was twenty-nine (I was fifty-one), Jewish, ex-Oxford, ex-Labour Party officer during the Kinnock election and everything else I cared to project upon her. I told her that I wanted a relationship with her and that I couldn't go through all the usual courtship niceties. She told me that for the first time in her life she had a man living with her so it was out of the question. We finished the meal, left the restaurant and suddenly I was pinned against a lamp-post and being kissed in a manner I thought would make me spontaneously combust. She got into a taxi and went off into the night.

The next day I flew to New York where Ted Mann, the Artistic Director of The Circle in the Square, wanted to talk about the Broadway production of *Maybe*. I sent her a postcard; I'm surprised it didn't catch fire. I couldn't think of anything but her.

When I got back to England she phoned me at the theatre. She would come up to Manchester for the weekend, see *Maybe* and stay with me in a hotel. I was in ecstasy; I felt for the first time in my life what I imagined love must be.

She came up and she saw *Maybe*, although I tried to persuade her to give it a miss. I saw her to the station and asked her to leave her chap and be with me. Although she eventually admitted to loving me, and I think she did, she never took that step. There followed about nine months of jealousy, agony and bliss. The affair was conducted in hotel bedrooms, mostly when I came to London on business, and Michael Meyer's flat.

The portcullis was nowhere, perhaps it would have been if she'd committed to me. I fully experienced the madness of love. I would have done anything for her including marriage, babies, absolutely anything; nothing else in my life mattered. I was afraid I'd find it difficult to rehearse properly.

Katherine was my first real Jewish girlfriend. I had held Marilyn Bloom's hand when I was very little, put my arm round Susan Rosenzweig a little later, had my first kiss with Rosalyn Gold and a brief fling with Barbara Lieberman at Oxford, but this was the first serious Jewish affair. It was oddly comforting. We shared a common culture; we were at home with each other. I was convinced we had met in another life and that if we didn't make it in this one we'd meet again in the next.

It was no good, she wouldn't take the jump. She said she felt overwhelmed by me, that she literally couldn't breathe when she was with me, that there was no room for her in my life. I thought she was crazy. No one could ever love her as much as I did. How could she spurn such love? We even translated a play together, Marivaux's *The Triumph of Love* – after all, she was sexier than Cogo-Fawcett.

It hadn't even been sexual attraction in that first moment, but now when we made love, it was the first time that it was literally that: making, expressing love. It superseded everything.

As the months wore on the jealousy and pain became more and more intense. Finally she broke it off and I was numb with misery. At the same time some other voice inside me was rejoicing: 'You've fallen in love at last, you've suffered, you're a human being after all.'

Six years later when I started another relationship that was extreme in a different way, I finally felt it possible to throw away the letters she had written me over that period. As I was going through them for the last time, I found one that I had written to her but had never sent. It was a violently angry letter, branding her as almost a criminal. Thank goodness I never posted it. I read it alongside a desperate letter she had sent me, telling me how unhappy the affair was making her, that it was even making her ill. That had been my reply: unbridled fury.

I had seen her from time to time over the intervening years and she phoned to ask me to have dinner with her. Over dinner she told me how right I had been. I had prophesied the end of her other affair. She now told me how unsatisfactory that had been in every way, including physically, and the only reason she hadn't committed to me was that she was afraid to tell her friends and family that she had failed with this other man.

Maybe wrongly, I sensed she could be signalling that we might try again. I told her about the letters. I told her that to have written my unsent letter, to have ignored her desperation as I did, meant I couldn't have loved her. She said I had lifted a great weight off her shoulders. She had been carrying the awful suspicion that she had made a terrible mistake and now I had released her.

She's happily married now, with twins, living in the States. We e-mail each other about twice a year.

You can argue till the cows come home as to whether I loved her or not. I can't see that I could have, it seemed so selfish, but the fact is it changed my life at a critical moment. I knew that at some time I could now do *Antony and Cleopatra* and almost immediately a raft of different kinds of plays presented themselves. The old cliché is true: ''Tis better to have loved and lost than never to have loved at all.' But now I've run through nine months and I have to go back.

CHAPTER 60

Meanwhile

The 1993–94 season saw the company beginning to go into an artistic slump; too many not first-rate productions. I directed Rod Wooden's new play that we had commissioned, *Smoke*. It was based on fascinating historical fact. In the fifteenth century in Rod's native Norwich there had been a rebellion against the king. It took two expeditions by the king's army from London to crush the rebellion and during that time the rebels set up an alternative Utopian society.

What Rod refused to do was to use the obvious narrative drive as the engine around which he could weave his cogent spiritual and political insights. This is what Gerry had done so cleverly with *Karamazov*. He had written a thriller that hooked his audience and, having hooked them, he slipped them the metaphysical Mickey Finn; this is, after all, what Shakespeare did. Rod refused. He made the narrative as opaque and impenetrable as he could. I think he had become seduced by European theatre with its experimental plotless style. At any rate we rowed and rowed, he made tiny concessions and the play failed.

Rod has refused to write anything like his *Your Home in the West*; in fact, he resents people's desire that he should do so. His chosen style has meant that his career as a dramatist has been in abeyance for years. Having met an expat Colombian who sang with a rock band in Switzerland, he fell in love with her. For political reasons she couldn't go back to Colombia. He did, and has stayed there ever since, writing wonderful stories about that beleaguered country. We stay in touch. He is a remarkable human being and a remarkable talent. I'm quite certain his life process will lead to something one day that we will all have need of.

I found that I could rehearse after all during my affair with Katherine, but my behaviour amazed everyone. During rehearsals I am very strict with myself. I go to bed early and use the weekends for recuperation; I don't stir. During *Smoke* I went down to London every weekend, even the ones when we didn't finish rehearsals till Saturday lunchtime. This astonished even me. It was the most extreme expression of love I could imagine. I'm extremely unsentimental but I even did that crazy thing of having a song. It was Ella Fitzgerald's 'Every Time We Say Goodbye (I die a little)'. Especially the lines:

> Why the gods above me
> Who must be in the know
> Think so little of me
> They allow you to go.

Katherine came and saw the show. I think she felt inadequate because she didn't understand it. Nobody did.

The year certainly didn't improve and a crisis was looming, exacerbated by *The Count of Monte Cristo* who finally found his way to the stage.

CHAPTER 61

The Count

It was clear that 1994 was going to be a difficult year. We had told our sons that we were separating, our house was on the market and we would both have to find somewhere to live. Johanna chose to stay in Manchester; I opted for a flat in London. Casper had told me it was time for me to step back and I figured if that was so I might as well be in London. Our sons seemed to take the news very well; it was only years later that they told me what a shock it had been.

Also, although Vanessa had decided she didn't want to do *Maybe* on Broadway, Tom and I offered to do *Uncle Vanya* if Ted Mann wanted us to. He did, so that was being set up.

On top of that Alex Bernstein resigned. He had stayed much longer than we had expected. He was one of those special men and it was a big blow. He arranged, too, for the Chairman of Norweb to take over and he made a big mistake. Ken Harvey was a nice enough man but he knew nothing about theatre. Moguls who don't understand theatre think it's like any other business, selling soap or motorcars or electricity. It isn't. For one thing subsidised theatre means that profit isn't the motive; for another the product changes roughly once a month. Breaking in this new Chairman was going to be a big job.

To add to all this, Greg asked me what had happened to *The Count*. What had happened was that I had forgotten about it. It had died with that New York phone call. Greg suggested I read it again. I did and as a result I asked David Threlfall if he wanted to do it and he did. This was a vast undertaking. Having been through the process once, I was aware of the task, which would include an eight-week rehearsal period, climaxing with both shows opening on the same night.

Monte Cristo was not a great success and I am puzzled as to why. I thought it a marvellous show. Simon Higlett solved all the scenic challenges, Fergus Early, imaginatively backed up by Emil Wolk and Liam Steele, created magic, illusion and spectacle in the movement. I had a fine cast, at the centre of which David gave a remarkable performance, or rather four performances. He was the young Dantès, he was the Dracula-like Count, he was the fat avenging Abbé, he was the languid silly ass of an English Lord. Actually, there was more: the haggard prisoner; the eastern potentate – the transformations were endless. Sometimes he did them too well so that people asked why the programme had missed out so many characters from the cast list.

Financially the production was a disaster. It cost an awful lot of money and the audience didn't buy into the two-night experience. When both parts were played on the same day the theatre was packed, people brought picnics to eat between the shows and at the end of the marathon we received a standing ovation. They simply didn't want to split the experience.

David was very upset by the comparative failure. He contrived to put his back out and we lost ten days of performances. Normally when something doesn't work I'm the first to hold up my hand but not this time. It was a special evening.

At the beginning of rehearsals I had resumed my weekend trips to see Katherine; I even agreed to direct a special Sunday concert for Yugoslavian refugees, but it was obviously coming to an end. We spent our last time together at the Cumberland Hotel and after the concert I wandered off by myself. My heart was broken. The song changed from 'Every Time We Say Goodbye' to 'I Get Along without You Very Well'.

With everything else that was going on, after *Monte Cristo* opened I had one day to find a flat in London before we moved out of our Bramhall house. I saw fourteen properties, all near Euston. The last was in Primrose Hill. Finding a place to live is the most fated thing I know. It takes a minute to be sure. I was sure. I was right. I've been there ever since. Of course I was right. Among many fine restaurants in the village there is the incomparable Lemonia where Tony, Theo and Stavros make sure the Exchange have a London office.

I also found a flat in the centre of Manchester. The moment of moving was looming. I started to spend nights in the flat to get used to the experience of living alone, which I had never done in my entire life. The day came and it was weird: like watching a movie with yourself in it. Joe was going to live with Johanna in her house in Manchester; Jacob was determined to live by himself. I said goodbye to Johanna and drove away in a trance.

I was scared stiff. What would I do all the time? So many hours had been filled with children and domestic problems. What would fill the void? How do you work a washing machine? I stayed with my parents that night and set out for Primrose Hill like Scott of the Antarctic. I moved in and went to bed in a strange state.

The next morning I woke up and thought I'd better get up because . . . er . . . er . . . oh! I don't have to get up. A delicious feeling of freedom crept over me, which has never left me. It was a peculiar moment of growing up aged fifty-two.

My relationship with Johanna slipped into the new gear amazingly easily. I visited her in Manchester and she coached me telephonically through my domestic ignorance. I must also pay tribute to the wondrous Mrs Welsh who runs the ironmonger's in Primrose Hill and was up to any panic-inducing crisis, like blocked sinks or replacing specialist light bulbs. Katherine also helped me buy things for the flat. That was bitter-sweet.

Monte Cristo was coming to an end. There was a particularly attractive girl serving behind the bar. She had a champagne personality and a cracking figure. She always seemed to be particularly chatty with me. I kept on bumping into her in the street. I decided to invite her out. She accepted. We started an affair that night.

Margaret Carney was a reincarnation of Stella Donelly, although she wasn't a theatre person. She was studying to be a physiotherapist and was just what I needed. She was warmth and affection, and she adored me. Being me, I reverted to the on-off pattern but the relationship was surprisingly durable, given that we came from two completely different worlds.

Monte Cristo closed. There was a wonderful last-night party. For all its problems, it had been a happy company who had been together for nearly six months. It left a good taste in the mouth.

CHAPTER 62

Crisis Again

It seemed to happen about every ten years and here it was again. An autumn season was planned that we thought would put the box office to rights, but it wasn't one I liked. It included an Alan Ayckbourn and that seemed to me desperation stations. Then things began to turn. I was up visiting the Edinburgh Festival when I heard the news that Michael Sheen, who had been a memorable Romeo for Greg, had agreed to come back for two plays: *Charley's Aunt*, which Emil would direct, and *Look Back in Anger*, which Greg would do. It felt right.

At Edinburgh that year Tom was doing his one-man play *Moscow Stations*. He advised me to go and see *Poor Super Man* by Brad Fraser, which was also on at the Traverse where he was playing. He had seen Fraser's previous play *Unidentified Human Remains and the True Nature of Love* and been very impressed. I took his advice and went with Sophie Marshall to see *Poor Super Man*.

It seemed for the first quarter of an hour like one of those in-your-face fringe works, where everyone went to bed with everyone else, male, female, whatever. I wanted to leave, then little by little it drew me in. Here was a writer probing sexuality and love in a profound and fearless way and, like Joe Orton, making us laugh while he was doing it. At the interval I assumed that the play would slowly dissolve into sentimentality. I was wrong. Brad Fraser was Canadian not American.

Back in London, I went to see the film of his earlier play, called rather more succinctly *Love and Human Remains*. It was a poor movie but sufficiently interesting to make me get hold of the play script. I was smitten. This was something I wanted to do. Brad was the playwright Katherine had opened me up to. I would never have gone into those areas before Katherine, BK.

We decided to do a very different spring–summer 1995 season. Both *Julius Caesar* and the Ayckbourn had failed at the box office. Instead of panicking we needed to get back our artistic self-respect. Since everything in the world, good and bad, is an outward projection of our inner selves, we determined on a season called 'Private Lives': Jim Cartwright's *Road*, *The Colleen Bawn* by Boucicault, Brad's play, Beth Henley's *Crimes of the Heart* and finally the Coward play itself. It seemed a good step in the right direction.

Whether or not it was as a reaction to this I don't know, but James Maxwell resigned. He said he had no objections to what we were doing but no real connection with it. He wanted to go back to being an actor and spend more time with his wife, Avril.

Effectively this meant there was no longer a group. A duopoly is not a group. In a group you can have all sorts of people of different talents. People who would normally not be artistic directors could be accommodated for their special gifts, as Max had been and as Greg was. Greg is the best Artistic Consultant ever but he is not and does not want to be a leader. This meant I was now where Armund had prophesied I would be. It was going to be on me. I was to be the bridge. Such were the traumas of that year that I don't believe I felt the full enormity of the situation. Anyway, the next season was planned and I was enjoying regular visits to New York to set up and cast *Uncle Vanya*, which was to rehearse in January 1995.

Margaret had moved into my Manchester flat, which was as near as I was to get to living with anyone again, and I was quite enjoying that too. The poor lady had a rather benign view of me at that point, because after *Monte Cristo* I wasn't in rehearsal. It was a respite that didn't repeat itself while we were together.

My last action before leaving for America was to help Emil Wolk get his production of *Charley's Aunt* on stage. There is no doubt that Emil is a comic genius and has no equal at physical clowning. His *Charley's Aunt* was Fancourt-Babberly meets the Marx Brothers. It was brilliant externally but he couldn't handle actors. I was called in by him to help the final week of rehearsals. The marriage between us worked, the show was an unconventional success. Michael Sheen inherited, via me, a lot of Tom's gags and 1994, that most horrible of years, ended on a high note.

CHAPTER 63

Back in New York

It was a relief to get out of England. It was like going on two months' holiday . . . until I got there. The cast seemed a good one. Tom had suggested I meet James Fox with a view to him playing Astrov, as David Threlfall, whom we both wanted, was under contract to the BBC. Tom had been in the movie *King Rat* with him and thought he would be right. I met him at Mon Plaisir and he seemed ideal; he looked right, he sounded right and he was charming. Ted Mann was delighted; his name would be good on the marquee. Amanda Donohoe, whom I hadn't really seen since the *Cymbeline* season, put herself forward for Yelena and I cast her immediately. Sonya was a fine New York actress, Kate Skinner, the great Elizabeth Franz played the tiny part of Vanya's mother and Werner Klemperer was Serebryakov.

The Circle in the Square was, as the name implies, a theatre in the round, or rather in the oval, so it was nearly home from home. It had been going through a rough time and *Uncle Vanya* was to revive its fortunes. However, money was very limited and although I had a great creative team, Loren Sherman (set), Mimi Maxmen (costumes) and the legendary Tharon Musser (lights), they were pretty constricted. Alongside Ted there was a new Artistic Director, Josie Abady, who was really my producer.

New York is freezing in January – you feel you should get a medal just for getting to the theatre in the morning – but we all met up in good heart. During the read-through the first misgivings appeared. Actors treat read-throughs in different ways. Some give it everything they've got, others hold back, no two people are alike. I always encourage them to take the opportunity just to say the words out loud and make contact for the first time with the people they are going to work with, not to take it as a test. The problem was that Fox simply didn't seem able to make sense of any of the lines.

We started to rehearse. Again, all actors are different, some hurl themselves at a part, trying out all kinds of approaches; some stalk their part, not committing themselves much externally until they are properly centred. James appeared to do precisely nothing.

Uncle Vanya relies on the central quartet, Vanya, Astrov, Sonya, Yelena. By week three it was obvious we had only three out of four. Moreover, rehearsing James reminded me horribly of rehearsing Michael David all those years ago in *Long Day's Journey*. He had to be bullied into showing emotion and he seemed to have no worries. Amanda Donohoe was suffering and everyone was concerned.

The crunch moment came. Josie Abady, who had watched me trying to rehearse the famous map scene between Astrov and Yelena, asked me if I wanted to replace James. This filled me with horror. I had cast him, it was my responsibility; besides, it would disrupt everything so near to previews. I told Josie I would work with him over the weekend. I did, he was better and I told Josie I'd stick with him. This was a mistake – better doesn't mean right, it simply means better. It also meant in this case that the centre of the play couldn't ever be right.

Everything was fine except this and apart from the lack of money for the physical production the cast were happy; we spent a lot of time together out of rehearsal. Tom was at his best and Amanda was a delightful new friend. We all felt we could get away with it.

I think Tom's performance as Vanya was one of the finest he has given. Sometimes I have had difficulty coping with Tom the stage actor as opposed to Tom the film actor. The former was developing mannerisms which the latter couldn't countenance. I was very straight with him about this before we started rehearsals and he responded magnificently. It was a profoundly soulful, moving portrayal, which also used his comic genius in the near farcical shooting sequence.

The previews started, the houses were full and, as one does, I tried to ignore the flaws in the production. To alleviate the pressure of opening night, the Broadway producers had decided that critics could come to any of the last ten days of previews. This basically meant that instead of being terrified for one night, the cast were terrified for ten nights. Opening night was therefore a celebrity occasion with no real meaning. At the end of the show Amanda collapsed on the floor. She said all she could see in her fellow actors' eyes throughout was fear. What she meant was that everyone knew their fate was sealed. The reviews were already written, especially the *New York Times*, which was make or break. I walked with Josie to the first-night party.

'Have you seen the *New York Times*?'

'Yup.'

'And?'

'It's shit. Forget it.'

By the time we got to the restaurant, everybody knew. It was ghastly. No matter that we had raves in the *New Yorker* and indeed from Clive Barnes, the ex-*New York Times* critic in the *Daily Post*, we were down and out. I flew back to England the next day, deeply upset and a bit low on confidence.

I was upset because I knew that almost all the production was first-rate and Tom was more than that, absolutely special. It seemed that every time I got near to a different sort of success, something went dramatically wrong. I hadn't yet faced the fact that with Max and Casper resigning, I had a very big new challenge to confront in Manchester. Destiny decreed that there would be no distractions.

CHAPTER 64

Back to England

On my return to England I had three separate professional problems. The immediate one was to pick myself up off the floor and prepare the Brad Fraser, which had to be cast in the one month before rehearsals. The second was to get an autumn–winter season together without Casper or Max. The third was to think about the long-term future of the company.

I returned to find that *Look Back in Anger* had been a great critical and box-office success for Greg and Michael Sheen. *Road*, the first production of our experimental season, opened as I arrived back and was terrific. I cast *Unidentified* in record time, helped by the fact that Andy Serkis and Paddy O'Kane agreed to play the leads.

I went into rehearsals still feeling drained. Unexpectedly, this had a very good result and taught me another directing lesson. Because I was tired, I didn't lean on the actors as heavily as usual, which allowed them to run with my basic take on the play and be more creative than they might otherwise have been. It made me realise that it is a good thing to give the actors as much rope as you dare. If they're good they'll repay you in spades.

I loved rehearsing the play. Brad is a huge challenge: myriads of short scenes in different locations; pauses strictly forbidden; a honed script as dense as a Gerry McLarnon; an apparently cinematic almost cartoon style disguising great seriousness; in other words a new theatre language. On top of that, sexual scenes of every variety and nudity. It's probably everyone's fantasy to be the director of nude lesbian love scenes. Forget it! Ten in the morning, nervous actresses, closed rehearsals, it's about as sexy as Birmingham City Reserves.

Like all the shows that season, except the Coward, there was very little advance booking before we opened but by the end of the run we were playing to full houses. So Brad's close relationship with the Exchange was born.

I then had another month before directing *Private Lives* for the third time with a terrific cast, Sian Thomas, Pip Donaghy, Lucy Scott and Colin Prockter. Even more Strindbergian, even funnier. Full houses. Our season had done what it had set out to do. It had returned our artistic confidence and, indeed, mine personally.

The other two problems dovetailed. Greg and I were aware that we would have to find more directors, both because we couldn't do all the productions, but also because if we were going to renew the group we'd have to find some new relationships.

Garry Hynes had done *The Colleen Bawn* beautifully and in the 1995–96 season we would have Robert Delamere back to do *Tartuffe*; a director whose work we had seen at Hampstead called Matthew Lloyd to do Iain Heggie's new play *An Experienced Woman Gives Advice*; Emil Wolk to work with Greg on the Marx Brothers' *Animal Crackers*; Dilys Hamlett to direct *Tess of the d'Urbervilles*; the Polish director Helena Kaut-Howson to do *Hindle Wakes*; and Josie Abady from New York for *The Philadelphia Story*.

I lined up two stars for the autumn, thus ensuring that the artistic revival would be followed up by a financial one. Before I had left New York, I had arranged with Amanda to do a play in October. I had always fought shy of Strindberg but I knew that Amanda, a sensual, intelligent and on-the-edge actress, would be a perfect Miss Julie. I also hooked Maureen Lipman to make her Exchange début as Mrs Malaprop in *The Rivals*.

The unexpected event that threw us all into great shock was that Max's new life did not last long. At the age of sixty-six he died of a disease of the liver. I visited him in hospital where he was lying very ill. He was a man who was ill at ease with himself, merciless on his shortcomings and equally furious with other people's. He is sorely missed, not just by me but by everyone in the company who knew him. The sound of his infectious, life-giving laughter is what everybody recalls about him. I remember him as being the most human of our group, the warmest and the kindest. Without him we wouldn't have survived our ego battles. Would that he had loved himself a little more. I did. It is said that his laughter has been heard in the theatre at night and that a white-haired man has been seen sitting in a seat at stage level. He is still our guardian.

Directing *Miss Julie*, my fourth production of the year, was hard. The play demands that every morning you take a deep breath and plunge into a dark, fiery abyss, and stay there for eight hours. Sometimes it was too much for Amanda and we had to take time out, but it was exhilarating too. My objection to Strindberg disappeared. His examination of the darkness in us was cathartic; you become determined not to go down that road. That is what makes him great. Amanda was absolutely mesmeric in the part, wonderfully backed up by Paddy O'Kane and Marie Francis.

It seemed that 1995 might actually end on an up note but then my lovely cousin/sister Gillian died aged forty-eight. She had had cancer for over two years and had dealt with it with her usual fearless, investigative mind. The illness almost seemed to purify her. I saw her often as she battled with the disease and before she died, when it had worn away her body but not her spirit.

Fortunately for me, she had an equally remarkable sister, Jaqueline, and my relationship with her deepened. I think we helped each other. It is one of my most important relationships to this day.

So 1995 was another horrible year; the only successes were some of the productions and what could they matter in comparison with real-life tragedies? Maybe 1996 would be better.

CHAPTER 65

It Depends What You Call Better

It was all beginning to work. An anonymous donor, who I will now reveal was Alex Bernstein, gave us a large sum of money to fund a Michael Elliott bursary for training artistic directors. After his auspicious début with the Iain Heggie, Matthew Lloyd joined us as a result of that award. Jacob had recommended we go and see a production at the Etcetera Theatre in Camden by one Marianne Elliott, daughter of Michael. She joined us too as an assistant. Emil and Greg had produced the funniest show I have ever seen – except mine, of course – with the Marx Brothers' *Animal Crackers*. Ben Keaton, Toby Sedgwick and Joe Alessi were sublime as the three anarchic Jews. Now Helena Kaut-Howson opened her *Hindle Wakes*, fusing Polish passion with the Manchester School. New blood and good new blood was flooding in.

It was also the launch of the John Major lottery and we had put in a bid. We were a few months short of our twentieth birthday and the place was in desperate need of refurbishment; it had a shabby, run-down feel to it. All the indications were that our bid would succeed and we were in consultation with the original architects, Levitt Bernstein. I had called in Casper as a consultant and even Richard Negri turned up to the odd meeting.

To cap it all Josie Abady came over from New York, and brought with her Jordan Baker, to revive *The Philadelphia Story*. Audiences were up again. We were clearly through our crisis. Then, at 11.15 a.m. on Saturday 15 June 1996, the IRA blew us up.

I was in London preparing for meetings the next week with the architects. I saw the news on Teletext. It said there had been an explosion and a plume of smoke could be seen one and a half miles away. I phoned the theatre but there was no answer. I called Pat Weller, our Executive Director, at home. She gave the historic answer, 'It's bad news, I think we're going to lose the matinée.'

The police had cordoned off the area of the city centre around the theatre but no one seemed seriously worried. By Monday the news was worse. We couldn't reopen that night. On Tuesday the bad news had accelerated. I was at the meeting with the architects. Pat kept on phoning. We might not be able to reopen for weeks, then six months, then eighteen months, then appallingly, if the damage was really bad, never. She wanted me up there immediately.

For the record, what had happened was that the IRA had planted a bomb in a van outside Marks & Spencer, which is very near the theatre. They had given a warning and the police had acted with spectacular efficiency. In spite of it being on a busy Saturday morning, they managed to evacuate the area and no one was killed, or even very seriously injured. Later, when I was allowed to view the bomb-site, I saw what a miracle it was. The television reporters who covered the atrocity said that they had never seen devastation anywhere like it, not even in Yugoslavia. It was once again for me a vision of pure evil – an expression of man's ability to suspend his own humanity in the sheer urge to destroy. If you want a comparison, imagine Regent Street, Oxford Street, Tottenham Court Road and Leicester Square laid low.

It's difficult to recall what sequence my emotional reaction took. On the train to Manchester I only had one thought: this was a golden opportunity. I put to the back of my mind the possibilities of being closed for ever and just saw visions of lots and lots of government money so that we could re-dream the dream.

The Library Theatre had generously offered the company asylum in their building. When I arrived they were huddled, shell-shocked, in the theatre's café bar. I was in a genuinely positive mood. 'We're going to get millions of pounds and we won't have to worry about the box office for years!' That may sound flippant, but not if you'd seen us waiting anxiously every day for the box-office returns.

We had a company meeting and I remembered the wisdom of the I Ching: 'Do not wrestle with evil, thus is its power increased. Progress in what is good, thus is evil weakened.' That is precisely what we did. The tour of *Tess of the d'Urbervilles* in our mobile theatre was coming to an end this Saturday. If we could find a home for it in Manchester we could open *The Philadelphia Story*, which had been rehearsing in the theatre when the blast happened, on time. Howard Bernstein, the Chief Executive of the City Council, was superb. He found us a perfect venue in the old Victorian meat and vegetable market in Castlefield. It was showing an art exhibition that was swiftly removed and preparations were made to turn it into an audience-friendly place, housing a theatre, in ten days.

At the same time the BBC came to our administrative rescue. They put up the entire company in Nissen huts, which were part of their complex on Oxford Road. They also gave us a studio to continue rehearsals of *Philadelphia Story* and we even played four public performances of *Hindle Wakes* in that studio within a week of the blast.

It was a hectic but exhilarating time. The company rose to the occasion magnificently. How people like Ean Burgon got our BBC offices IT'd up or Irene Muir rode roughshod over the problems in Castlefield I'll never know. At the helm, masterminding it all, was Pat Weller. Absolutely the best Executive Director I had worked with, now she was indefatigable, controlling the whole operation.

When *The Philadelphia Story* opened ten days after the bomb on its original scheduled opening date, I have to say I was profoundly proud of what our people had achieved. 'Progress in what is good' is precisely what they had done; a great production in a great new space by 150 people who a few days earlier had been fearful and professionally homeless.

– ii –

There was a downside to it, of course. The funding bodies insisted we lay off anyone who was effectively redundant. This certainly meant the majority of the catering staff and reluctantly we had to do it. Ambulance followers tried to make a case against us but our hands were tied. It was perhaps the one big negative of the bomb.

The big thing now was to go for the long-term objective as quickly as possible, re-brief the architects and put in a bigger bid. There were other major problems. The Pru wanted us out of the building, which was a prime retail site, and the Arts Council had to be persuaded to go on subsidising us, even though our income would be decimated, and we needed to rush through the lottery bid or the time lapse could be equally fatal.

Howard Bernstein was on our side against the Pru and eventually all was well, but not before some heart-stopping moments. After the bomb went off, no one was allowed into the building for quite a while. Every time it rained we were in misery, imagining the water pouring through the shattered glass domes and wreaking havoc on the theatre beneath. When we were eventually allowed in, the amazing thing was that the auditorium was untouched; we could have played *Hindle Wakes*, whose set was still there, that night. It was the rest of the building, especially the theatre exits and entrances, that had been affected. This was because, as I've said, the auditorium is hung from the four great pillars since the floor couldn't take its weight. Thus when the after-blast happened the auditorium rose slightly and settled back unharmed. The Pru sent in forensic scientists to establish whether the bomb had disturbed the foundations of the building. If it had, that would have been the end for us. It hadn't, but to establish that fact they had to cause almost more damage than the bomb itself, ripping up the old parquet flooring and tearing out the walls.

After the bomb went off Thelma Holt had phoned me. Her message? 'I knew you were clever, but I didn't think you were that clever!' She too immediately saw what a bonus this could be for us. It was she, as Chairman of the Arts Council Theatre Committee, Lord Gowrie, the Chairman of the Arts Council, and Moss Cooper, the lottery official, who eventually got us what we needed, but it was a struggle. The Arts Council since the days of Joe Hodgkinson had become a bureaucracy and the lottery, as a new government venture, a bureaucracy times ten.

I had to persuade them to move fast or all would be lost. The master-stroke was getting the temporary theatre up and running so quickly. Either they had to agree to keep funding us and give us an immediate interim lottery grant or close us down. I seemed to be endlessly in London thumping tables, and dashing back to Manchester as the politicians made their visits for press opportunities. It was exhausting.

— iii —

On top of all this there was the usual business of running a company. We had a new season to announce. Fortunately quite a lot of that had been fixed before the bomb. Matthew would do *All's Well that Ends Well*, Marianne, who had been swiftly promoted, Priestley's *I Have Been Here Before* and I was already slotted to do *Lady Windermere's Fan* with Gabrielle Drake. The last show of the season would be an Emil Wolk extravaganza, *Wolk's World*.

Again, at the same time I had to work with the architects on the new bid. Of course, I had terrific back-up from Michael Williams and from Pat, who continued to be prodigious, and in truth it remained an adrenalin-inducing challenge that I relished.

Margaret had seen me wonderfully through that initial time. It was actually good to have someone to come home to. I think she never knew how important she was to me over that period. However, Pat and I had stood shoulder to shoulder through the blitz and gradually we began to drift closer together. This is a relationship I'm not going to talk about because it has ended too recently to be properly understood by me.

— iv —

The success of the temporary theatre interplayed with the new design process of the architects. I made them come up to experience it, it was so relaxed, egalitarian and unstuffy. The architects also wanted a big idea and I decided that we should have a studio and, despite Casper's suggestion of creating a new auditorium outside the Exchange, a studio in the main building.

In the early days of the company we had resisted the idea of a studio because in other theatres it tended to be a space where all the interesting plays were done, while the main house accommodated big boring revivals. Now it seemed to me, with our blossoming education department and the need to nurture new writers who couldn't yet be exposed to a 750-seat theatre, there was pressure to have a second space; it would also provide a training ground for new talent. Laurie Dennett was asked to dream up the space. In fact, our three main designers, inspired by Richard's teaching, Johanna, Laurie Dennett and David Short, formed a designers' committee to consult with the architects as they decided what to do, if anything, to improve the auditorium.

All this was heady, if slightly alarming, stuff for me. In spite of Casper's help, it seemed to be my call and certainly I had to watch the architects every inch of the way.

— v —

I did *Lady Windermere's Fan*. It was the first rehearsal period where I allowed myself to be interrupted if there was a political or architectural crisis to be dealt with; I hope it's the last one. It was a great success and Bill Kenwright transferred it to London at the Haymarket via Windsor, where it enjoyed a good run. But apart from a peculiar failure of a new play called *The Candidate*, which coincided with the General Election, I had to stop directing because there was too much else to do.

CHAPTER 66

The Royal Exchange, Mark II

The political battle was over and we were to receive £17 million from the lottery. All lottery recipients had to find matching funding and that was taken care of by our insurance money. The big remaining question was what to do with the building, particularly the auditorium.

At last we could have proper offices and dressing rooms. With the studio being housed where our very cramped workshops used to be, the lottery money enabled us to erect a custom-built super workshop and extra rehearsal room in the Northern Quarter, five minutes from the theatre.

Our team of designers and we ourselves decided to do little to the auditorium. It remained bang up to date, if not ahead of its time. Technically it was made state-of-the-art with the dubious advantage of everything being computerised and we changed the colour of the balcony fronts so that they were less of a barrier to the audience. The floor was the problem. Richard had kept the original Victorian parquet so that the audience arriving and the actors shared the same earth, the same world. His idea was that this stage floor would serve all the plays, as the Elizabethan and Greek theatres had always used the same floor.

We had all tried to do it that way, but as time wore on we used the parquet less and less. A good deal of the budget was spent on special floors, some built high, some elaborate, some even revolving and trapped. The parquet had been ripped up by the Pru, so we tried to find a common floor anew. After much experimenting, we fixed on a very expensive oak, which seemed excellent in sample but in fact was upsettingly wrong when finally installed. It was the one big failure but in truth, was it ever likely in our time to find a piece of earth on which we could all stand?

The relationship with the architects was far from perfect. Malcolm Brown, who had masterminded and supervised the original, had been very ill and his replacement was not in the same class. Although we had Malcolm's advice, it was difficult to get the relaxed feel that we wanted. They seemed addicted to battleship grey everywhere and the constant skirmishing was wearisome.

Over the years various 'carbuncles', as Casper called them, had sprouted in the hall, obscuring the purity of the auditorium. Casper pushed hard for these bookshops and craft centres to be placed in the side run of the building, to leave the theatre free. I'm not sure it was the right idea because it left the building less attractive to visitors in the day. The interior of the hall was beautiful but also a little imposing.

However, in spite of all this we were pleased with progress and the building was on schedule to open at the end of 1998. The company had found a new saviour in the form of the Hallé, who were to have a new home in the Bridgewater Hall, thus vacating both the Free Trade Hall for rehearsal and their offices, much nearer the Exchange, for our staff. We gratefully bade the BBC farewell and removed once again.

CHAPTER 67

Resurrections

The theatre was being resurrected and the group might be on the same path. Matthew and Marianne were earning their spurs with largely good productions and we had an interesting new Literary Manager in Sarah Frankcom, another person Jacob had spotted as a director on the London fringe and recommended to us.

For me there were two other artistic resurrections to work on, even though I wasn't to direct again till 1999. Kent Nagano was then the resident conductor of the Hallé and he liked my work. He phoned to ask me if I was interested in directing at the Houston Grand Opera. A friend of his, Tod Machover, had been commissioned to write an opera for Houston and Kent had recommended me to him. I was a bit wary. I hadn't touched opera since Oxford and *The Sicilian Vespers*, and my visits to watch it had too often left me giggling. What was the new opera to be? The answer was Tolstoy's *Resurrection*. It was a novel I knew and loved. It was his last great novel, after he had turned to Christianity and, although it was flawed – not a bad thing if you're going to adapt it – its theme of hope in a corrupt and materialistic world was very potent.

The story is of a prince, Dmitri Nekhlyudov, who is summoned to serve on a jury. Up in front of the court is a whore, Katusha, who is accused of murder. Dmitri recognises her as a servant girl whom he raped as a young man. She is sentenced to Siberia, although she is probably innocent, and he follows her there. She still loves him but refuses to accept his offer of marriage, preferring to send him back into the world to do the good that only a man in his position could.

I was hooked. Things moved fast. Tod was due in Europe almost immediately. He would fly to Manchester, meet me, give me a copy of the libretto so far, fly off to Europe, then back for another meeting. Tod is a smallish, Jewish, wild-haired, human dynamo who seems to be endlessly flying over the pond. He is a professor at MIT, experimenting with music and computers, besides being a composer. He also has infectious enthusiasm and is totally charming. One of his daughters, Hana, is my godchild.

Anyway we met, got on well and off he went, leaving me the libretto. I thought it was awful. The librettist, Laura Harrington, clearly had no real connection with the novel, she had simply used the epic story to write what she thought of as spectacular scenes that smacked more of *Phantom of the Opera* than Tolstoy.

When Tod flew back I told him how I felt and said sadly that I couldn't put myself forward. Tod's reaction was great relief, not about my withdrawal but because he didn't like the libretto either. Would I be prepared to meet with him and Laura to discuss it?

I was due to be in Toronto in a couple of weeks and we agreed to meet up there. In those two weeks I reread the novel, which is a massive sprawling thing, and tried to make the story of Dmitri and Katusha the spine of the drama, learning from McLarnon rather than Wooden, that on to the spine could be grafted the socio-political, spiritual themes that make this novel so remarkable.

The Toronto visit was an interesting one. I was going to meet Brad Fraser. Reopening the theatre seemed like an ideal time to commission new plays. I had read that Brad had given up the theatre and gone to work for Disney. His argument was that theatre didn't pay enough 'to fuck you around' but Hollywood did. All the same I phoned him – I had talked to him prior to doing *Unidentified* – and left a message on his answering machine asking if he'd consider a commission. To my surprise and pleasure he rang back and said he would. He wanted to write a play about Lizzie Borden, the famous parental axe killer. His new play, *Martin Yesterday*, which he was directing himself in Toronto at Buddies in Bad Times (it's what the theatre is called), was about to open, so I could meet him and see the show.

I saw the play, liked it (but not really the production), met Brad and we had a very long meal. He must have been surprised at this rather older than he might have suspected director and I was surprised at this over-six-foot giant, more conventional in dress than I might have expected. Anyway we sparked; it felt like meeting my brother. He had gone off Lizzie Borden and wanted to write a completely original script called *Snake in Fridge*. It was to be about twenty-somethings and would deal with a group whose varied sexual orientations would be more like *Unidentified* than his increasingly gay plays, of which *Martin Yesterday* was the latest example. This would mean that the new play wouldn't be ready for our reopening season, but in the meantime would we consider presenting the British première of *Martin Yesterday*? I was sure we would be interested and a very firm friendship was formed, which is just as well because it had to weather some considerable storms.

The next day I met Tod and Laura, took them through my proposals, which they liked, so we agreed to go forward together. It was a welcome diversion from things back home and involved frequent trips to Texas, and indeed Big Sur, where Tod was holed up writing the piece.

In the opera world everything happens early. You are contracted about two years before rehearsals start, as indeed are the singers and the conductor. The set and costume design also had to be ready much earlier than for the theatre. Simon Higlett, who was designing for me, had to work without hearing much of the music and he had an enormous job. Still, with the terrific back-up we had from the Houston team we made progress.

What I didn't know was that right up to the summer of 1998 David Gockley, the Houston boss, might have pulled the production, had he not liked what we were creating. In that summer we met in Sante Fe, where Tod would play and sing the entire score to David and the wealthy Texans who had put up all the money for the commission. By this time I had more or less taken over the libretto and it was a tense few days, but in the end Gockley gave the green light and the relief was profound.

The other resurrection was Casper's idea. He suggested, actually insisted, that I should direct David Threlfall in *Peer Gynt* for the reopening season. I had never done Ibsen; Michael and Casper had commandeered him although Greg had managed to sneak in his wonderful *Doll's House* with Brenda Blethyn. I wanted to do one badly, but after Michael's superb production at the Old Vic with Leo McKern, I found the idea daunting. Moreover, when I read it I was completely put off by the way women are treated in the play. There are three temptresses, Anitra, the Green Clad One and the Troll Princess, and then the pure and faithful Solveig who waits patiently for him to live his odyssey and welcome him back at the end. This seemed to me to perpetuate the whore or Madonna view of women, and I didn't want to do that at the end of the twentieth century. Casper wasn't pleased. Women had always symbolised the soul. That was just how it was: Solveig was Peer's soul. It didn't help me. Then I had, I think, a brilliant idea. If the same actress played all the temptresses and Solveig they would together become woman for Peer and at the end all be contained in Solveig. I agreed to do the production.

Casper also said that the last act of the play, when Peer meets the Button Moulder and the Thin Man, is an after-death experience. Peer dies in the shipwreck. This I found very appealing and I knew I would take it one stage further. At the end of the play I would have Solveig lead the naked Peer back into the world, to a new incarnation, a resurrection if you like.

Although I wasn't directing, preparing these two huge projects, *Peer Gynt* and *Resurrection*, was a welcome balance to the endless checking up on the progress of the rebuilding.

CHAPTER 68

Au Revoir

The big story of 1998 should have been the reopening of the theatre but for me it was the death of Casper. He was sixty-nine. I had suspected that all was not well with him for some time, but he was a very secretive man, and finally I had to confront him and ask for the truth; there were too many rumours flying about. He had pancreatic cancer, the most hidden form of the disease. By the time it is diagnosed it is too late for a cure.

Judith, the character played by Clare Higgins in *Blood, Black and Gold*, had cancer. Casper had given me an explanation of what cancer meant: when the person ceases to renew himself, the body cells multiply to compensate. That this should happen to Casper was a profound shock to me. He was a man for whom a serene old age, with increasing spiritual wisdom, seemed natural. I knew that was what he was expecting, or at least hoping for.

Shortly after he told me he went with his second wife, Karin, to Finland, ostensibly for a visit but, eventually it became increasingly clear, to die. I spoke to him only by phone; his voice had become like a quavering old woman's. He was less and less the Casper I recognised. Dilys and I wanted to fly to Finland to see him. He refused.

Casper never believed he was appreciated or loved. In a terrible letter he sent me, probably under the influence of morphine for he was in dreadful pain, he revealed the extent not only of his perceived lack of appreciation but also of his bitterness at that lack. It made me weep. I am weeping as I write this.

I had tried so hard to express my love for him and now I tried again. I don't know if he believed me. I also promised that as long as it was in my power I would keep the flame alive at the Exchange.

Casper's death left me professionally, and I suppose spiritually, alone. Since that moment, in some sense I have had no one to talk to. It also left me with the question of why the Exchange seems to give its Artistic Directors such a curtailed existence. It demands complete dedication, which sometimes appears to preclude a proper private life, but when the person realises it the poisoned arrow is so far into him that it is as fatal to pull it out as to leave it in.

As I write this I am sixty-three, near the end of the eighth cycle and soon to begin the one that none of them survived. It is not death I am scared of; it is to maintain personal growth. Michael died at fifty-two, Max at sixty-six and Casper at sixty-nine. They were remarkable men. They were my family.

But Casper had taught me well. At the same time as I was dealing with the shock, I could see that from another point of view his timing was exquisite. He knew his days were over at the Exchange, that he had nothing more to offer. It was time for me to become truly the bridge that Armund had forecast I would be.

CHAPTER 69

The Reopening

I thought I had the renewal of the group well in hand. In 1998 Matthew Lloyd became an Artistic Director and Marianne Elliott an Associate Artistic Director. Matthew seemed to me to be an Artistic Director in the way I was. He too was a wheeler-dealer. Marianne, as well as obviously being a potential star director, had terrific leadership qualities, as her father had had, and she was a woman. I was pleased. I shouldn't have been. I ignored very strong warning signals.

Marianne had assisted Matthew on the Heggie première and she didn't like him. She told me as much. She advised me against the appointment. I did like Matthew. He seemed completely devoted to the company. Like all of us he had personality quirks. He was a very reserved person who went berserk on his opening nights but was otherwise quite difficult to get to know. That didn't worry me. I brushed Marianne's worries aside.

My mistake was not to imagine the group after I stepped back from it. Since, for the group to work everyone had to respect each other, what was the point of going forward with two new people who didn't get on? It was a clumsy move but in these matters I was a beginner. I thought I got on with everyone, Marianne and Greg were very close, and Matthew seemed very committed and did not seem to have problems with anyone.

It was also the year Ken Harvey chose to resign as Chairman, rather precipitately. He was offered a lucrative job down south and went. He thought he knew who his successor should be, a successful accountant, but for me it would have been out of the frying pan into the fire. Paul Lee, the Managing Director of what is now Addleshaw Goddard, a leading law firm, who had chaired our Development (fundraising) Committee, agreed to take over and is still there now. He cares about the work and is as shrewd as they come. We have needed him these past few years.

This was the group that opened both auditoria in December of that year. The build-up was as it was in 1976, exciting and frantic. The architects continued to give us problems.

One example will be enough to show what was happening throughout the whole building. We were back in the theatre and the builders were due to hand over all but the hall on the following Monday. Michael Williams, who had been a superb Project Manager again, came to see me. 'I think you should come and see the dressing-room floor.'

'Why?'

'Just come and see it.'

We went down to the first floor and entered the dressing-room corridor. It looked like a prison block. The corridor was lit by fluorescent lights encased in wire boxing. We proceeded to one of the dressing rooms. 'Go in,' said Michael.

I opened the door but it quickly jammed. 'I can't,' I said.

He squeezed past and I heard him moving things about. 'Come in.' I entered. The rail for hanging costumes was so large it had blocked the door. 'Sit down at a mirror,' he ordered.

I couldn't, the rail was blocking access: 'I can't.' He moved the rail so that it blocked the door again. I sat down.

'Get up carefully,' he advised. I got up and banged my head on the underside of the bunk bed that every actor had. We left the dressing room. 'Now we'll go to the Star dressing room,' he said. The Star dressing room looked like a boiler room. A huge round tube conducting the air-conditioning went along the ceiling and all the pipes for the shower and basin were exposed. The final laughable mistake was that each dressing room was identifiable by its door, red, green, blue etc. The painters had painted the colour on the inside of the door, the outside was a uniform battleship grey. It was a Fawlty Towers of a fiasco. The whole floor had to be redone.

Still, in the end the place looked very well and the opening attended by Prince Edward, our very involved and supportive patron, was a great emotional success. We also had one night when we invited actors, directors, designers, writers, stage management, workshop, wardrobe etc. etc. from our past to come and celebrate with us. It was a terrific event. They had all made the Exchange the success it had been. They were its legacy for the future.

CHAPTER 70

First Year Back

The first year back was a good year for me, but a mixed one for the company. Opening or reopening a theatre puts an onus on the first production. I solved that by starting with *Hindle Wakes*, which had been stopped in its tracks by the IRA. It was a good play for Christmas and pushed all the right emotional buttons with our audience.

The nine plays we presented in 1998 had no fewer than five premières, the nearest we had come to fulfilling our aim of announcing a season of premières. It was a mistake. I had thought, correctly, that our audience would be right behind us when we reopened, so had imagined, wrongly, that this would be the moment to take risks. I encouraged my colleagues to do so.

The trouble was they were the wrong risks. Almost none of them came off. On paper it was an impressive list of authors: Brad Fraser, Peter Barnes, Alex Finlayson (whose play *Winding the Ball* had been a success), Jim Cartwright and finally, not really of the same ilk, a spoof of *Dracula* that Emil Wolk and I were to concoct.

In *Martin Yesterday* Brad censured the irresponsibility of the gay world in an AIDS society; thus he managed to antagonise both the anti-gay and the gay audience. Marianne did a fine production with first-rate actors but the play aroused fury. Pat Weller was phoned by an outraged woman who ranted at her until Pat said, 'I can't talk to you, you're a homophobe.'

'No I'm not,' came the reply. 'I'm married to a man.' This was funny, but the wish that the whole cast might contract AIDS and die was disgusting.

I didn't see Peter Barnes's *Dreaming* as I was in Houston. I hadn't cared for the play much and I gather the production didn't help. Alex Finlayson's *Tobaccoland*, which Trevor starred in, just didn't come off. *Prize Night*, Jim Cartwright's play, was finished very late, so late that Jim had to play the lead. Greg strove valiantly with the unfinished script, and there was just enough of Jim's brilliance to prevent it being a disaster, but it wasn't right.

Thus at a stroke we lost the confidence of our audience for new work, always the most risky side of any company's output. We are gradually recovering it.

The other productions went some way to compensating for the drop at the box office, although Richard Wilson in *Waiting for Godot* failed to fill the theatre. This was odd as Richard was at the height of his fame from *One Foot in the Grave*. On the other hand Marianne did a stylish *Nude with Violin* by Coward starring Derek Griffiths, and indeed Marcia Warren on top form, which pleased the audience, and Tom reinvented *King Lear* in a heart-rending and extraordinary performance. My *Peer Gynt* I'll come to later.

The other disappointment was the studio. It proved to be a terrific space and the visiting companies were an immediate and continuing success. The failure was with our own productions. Matthew, whose particular interest the studio was, had very recherché taste and despite our attempts to persuade him to the contrary our initial production there, which opened on the same day as *Hindle Wakes*, was Kevin Hood's *So Special*. It was the first of several failures and we performed less and less there until the situation was dramatically reversed three years later. In fact, I don't think we really recovered artistic consistency in the main house either for about five years, although there were many fine things that were done during that time.

With hindsight, our artistic output reflected the state of the Artistic Directors, of whom Marianne soon became one. Even with the right group it takes time to adjust to changes in the team; with the wrong one it never happens. This was the wrong one. A successful group, while retaining their ego ambitions, must also be serving something beyond the individual, to which they subscribe with their hearts. I won't say I realised what was going wrong quickly, but eventually I did understand and had to act drastically.

CHAPTER 71

First Ibsen

When my cousin Jaqueline saw my production of *Peer Gynt* what she said was, 'It's your autobiography.' She was right, but it is the autobiography of most men: the love/hate relationship with the mother; the fickle relationships with women, sexually driven; the abandonment of your own soul to pursue power and wealth; and finally facing death and infinity.

It is even longer than *Hamlet* and, unlike *Hamlet*, was not written to be performed. Therefore the director makes up his own version. I worked from Michael Meyer's translation, which had in turn been cut by Michael Elliott for his productions with Leo McKern and Tom. Naturally I was in touch with David during the process.

I had always intended to have Johanna as my designer and Fergus Early as my choreographer, but when the dates were finalised neither was available. Johanna found me a new choreographer. When we were in Richmond Christopher Bruce, he of the Rambert, lived in the next road and we were introduced to his son Mark in his pram. Now Johanna saw Mark's work at The Place. I went, realised this was a highly individual talent, which was exactly what I was looking for, and he came aboard.

There was a young designer apprenticed to the Exchange who seemed to me original and exciting, and I asked him to do it. I think he was paralysed with fear because week after week he would come to my flat with nothing concrete to show me. Eventually I had to jettison him and asked Simon Higlett to save me, which he did. By the time he took over the production was very advanced in my head and in Mark's. Simon therefore worked to a much tighter brief than usual and this probably worked well since the production was so personal.

There was only one actor in the world to play the Button Moulder and to my great delight Espen agreed to double it with the Troll King. John Bennett returned to do the Thin Man and, together with John Ringham, gave the whole thing real weight.

The question was where was I going to find this amazing actress to play all the women and sing like an angel? The very first person to audition for the play in Tottenham Court Road was Josette Bushell-Mingo. I vaguely knew her for her entrepreneurial skills in furthering black artists, but I had never seen her perform. At ten o'clock in the morning she sang the blues and I was knocked sideways. I reminded myself that she was extremely unlikely to be a good actress as well. She was a terrific actress. That evening she met David and agreed to take on the part.

Peer Gynt has a huge cast. Mark wanted a core of his dancers to centre the big set pieces like the Troll scene. He also had the inspired idea of having three birds (dancers) flying above the actors and mirroring Peer's relationship to his soul. He proposed that his troupe audition for me. I decided to risk them playing the small parts. Risk them? They were superb. They were so eager to prove they could act that every nook and cranny of the play came alive.

Thus began another exciting rehearsal period, even more so than *Riddley Walker* or *Hamlet*. There was one black cloud. I had cast a Yugoslavian actress as Peer's mother, Aase. A refugee from the war, she was admired in her own country and seemed to have the emotional equipment for the part. It became clear that she couldn't deliver. This was horrible. The poor woman had suffered enough and she was a friend of David's Yugoslavian wife Brana Bajic, whom he had met doing *Monte Cristo*. Finally I remembered the James Fox débâcle and decided I had to act. After I had done it and told the company, Josette came to me and thanked me on everyone's behalf. 'Now we know how much you care,' she said. Tilly Tremayne answered the bugle call and took over.

I'm not going to detail the production, which we set so that the tricky Peer in middle age act was in modern times, but I'm going to give two examples of how far we went out on a limb.

The Troll scene had the company all dressed in evening dress. There was nothing grotesque about them except that they went about on all fours. What more do you need to say about the celeb society? The madhouse I peopled with a cross-section of the twentieth-century lunatics from Freud, Marx and Einstein, through Tony Blair with Margaret Thatcher's mummy on his back, to Chris Evans. It all worked, as did Casper's idea of the last act taking place after death.

Michael Meyer came to the first preview. I arranged to meet him in the restaurant after I had given the cast notes. I sat down opposite him. He had finished his meal. 'Well?' I asked.

'I'm very disappointed.'

My heart plummeted. 'Why?'

'My steak was very mediocre.' Actually he was delighted. He said it was the best *Peer Gynt* he'd seen, even better than Michael's at the Old Vic. He gave two main reasons: Josette's performance, which made Solveig into a creature of flesh and blood rather than a male fantasy. But the main reason was that David had brought off the three ages of Peer. Leo had been marvellous in middle and old age but not so convincing as the young Peer.

He was right on both counts. Josette's ability to switch between the male black fantasy *Three Degrees*-esque Anitra, to the physical animality of the Troll Princess to the total purity of Solveig was breathtaking. David . . . well all I could say to him on the first night was, 'I don't know where the boundary was between you and me.'

All he could say was, 'Casper was here.'

Peer Gynt received wonderful reviews. It was the third production that I felt I had really pulled off, joining *Hamlet* and *Riddley Walker*. I think it gave me a final boost of confidence as a director. It launched me into the current phase of my directorial career so that I could say that although I could and should do better, I now knew I was a good director. It was the last time David and I worked together.

CHAPTER 72

Houston

After *Peer*, where we had rehearsed for six weeks, three sessions a day from ten in the morning till 8.30 at night, going to Houston to direct the opera seemed like a holiday.

I had prepared very carefully. I couldn't read music, although I could understand a score by listening to it, so Tod had gallantly put down a tape of the opera and I knew every note of it by the time rehearsals started. Of course I was nervous: this was an entirely new world that I knew little of. In the event, Houston was the most benign experience to begin my professional opera career.

David Gockley, the General Director of the opera house, had been there for almost exactly the same period I had been at the Exchange. He was a dedicated man of great commitment who ran a tight ship full of good people there to make it work. The conductor was the newly appointed resident, Patrick Summers, and he was the ideal partner for a rookie director.

If you included the chorus, the company was eighty-five strong and I asked that they attend the first meeting, as in the theatre. This was most unusual, apparently, but David agreed. It was a good move. I gave my spiel and showed them the set. They knew what they were part of. The chorus at Houston is semi-professional. You rehearse them in the evenings and at weekends, and you couldn't have selected a more physically weird set of people to go on the march to Siberia. Nevertheless, they were always willing and in the end were a big part of the production's success.

I found the principals a delight to work with. Joyce DiDonato and Scott Hendricks, who played Katusha and Dmitri, were not long out of the opera school. Scott had replaced the original Dmitri after a fortnight, a well-known singer whom I had been flown to Berlin to meet. Physically he appeared perfect, which was all I was meant to find out. In rehearsals he seemed very weak. I knew I had to suffer him. The singing was primary. Then Patrick Summers came to me and told me he couldn't sing the score either; he would have to be replaced. This time, unlike *The Good Companions*, the conductor did the dirty deed. Scott took over and was terrific. They were anxious to learn about acting and I was happy to teach. Since I had largely written the libretto I rehearsed the text like a play before they sang it. It worked well. Well, usually it did. A great deal of the piece is set in the Siberian prison, where Dmitri and Katusha have intimate scenes surrounded by other prisoners. Naturally I rehearsed them to be as discreet and quiet as possible. We achieved a wonderful, believable atmosphere. Then we had to do it with the music. No possibility of quietness; their voices had to fill a 2,500-seat opera house. We concluded that the other prisoners were probably deaf.

I say it was like a holiday and so it was. After the theatre, directing opera is only half a job. You are not responsible for the rhythms of the performance and there is no elaborate analysis of the text. Emotionally the music tells you everything. More than that you get a lot of time off. Singers have to have purely musical rehearsals and days off in between to preserve their voices. I saw every movie that came to Houston for six weeks and must have eaten at most of the excellent restaurants.

What you don't get as a director is that gradually mounting excitement, culminating in the adrenalin rush when you get into the theatre and everything comes together, as you travel towards the previews and opening night.

Once on to the stage in Houston you hardly get to rehearse at all. It's too expensive. In addition to the company, there is an orchestra to pay. The emphasis is entirely on the music and you sit and fret, especially since there are still the days off.

Getting on stage means a lot of adjusting for the director because it is the first time he can see properly what he is doing. How was I going to put my changes into practice? I had an absolutely terrific assistant called Garnett Bruce. He had saved me from catastrophe endlessly, from advising me how to handle musical situations, helping me rethink what was needed in the libretto so that my rewrites fitted the music to making sure I ate at the right restaurants. 'What do you want doing?' he asked. I took him through my list, which was mainly the chorus on the march to Siberia. 'Leave it to me.'

That night everything was changed exactly as I wanted. I found out how he did it. He stood in the wings and bellowed at them through a megaphone like an RSM. Amazing.

On opening night I was warned that the audience would rush for the exits at the end of the show to get their cars for the often long drive home, but when I went on stage, as one does in opera, for my bow, the house was still full and on its feet, cheering.

Why has *Resurrection* not been done all over the world? Apart from Boston, Tod's home town, no one has put it on. It is a wonderful score. The only criticism I read was in the German press, which found the score and the production too conventional. Utter rubbish! Tod achieved, at the greatest moments in the opera, a lyrical intensity that affected people's hearts. To hell with gratuitous experiment!

I am now working on a new opera with Tod, of David Almond's beautiful novel *Skellig*, which premières at The Sage, Gateshead in 2008. The Houston experience is my paradigm for how to conduct the rehearsal process. I hope we have a conductor as congenial and collaborative as Patrick Summers and that Tod gets the recognition he deserves.

CHAPTER 73

Catching Up

While I was in Houston, Richard Negri died. He at least made it to the ninth cycle, he was seventy-two. I knew him least well so it did not affect me so deeply emotionally, but every time I go into the auditorium to rehearse I bless his name. He has never really had the recognition he was due for that genius of a creation. He also gave me the title for this book. I was doing an all-nighter, lighting a difficult show. It was about three o'clock in the morning. I was sitting there with the lighting designer, exhausted, fraught and dispirited. Richard appeared, looked at us and said, 'Cheer up! The worst it can be is a disaster.' Perfect. I cheered up immediately.

I was now writing *Bats* with Emil and trying to work on two new plays that I was to do the following year. Simon Robson had played Lord Darlington in *Lady Windermere's Fan* and he asked me if I'd read a play he'd written. My heart sank. My life is full of people I know and like, telling me they've written a play. Unexpectedly, I liked *Ghost Train Tattoo*. It was obviously autobiographical and dealt sensitively and interestingly with the growing up of a boy from puberty to adulthood. It was meant to be one of a trilogy. I persuaded him that one play would be enough and began to work on condensing the material.

Sarah Frankcom, who was proving to be a first-class Literary Manager, gave me a play to read called *Snapshots* by Fiona Padfield. This was, like Simon's play, also a time-shift drama about two sisters, their childhood and traumatic adulthood. It dealt especially with giving birth, the possibility of rejecting your own child, marital breakdown at the hands of a sexually preda-tory husband and paedophilia. It was like being introduced to a female world that I didn't know but felt through the power of the writing had to be true.

Fiona had just given birth to her second child, who was suckling at her breast when she came to meet us. I felt we should do the play and Marianne said I should direct it. That terrified me. What did I know of these matters? As so often, terror gave way to intrigue and I arranged to meet her in London next time she came down from her Welsh cottage on a hill, where she lived with her husband, children and goats.

Before I met her, Sarah suggested I read her first play, *Stripper*. It was a powerful, alarming piece about a middle-class young girl who becomes a stripper and forms a dangerous relationship with a punter who is a German masochist. Then Sarah told me that she had given it to me to read because it was autobiographical.

When I talked to Fiona, it was difficult to square her play with her distinctly girls' public school persona. We got on well and she agreed to the rewrites I thought were needed. We got into the habit of meeting whenever she came to London. Like my first wife, she came from Woodbridge in Suffolk. I had been warned.

One other very important thing happened after I came back from America. I went with Pat for a holiday in Turkey, visiting Kalkan and Fethiye, and I fell in love with the country. I felt well there in a way I hadn't for a long time. I investigated building a place out there. It was remarkably cheap and you could pick your spot by the sea, or on a cliff, where you wanted. It seemed an idyllic idea. I decided against it, partly because of the way women were treated in Turkey, partly because of the instability of the government, but mostly because it was just too far away to be practical.

Back in England I was restless. I wanted that sense of well-being. I had always talked with Johanna about one day buying a house in France, which we both loved. Then came our divorce and I waited for someone else to share my life with. I had become more and more accustomed to being alone, and living with someone became less and less of a possibility, and with it the dream of France. Now I thought, 'Do it or you never will.'

In September I went to look at properties in the area I loved, the Midi and south west from Albi to Gascony. Johanna agreed to come over to advise. We spent a week looking all over the area but when I walked into La Fontaine, an old farmhouse in the village of Dunes near Agen, it took me about ten seconds to know that this was it. I told the estate agent I was going back to England and I would be in touch quickly.

I went home and panic set in. Suddenly it seemed a terrifying prospect, taking on a place in a foreign country. I bluffed myself. I phoned and made an offer well below the asking price, for £75,000. I put down the phone, convinced it would be refused. Within five minutes the phone rang. The offer was accepted. I rushed to the bathroom and threw up. It turned out to be a life-saver.

Dunes is a thirteenth-century Bastide village. La Fontaine is about 150 years old, just outside the village, completely secluded and three minutes' walk from the *boulangerie*, two restaurants, the post office and Huit à 8, the mini-market. The interior had been completely modernised in terms of facilities by its owner, an Englishman called Rod Arnold, but preserving the character of the place. It felt benign. I later found that Arnold had sold it at a knock-down price because he knew he was dying and didn't want his wife to inherit it. It's an ill wind . . .

In France buying is easy. You go to the *notaire*, both parties sign, the seller can't back out but the buyer can if he finds out during the searches that someone is going to build a motorway or something nearby. I arranged to come back to take possession in early September after *Bats* had opened.

CHAPTER 74

Absolutely *Bats*

Bats was a *Dracula* spoof in the *Three Musketeers* mould. Emil, as well as writing it with me and staging the physical sequences (which were many and elaborate), played Dracula, and Ben Keaton, so brilliant as Groucho, was equally brilliant as Van Helsing. I'm not going into detail about the show but like the Dumas it had the audience in fits. The physical side was breathtaking, the two leads together were dynamite. Johanna's Gothic killer of a set was brilliant and all in all it seemed very satisfying to me to have started the year with *Peer Gynt* and ended it, via operatic Tolstoy, with the ability to make people just laugh and laugh and laugh.

The week before rehearsals started Fiona phoned me to say she was going to be in London on Saturday. I told her that I was going up to Manchester on Sunday so I'd be in a bit of a flap, but if she didn't mind my cooking rather than a restaurant she was welcome to join me.

We had a pleasant dinner – I think I cooked salmon – after which she suddenly said, 'Will you come over here and kiss me please?' I had never for a moment fancied Fiona. I liked her, I admired her talent and she was a good-looking woman, albeit nearly half my age. I didn't want to hurt her, so I went over to her, gave her an affectionate kiss and rang for a taxi to take her wherever she was staying. She wasn't pleased.

'What would your husband think?' I asked.

'He told me to come down and fuck you,' was her answer. The taxi arrived and I said goodnight.

I started rehearsals and when I was back in my flat one evening she rang. 'You've got nothing to lose. If you don't like it, you can end it,' she said. Something strange happened to my body and it wasn't sexual excitement. I went red-hot from top to toe. It was a sort of excitement that I didn't understand and couldn't control. I said she could come and stay with me next weekend in London. By the way, this wasn't infidelity, I was alone at that moment. It was an 'off' time.

The following weekend I embarked on a crazy affair with Fiona. She came to the play's first night. I went to France to take possession of my house and returned to spend the Millennium night with her. This is how crazy it was. I went down to Wales and stayed in a B&B where she would join me for part of the night. I spent the days with her, sometimes in her house with her flu-ridden husband, who was marginally more unsettling than his fictional counterpart in *Snapshots*, and her two small children. On Millennium night we were in a bed in a friend's cottage with her daughter sleeping between us because at the last moment Fiona wanted her with her. During the weekend, completely bats, I seriously discussed with her setting up home together with her kids.

What had happened to me? I think I know. Deep down I still felt that no woman really wanted me. For someone to state so clearly that she did bypassed all my radar systems and defence mechanisms; I was completely routed. It had happened a couple of times before, in less ultimate circumstances, and on each occasion I was unable to say 'no'. And, equally, on each occasion the relationship didn't last. I was starting the Millennium, agreeing to sell Primrose Hill and take on a new family, a very young family, with the woman whose play I was soon to direct at the Exchange. At one point she brought her children to my not very large flat in Primrose Hill and we somehow existed with each other, knee-deep in nappies, for nearly two weeks.

My parents, my sons, were horrified. As is my wont, this only made me more stubborn, on the outside at least. I put my flat on the market and we started house hunting. Two days of that and I knew it was madness. Fiona was a volatile woman who careened between one view and another. At one moment she liked a house and was furious when I wouldn't commit to it instantly, half an hour later as we drove away she said she could never have lived in it. I said I'd remain her friend but that living together was not going to happen.

This was roughly the status quo when I started rehearsing her play. I was fifty-seven and had acquired a certain veneer of experience, and I was at a good moment as a director. Why is it that what happens to us in our sexual life often seems at odds with what our apparently wise consciousness thinks it wants?

CHAPTER 75

New Work, More Tensions

It was a relief to get back to doing new works and I did three in 2000. There is something particularly exciting for the director and the actors at rehearsals, knowing they are creating their production for the first time. You're not taking on centuries of *Hamlet*s or *Peer Gynt*s. It is a complete voyage of discovery.

I did *Ghost Train Tattoo* and *Snapshots* in repertoire with the same actors and minimalist settings: two for the price of one. Sarah Frankcom, who was obviously an outstanding Literary Manager and was finally establishing our credibility as a new writing centre, had been a director; that is where Jacob spotted her. When we interviewed her for the job, she was quite clear that she had no ambitions to continue down that path. Indeed, we wouldn't have given her the job if she had; it's no fun having a repressed director breathing down your neck. However, I asked her to be my associate on the two plays. We were going to rehearse both at once, three sessions a day, open *Snapshots*, continue rehearsing *Ghost Train* during the day and open it ten days later. I needed help. It was a good move.

Fiona was living with me in my Manchester flat when we started rehearsals. I like the author to be around while we go through the play for the first time, then go away until the run-through stage. Fiona, giving readings of the parts, was quite terrifying. The ferocity of the emotions was so intense that it was as if a dybbuk had taken her over. There was no dividing line between her supposedly fictional play and her traumatic life.

Snapshots centred on three people, the two sisters played by Amy Marston and Jessica Lloyd, and their gardener (a version of Fiona's brother), played by Terry Wilton, who was fast competing with Colin Prockter for the most times worked with Braham Murray medal, and the husband played by Richard Lynch. For *Ghost Train* they were joined by my son Joe playing the Simon Robson role, Gaby Drake amazing everyone with a wonderfully lower-middle-class performance as the second wife, and for the first time I worked with Joanna David who played the first wife-mother. They were all terrific and, despite the gruelling hours, we were a great team.

Snapshots opened first to a critical reception rather like the one David Beckham received when he was sent off against Argentina. There was real hatred in some of the attacks, the glaring exception being Lynne Walker in the *Independent*.

We knew the play wasn't a laugh-a-minute crowd pleaser, but we were stunned. Our morale was saved by a significant minority of the audience, who wrote in to express a profound appreciation of the fearlessness of the play in addressing issues of motherhood and sibling rivalry that were taboo to so many. These were professional women – nurses, doctors and therapists – who were grateful to Fiona.

By this time Fiona and I had parted. My White Knight capacity had exhausted itself. The evenings between rehearsals were precious for recuperation and not a time for reliving the play almost literally, because she was still wrestling with both her sister and her husband. Fiona may be fragile in some ways but she's as tough as they come in others. As a mother she's like a lioness with her cubs and she took the critical onslaught on the chin. Having experienced my own form of being roasted several times, I was desperate that this wouldn't stop her from writing. It hasn't and one day when she stops writing about herself so directly her talent will express itself properly.

Ghost Train had a much kinder reception but in truth these two plays did little to restore our audience's confidence in our new work.

The company was still very uneven in achievement. Marianne's production of *A Woman of No Importance* was the high spot of the spring–summer season; Matthew's *The Way of the World* the low spot.

The Congreve is a fiendishly difficult play to pull off. It is High Restoration with its extreme complexity and sophistication of language, and it requires about ten top actors at the top of their form. I warned against it but Matthew was an Artistic Director and had carte blanche. It didn't come off.

I was now seriously worried that this new group wasn't working and I talked to Paul, our Chairman, about my reservations over Matthew. The group have to like each other and this one didn't, and each person has to appreciate everyone else's artistic talent, even if they have some inevitable reservations. There was undoubtedly a problem now with Matthew.

– ii –

I went to France that summer for the first time and just before I left Michael Meyer died. I didn't know Fred Astaire but when he died I felt as though something very important had left the world. I felt the same about Michael and so did many, many people. He had been a true friend. I don't know how I would categorise my relationship with the other Michael, Casper and Max, but neither friend nor colleague captures it. Michael was a friend, a person who sustains you through his affection and warmth, a person who you can always turn to and perhaps most of all a person who will put up with you no matter what. I spent the first days in France writing his obituary for the *Guardian*.

La Fontaine became immediately like another person in my life. It has taken me all of six years to form a proper relationship with it. Each year I would get ill there with vertigo or gout or swallowing disorders, and I blamed it on La Fontaine. Two years ago I came very near to selling it. Then it became clear that it was I who was at fault. The driven lunatic, which I still in some measure was and probably still am, couldn't cope with the peace and rhythms of nature. There was a terrible jarring. I realise now that the hidden purpose of La Fontaine is to help me through this transition into the ninth cycle, to bid farewell to certain energies and encourage other ones, which I hope will be equally creative.

Anyway, France fits into this chapter on new work. Every August, Dunes is en fête for four or five days, there are sideshows and dances and firework displays, and markets of local produce, and there is a fête champêtre where the whole village sits down together and for a ridiculously small price eats and drinks itself, with an innocence I doubt could happen in England, into gentle oblivion.

The Mayor, Monsieur Astruc, asked me how I had enjoyed the fête. I told him I had loved the meal but not much of the rest of it. He should have a show, I suggested, which could be performed in the village square on the temporary stage that served for the dance band. Might I think of something? I would try.

I had worked with Derek Griffiths now for over twenty-five years and I had mentioned to him that I had bought a house in France and he'd be welcome to visit. Although we were very close creative colleagues, I hardly knew him at all privately and I was amazed when he phoned and said he'd like to come out. I was rather worried about what we'd find to talk about, but pleased because I'd come with Johanna and when she went I had my only panic attack ever in the supermarket Géant. What was I doing here on my own?

Derek arrived and was captivated, as all my visitors are, by Géant the supermarket. No one seems inclined to visit the thankfully few Michelin-starred sights when they come here, they all want to visit the Aladdin's cave that is Géant. Anyhow we got on very well. Then one day he asked me if I had read *The Celestine Prophecy*. I told him I had and it was a load of rubbish. He seemed relieved. Then he asked me if I knew of a book called *Seth Speaks*. Indeed, I had a copy. It was the creator of *Dr Heart*, Peter Mueller, who had introduced me to it as one of his central inspirations for the show. It is, to put it simply, a book inspired by the spirit world. Derek was amazed that I knew it. It transpired that he had psychic gifts, had explored his past lives and was fascinated by the whole area. He had never talked to anyone about it for fear of ridicule. I had known him for years and hadn't been aware of any of this. He had known me for years and knew nothing of my interest in the 'other world', nor the connection of Armund, Casper, Michael and Max to esoteric matters. Suddenly a twenty-five-year relationship moved to a different level. A couple of years later he bought the field next to me; building is due to start some time in 2007.

I suggested to him that we might get a show together for the fête in the following year. Long ago he had a run-in with my old friend Julian Chagrin. Julian had accused him of pinching material from the one-man show we had devised together, *One Is One*. I had always told Derek that the two of them would get on. Derek also had a one-man show; what about getting Julian over and concocting something between them? Both shows relied heavily on mime, which would be ideal.

Julian was now living in Israel. In the mid-seventies his first wife, Claude Chagrin the choreographer, who had done the movement for, among other things, *The Royal Hunt of the Sun*, had divined that the world was about to be hit by earthquakes, floods and other natural catastrophes. The only unaffected place would be Christ's birthplace. They sold up and ended up in a caravan in Bethlehem with their three children. Fortunately for Julian, she soon left him but he had remained in Israel and married again, a Jewish version of Claude, Rolanda. I always regarded this as a tragedy. Julian was, rather like Emil, a comic genius who should have stayed in England. I had visited him about five years previously. He too was immersed in esoteric things and introduced me to the Five Tibetan Rites, which I have done practically every day since. Julian and Derek together was an irresistible idea. I contacted him. He agreed, if the village council would pay his air fare. He hadn't any money. They did and we were set to go.

There was one other new work in Dunes, not theatre but another of my loves: food and wine. The south west is full of marvellous restaurants at ludicrously low prices which, for all the blather about food in the English press, make London look ridiculous. The French office of the Royal Exchange was quickly established at L'Auberge en Gascogne in Astaffort, which boasts a chef, Fabrice Biasiolo, of striking originality to equal anyone anywhere. However, I was to achieve a greater intimacy with restaurants than being a mere food critic.

When I had moved into La Fontaine the previous winter, it was filthy and the previous owner sent round two women to clean it. They arrived like the SAS and attacked the house. It took them two days to erase the past.

There was a cheap restaurant in the village called La Gousse d'Ail (The Clove of Garlic), which I visited for lunch. It wasn't a very good lunch but for ten francs you got four courses, wine and coffee *service compris*. On the second day one of the women, Muriel Lellouche, said that they had brought lunch with them, and I'd be welcome to stay and share it. I opened some wine and we talked for hours. She and Monique were a great couple. Monique was thin, dark and rather beautiful; Muriel was somewhat plumper, a bundle of energy with a mordant wit and infectious enthusiasm. I was in the middle of my Fiona time and we discussed marriage (Muriel was divorced), sex, children, life, the universe; it was great. Muriel agreed to become my cleaner. She needed the work to support her daughter Julie.

When Derek arrived the next summer, we went up to have lunch at the restaurant but it was closed. Next time Muriel came round we told her. The time after that she announced she was going to buy it. It turned out that her ex-husband was a restaurateur and she had been in the business for years. We asked how much it would cost and were told that, including the flat above where Muriel and Julie would live, it would cost £15,000. After Muriel had gone, Derek and I looked at each other and agreed. The next time Muriel appeared, we said that if she had difficulty raising the money we would put up £5,000 each. She thanked us.

That was in the first part of the summer. I had to go back to England and while I was there I phoned her to make sure that all was well with La Fontaine. I asked her how the restaurant was going. It wasn't. The bank had only been prepared to lend her £5,000. Why hadn't she told us? Because she hadn't taken the offer seriously.

Within the hour Derek and I transferred the money to her account and La Goulue opened later that year. We owned a restaurant. La Goulue was inspired by the Toulouse-Lautrec painting; the word means 'the gobbler' with the rude connotations of one who gives oral sex, quite in keeping with Muriel's sense of humour.

Suddenly I was part of the village. That was the other side of Dunes; it took me out of the enclosed world of the theatre and back into the real world. I made other friends, steering well clear of the English who seemed devoted to not belonging and not learning the language. There was Jean-Luc Bouin, the builder, who lived with Muriel and is now with Mireille; Josè Hermoso, ex-marine, gunrunner and jailbird, but with a big heart, on whom I modelled Iago later; and Monsieur and Madame Gomez, who look after my house and garden. They all became friends. Going back to Dunes each time is like turning on *The Archers* again, except with a more international cast list. My kitchen became a therapist's couch as I caught up with who was living with whom or who wasn't living with whom. I can't imagine the equivalent happening in England. The hermetically sealed enclosure of the theatre world was broken, although naturally it fed it. My life was acquiring another dimension. I had not realised how desperately I needed it.

– iii –

When you commission Brad to write a new play, in the contract you have to agree to workshop it first. I had never done this. I was suspicious of workshops. What did writers do before this modern invention? Still, I had to, and Brad came over for it.

Snake, as Brad had promised, was about twenty-somethings. It involved a snake who ate people, a body-building fanatic who killed people, a stripper and her sister who was mentally retarded, only wasn't, and a young man who got himself involved in the web-cam end of the porn industry and who was two-timing his innocent Chinese girlfriend to give under-the-table fellatio to his lady boss. That's just a taster. I thought it was brilliant. What Brad does is to take the things bottled up in all of us and externalise them in a vivid, heightened way, always laced with humour, nudity (although not so much here) and a very poetically rhythmic way with swear words. Released by Katherine and stoked up by Fiona, this was just where I needed to be.

The workshop was due to last a week, culminating in a public reading on the Saturday night. Halfway through the week, Brad announced that he would like the cast to read the play once with Manchester accents. I was bemused. Brad's style is very quick-fire North American dialogue, nothing akin to the rather more stolid, flat Manchester accent. However, we did and awful it was. He then announced that that was the way he wanted it done. I reeled.

It appeared that he wanted to invent a language that was universal. He had been intrigued by seeing *Unidentified* in various different countries and how the actors had grappled with the North American dialogue. I thought he'd gone off his rocker and told him so. I insisted the public reading would be done Canadian and he allowed it. The reading was a success and Brad had got what he needed from the week. Indeed, he was brilliant at using the workshop to rewrite. I had to respect his method. Off he went, back to Toronto.

A second workshop took place at CanStage in Toronto. Brad's agent had seen Marianne's *Martin Yesterday*, thought it outstanding and brokered a link between CanStage, which is Canada's nearest equivalent to a national theatre, and the Exchange. We agreed to co-commission six writers, three from each country. Brad was one of the Canadians. I went over to watch the workshop, which was taken by Brad.

The workshop done, I was due to go back to England to start casting and designing the production. Then Brad told me he hadn't changed his mind; he wanted the show done in a Manchester accent. I said I wasn't prepared to do that. He said then I wasn't the right director for the show.

I got back to England and was phoned by his agent to be told that Brad would withdraw the show. I told him that we had commissioned and paid for it, and we would go ahead. He had no right to change the show that we had accepted in good faith.

A few days later Brad called me or wrote to me, I don't remember which, to say that he had talked to friends of his, whose advice he respected, and they had all told him he was wrong. He apologised unreservedly. Phew! This was a pattern that would repeat itself during our friendship, which remains miraculously intact.

Not only were there more swear words per square foot than I had ever heard in a play, but there were more scenes too: eighty-five in a two-hour play. We were in the round, remember. The script, which Brad had written specifically for our theatre, called for a three-storey house with basement and attic. Outside that it asked for a strip club, a diner, an office, a park, a restaurant, the alley outside and a functioning lavatory. Johanna's set was miraculous. The brief was, as usual with Brad, that there couldn't be a split second between scenes; as in Shakespeare, the last line of one scene was followed by the first line of the next. Johanna designed one of those sets that a director simply had to put the actors on and it took care of them. Things flew up and down, were lit through, rose electronically, all without distracting for a second from the play. It was a tour de force. The company was pretty nigh faultless. Brad, thank God, was thrilled. He usually directed his plays himself, but he was very pleased; so was the audience.

The play has been done only twice since, once in San Francisco and once in New York, off-Broadway. The director of the San Francisco production came to see it at the Exchange. Apparently he asked in horror, 'Doesn't Brad

Fraser mind all those laughs?' The New York production, according to Brad, was a disaster. It's never been done in Canada. I'm fond of Marty Bragg who runs CanStage but they didn't even send someone over to see it. *Snake in Fridge* is a terrific play. We can't afford to waste terrific plays.

CHAPTER 76

Upheavals

– i –

Matters with the group were now at crisis point. Matthew was a good director, but he was probably in the wrong place and his next production was no improvement on *The Way of the World*. We met to plan the spring–summer season of 2001 and it was a difficult meeting. Matthew was playing the carte blanche card strongly. He wanted to do *A Moon for the Misbegotten* and a Feydeau. *A Moon for the Misbegotten* Greg and I had always wanted to do and Feydeau, after what we had thought were inadequate comedy productions, didn't seem a good idea. However, both projects were perfectly good programming and no one wanted to provoke a crisis. Everyone stayed silent and the season was fixed.

The three of us hadn't really talked of our feelings about Matthew and I decided we had to. We were in the middle of what was for the most part a mediocre season, which was by no means only down to Matthew, and I thought we couldn't let things drift.

I was worried beyond that. Marianne's attitude to the company was ambivalent. She knew what it was all about – how could she not, being Michael's daughter? – but she had always regarded it with some suspicion because of how it had come between her and her father as a child. There was no cohesion among us.

Casper had told me that it was crucial to bring in Jacob, my son. He had formed a close relationship with him and insisted that he was a key to the future. I told Casper that was something I simply couldn't do. Casper saw that and said it would have to wait until I left the company but that it would have to happen. At that time we both thought my stepping down was in the near future.

I now realised what Casper had meant. Jacob had been weaned on the Exchange and his connection to it was direct and pure. At this time the company had need of that quality. Jacob had been a professional director for seven years at Ipswich, Chichester and Nottingham, as well as running his own fringe company, State of Unrest. I decided to bring him in. He had no idea that I was thinking on these lines. It was a difficult decision and I knew it would be a controversial one. He was to start in October 2001, also on the Michael Elliott bursary; in fact, he was the last recipient before the money ran out.

The three of us felt that *A Moon for the Misbegotten* was an underpowered event and in one crucial case miscast. The decision was taken among us that Matthew must go. We had to wait until the Feydeau – which was, bizarrely, my translation of *Le Dindon*, titled *The Fall Guy* – opened.

The Feydeau didn't work either; in fact, after watching the run-through and the first preview, I even thought I might have to take it over but there were enough good performers for me to think that would cause even more trouble.

I had to talk to Matthew by myself, as Greg and Marianne couldn't face it. Indeed, they left the theatre and switched off their mobiles, not something I greatly appreciated. I tried to make the meeting as easy for Matthew as possible. I genuinely liked him and knew how much it would hurt. I told him the truth. The group wasn't working and he seemed to be the odd one out. There was no shame in it. He could resign, saying how much he had enjoyed the five years but that he hoped now to run his own organisation. He wouldn't have it. He insisted he'd been sacked and that was what the world should know. He was very courteous, shook my hand, wished me good luck and went. Why am I recounting all this? The next week he had a meeting with our Chairman to finalise the notice. We were all on the same contract, which was a rolling one, with a get-out clause of one year on either side, so his would be a generous settlement.

He told Paul Lee that I had got rid of him in order to get Jacob into the company and he would go public with that story unless his payment was substantially increased. Since I had been talking to Paul about the group situation vis-à-vis Matthew for two years, and as Jacob was already joining the group anyway, Paul knew this was rubbish and dismissed the threat. That is why I have told the story in detail; it was a pernicious slur with not an iota of truth in it.

– ii –

The next upheaval was around David Threlfall. He had been appointed an Associate Artistic Director in 1998. I thought he could fulfil the same contribution that Max had made as a representative of actors among us. Again, it was not a popular appointment with Greg or Marianne, but I was trying to re-create the group in its old image. This was, of course, wrong. The whole point of a new group is that it would be different from the first one, which in any case couldn't be reproduced, and carry things into a different sphere.

The autumn–winter of 2001 was our twenty-fifth anniversary season and I wanted to use it to bring back some of our stars to re-establish our profile and improve the box office. After months of sweat and tears, we set up a formidable series of productions. Tom would play Prospero for Greg, I would direct Amanda Donohoe in *Hedda Gabler* and Pat Routledge in *Time and the Conways*, and Greg would round things off with Pete Postlethwaite in *The Homecoming*.

Tom phoned me to say that he really didn't want to do Prospero so soon after Lear, but he did want to celebrate twenty-five years, so would I do *Uncle Vanya* again and might David do Astrov this time, as he had hoped to on Broadway? I always felt that Tom should repeat his wonderful performance and I agreed, adding that David's wife, Brana, would make a perfect Yelena. I phoned David, he agreed and began to make arrangements to move his young family up to Manchester for the duration of the engagement.

I then came to my senses and realised that three big shows on the trot, besides looking like megalomania, would just about do for me. I asked the chaps if they'd be prepared to do the play with Greg if he agreed. They said yes, Greg said yes and we were all set.

I will try to describe what happened next as dispassionately as I can. David phoned me to say that he was going, the next week, to do a pilot for CBS. He then informed me that he had to sign a contract committing himself to the whole series if the pilot was a success. This would mean a complete clash with *Uncle Vanya*. David's agent had agreed his contract with us and I pleaded with him not to sign with CBS. He had already signed. He had not told his English agent about it, but had done it through his American agent.

I was deeply upset. Not only was he an Associate Artistic Director of the company, but he was a close personal friend and creative colleague. He was doing it for his family was his explanation. I was furious and hurt.

I handed the matter over to Greg and Tom. David wanted them to wait until after the pilot before they looked for anyone else. If only he had asked Tom before signing, I suspect Tom would have said yes, since very few pilots get made into series. In the event, both of them were understandably upset and decided to recast immediately. Furthermore, neither of them knew Brana and they didn't want the wife of the actor who had insulted them in rehearsal. She was not under contract yet. I had nothing to do with that decision. If it had been me, because I had worked with and was fond of Brana, I might have done differently, but if I had been Greg or Tom I can't honestly say I would have.

Thus ended my relationship with David. He resigned from the company, blamed me entirely and cut himself off. I have tried everything to effect a reconciliation, it seems such a criminal waste. When, by coincidence, he was playing Skellig at the Young Vic, just as I was starting to work on the opera version with Tod Machover, I ambushed him in the bar. We had dinner in Manchester while he was filming *Shameless*. He wouldn't give an inch. I was one hundred per cent to blame, he not at all. He would never appear at the Royal Exchange again. He must know that he precipitated the entire fiasco and he had been told by enough people that I had nothing to do with the dropping of Brana. I suppose he is in denial. I am far too fond of him as a person, and admire him too much as an actor, not to keep my hand out to him whenever he wants to take it.

— iii —

Derek Griffiths had played Truscott for me in my second production of *Loot* with a stunning, sexy, witty performance from Gaby Drake as Nurse McMahon, so when Julian Chagrin arrived in Dunes to start rehearsals for our show at the village fête there were two Truscotts at La Fontaine.

We had a hysterical week of rehearsals. Laughter is a great tonic and boy, did I need to laugh after the Matthew–David sagas. Away from rehearsals was as funny or even funnier. Derek seems always to like to reduce anybody from a lord to a road sweeper to the same level, quite a low one. So it was that three reasonably intelligent, mature men in their late fifties walked back from rehearsals one night indulging in a farting competition. Don't ask me how he does it and don't ask me who won. As I predicted, Derek and Julian did get on well and the whole preparation was a delight.

Dunes had never done anything like this before and no one had any idea if there would be an audience. The Mayor had arranged a newspaper article in *La Dépêche du Midi*, but that was about it. The show was due to start at 9 p.m. There was hardly anyone there. I went behind the stage and told the chaps that we didn't have much of an audience, so do your best and we'll have a good meal afterwards at our restaurant La Goulue. At 9.10 people started coming into the square from all four corners. It was one of the most exciting sights I have witnessed, rivalling the first night of *The Black Mikado*. Suddenly there weren't enough seats. The Mayor panicked. Minions ran about finding more chairs. The Mayor was delighted. They came from nearby villages, they came down the motorway from Toulouse, goodness knows where they came from. Eventually in our little village square there were over 300 people.

It was an evening of pure unadulterated magic. It was the real roots of the theatre and I'm not being sentimental. It took me back to Century Theatre and *Hamlet* in Newbiggin-by-the-Sea. There were people – mostly there were people – who had never been to a theatre in their lives and they loved it. Derek and Julian are two very special performers and you could see them react to their audience. It was the kind of laughter you'd kill to hear in any performance.

Afterwards, as we sat out on the terrace of La Goulue, we all agreed that it was as fine a night as any of us had experienced in our careers.

CHAPTER 77

Twenty-fifth Anniversary

The IRA had deprived us of a twentieth anniversary, the twenty-fifth anniversary season did its job. Of course, I thought Tom's *Vanya* had been better in New York – I would, wouldn't I. The mannerisms were creeping back, but it still had that soulful essence and Robert Glenister's Astrov was superb. My two shows were, for different reasons, traumatic.

There had been trouble getting the rights for *Time and the Conways*. Jude Kelly, who was doing a Priestley fest at West Yorkshire, gratuitously blocked our production on the grounds that it would clash with hers of *Johnson over Jordan* with Patrick Stewart. This was nonsense. By the time our Priestley opened at Christmas, *Johnson over Jordan* would have finished its run at West Yorkshire and if it got a transfer would be well established in London. I was later told by a senior member of staff in Leeds that in spite of all her protestations of innocence, it had been sheer bloody-mindedness. Anyway, Pat Routledge's agent (not yet mine), Penny Wesson, went direct to Tom Priestley. He was persuaded and all was well.

That is until, as I was about to start rehearsing *Hedda*, Pat became ill and had to withdraw. I immediately turned to Gaby, who agreed to do it. That was a relief. I could concentrate on *Hedda*.

Here is an extraordinary story that came out of auditions. The next person to audition was for the part of the old nurse, Berte. The actress's name was Eileen Essel but in walked Gerry's wife Eileen McLarnon. I gaped. This was the story.

Before Eileen married Gerry she was an actress. She gave up acting to teach, in order to support Gerry in his writing. I knew her as a delightful hostess, and devoted mother and wife. It can't have been easy. Gerry was married to his work, obsessively so. Gerry had died peacefully, thank goodness, at a ripe old age a few years ago. Eileen's son Fergus was an actor. He was in a play-reading and one of the actresses had to drop out. He asked his mother to step in and save the day. She was reluctant; she hadn't acted for over fifty years, she was in her eighties. Eventually she agreed and the reading took place. Afterwards an agent approached her and asked who

285

represented her. He took her on and she immediately got a job in the Ali G movie. Now here she was to audition. She was terrific and I cast her. There's more.

In the last week of rehearsal our casting department received a call from Hollywood. They wanted Eileen to fly over to screen-test for a film with Adam Sadler and Drew Barrymore. We were coming up to opening and I refused. They sent a camera team to the theatre. She got the job. She's hardly been out of work since, on television and the movies (she's in *The Producers*). If ever anyone got a just reward for genuine selflessness it is Eileen. She was terrific in *Hedda*. The only problem I had with her was getting her to act old.

Rather as with *Miss Julie*, I had always said I'd never direct *Hedda*. It seemed to me of all Ibsen's oeuvre the most poisoned play. However, Amanda was ideal casting. What was exhilarating about rehearsals was that I discovered that Ibsen's exploration of the darkest sides of the relationship between men and women was so extraordinary that it validated the play. And, more than that, Hedda's suicide, which I could bring on stage in the round, became a triumphant self-sacrifice leaving Tesman and Miss Elvsted a future. The poison was drawn.

Rehearsals were not easy. Amanda was filming in the States and they overran. She arrived late and totally unprepared. Hedda is hardly ever off stage. It is a gruelling part to learn and to rehearse. Amanda, who I knew was highly strung, threatened to crack under the strain and we got to opening night by the skin of our teeth.

She was superb, quite magnificent. She is very beautiful and highly intelligent, and probably a little self-destructive. You knew completely why no man could resist her and she drew you remorselessly into her inner hell. You could feel the Trolls in her. So you could in Terry Wilton's terrifying Judge Brack; this was one of the most outstanding performances he had given for me. It was a grade A cast. It was a pleasure to work with Avril Elgar again and Jim Clyde, and Kate Islett as Mrs Elvsted, and especially with Simon Robson who created a Tesman who was not a cretin but simply a blinkered, rather brilliant academic. Alas, it was to be the last time I would work with Amanda.

Hedda had been very tiring. As a director, the by-product of rehearsals is that you are continually in therapy. The subject matter of every play awakens processes in you which invade you in very secret places. I went into rehearsals for *Time and the Conways* with scarcely a pause.

Fortunately I knew the play well and I had a great cast with no weak links whatsoever. I had now worked with Gaby so often that I knew how versatile she was, but could she play the old Mrs Conway? She could do the young one standing on her head. When we came to rehearse the second act she asked me how to approach it. I told her she just had to jump. It was going to be an extreme character performance and there was no way she could gently stalk it. There and then she jumped and this crabbed, arthritic monster appeared in the rehearsal room from nowhere. She never ceases to amaze me.

There had been one serious weakness in the previous production. Kay and Alan are the spiritual centre of the play. Chris Gable had been exactly right but our Kay had been disappointing. Sarah Kirkman had played small parts at the Exchange. In *Lady Windermere's Fan* she had understudied the lovely Rebecca Johnson as Lady Windermere; I had seen the understudy rehearsal and couldn't fail to be bewitched by her soulfulness. Her Kay was very special for she is a special actress. I fear her qualities are not fashionable but there must be other parts like Kay that are just waiting for her. At any rate she and Laurence Mitchell cast a magic spell together. It is Priestley at his most sublime and they brought it off.

I was done in more senses than one and Greg finished the autumn–winter season with *The Homecoming*, or the Pete Postlethwaite play as people called it at the box office. It was a sell-out, as was most of the season.

CHAPTER 78

A Last Upheaval (So Far)

The anniversary season was a distraction from the progress of the group and the company. Even before Matthew went there had been an important casualty: our PA, Angela Mitchell. She had gone because of the divisiveness among the Artistic Directors, in her words 'playing one off against the other'. It was a serious casualty because she was an excellent PA and that role is crucial in a group company. The only good news was that her successor, Jayne Fenwick-White, turned out to be the nonpareil.

Matthew's departure and Jacob's unconnected arrival in the autumn changed the artistic dynamics, it seemed for the better. The season to begin 2002 had already been chosen and once again it veered from the pretty good, with Lucy Bailey's conceptually if not thespianly exciting *Dream* and Helena Kaut-Howson's *Marriage of Figaro* (in the Murray–Cogo-Fawcett translation) to Marianne's pretty awful *Design for Living*. She was meant to be doing Debbie Horsfield's musical version of *Sex, Chips & Rock 'n' Roll*, but the music was both alarmingly incomplete and alarmingly inadequate, so it was postponed.

We knew we had to find a new way forward. My alarm bells had gone off when my, I think, good production of *Loot* with Derek and Gaby, who were Exchange favourites, failed to do the business. The problem seemed to be that we had two audiences: the conservative, classical one and the adventurous, new play one. How could we address this difficulty?

The new dynamic of the group seemed positive. Marianne and Greg, who had co-directed an excellent production of Lorraine Hansberry's *Les Blancs*, had a close relationship, as did Sarah and Jacob. These two now took responsibility for the studio, which had become almost non-existent in terms of Exchange productions. Following her excellent work with me on the double-header, Sarah had directed *Still Time* by Stephanie McKnight in the studio, and it became clear that we might have a special director on our hands.

The idea we came up with was to cross-theme the studio and main house. The first season in the autumn of 2002 illustrates what I mean. In the studio there were two plays about contemporary South Africa, and to complement them in the main house I surprisingly found myself doing *Othello*. Following that in the main house, Marianne would direct the première of Simon Stephens's *Port*, about Stockport, while in the studio Sarah would direct the first of our CanStage co-commissions, *Habitat* by Judith Thompson, both about the rites of passage of young women. It caught the audience's imagination and the upturn in attendance figures and in crossover bookings was encouraging.

Then Marianne announced that she had been offered a job as an Associate Artistic Director at the Royal Court and was thinking of taking it. At the time I was devastated. We were just beginning to make some headway after Matthew's departure and now it was going to go for nothing. I should have seen it for what it was: a clear indication that the Exchange had no real importance for Marianne. I didn't realise it and instead, with my heart in my mouth, I offered to resign immediately if Marianne would stay and run the company with Greg. After several days she decided she would leave, called a company meeting to tell them she was going because she didn't want the responsibility of being an Artistic Director, but wished to concentrate on directing, and shortly afterwards went.

Now I was used with Adrian, Nick, Phyllida and indeed James Macdonald to people moving on. I had no objection to Marianne going, although I was disappointed, but the manner of her going was deeply upsetting. As I have said, artistic directors have rolling contracts with a year's get-out clause on both sides. This is to protect the director from being suddenly thrown on the streets and the company from the disruption of a director's departure. Without even asking, Marianne simply went. It was ruthlessness worthy of her father.

Her explanation to the company probably was a partial truth and her husband was an actor living in London, but I think the real truth is that she is very ambitious. There is nothing wrong with that but I suspect that her inheritance is not so easily ducked. There may be another page to be written.

She also seemed to have chosen a very damaging moment. The Arts Council was about to do their five-yearly in-depth appraisal of the company, and now we were back to a duopoly. At least her last production, *Port*, was her at her best. She is a major talent.

Encouragingly, Sarah and Jacob had done excellent work in the studio, as had a new director found by Jacob called Michael Buffong with his production of Aubrey Sekhabi's *On My Birthday*. The other play of the season I shall say something about was my *Othello*.

*

I hadn't done a Shakespeare since *The Tempest* six years earlier and I certainly didn't expect to do *Othello*. I loved the play but I had wanted to do it in negative, that is to say a white Othello and the rest of the company black. Every version I had seen of the play made Othello seem a bit gullible and stupid, a blundering black man for whom you could feel sorry but not much more. I felt that by putting the audience in Othello's position they would see what it was like to be a minority of one racially. I had nearly done it with Trevor Peacock as Othello and Hugh Quarshie as Iago, but Hugh backed out thinking it would send a dubious message racially. Years after that Jude Kelly did such a production in Washington. *Othello* was off my list.

Then I saw Paterson Joseph in *Les Blancs* and knew that this was a real Othello. His performance in *Les Blancs* was one of the finest the Exchange had seen. I put it to him over lunch that he should play the Moor. He was dubious, for my very own reasons. He was also, like a lot of black actors, fed up with the fact that after years of white actors blacking-up, now *Othello* was the only major Shakespeare black actors got to do. However, I persuaded him.

I also persuaded Andy Serkis to play Iago, and for the first time I can remember there were a great Iago and a great Othello on stage in the same production. Additionally I had the bonus of tempting Lorraine Ashbourne, Andy's wife, to play Emilia. I had always thought Lorraine was going to be my leading actress for years but instead she had babies, which I suppose is reasonable.

There's not much to say about the production. *Othello* stands or falls by the acting, and Andy and Patterson were outstanding. It joined *Hamlet*, *Riddley Walker* and *Peer Gynt* in my personal *Brand* category, until disaster struck. Like David Threlfall before him, Andy was laid low by a bad back and missed the last three weeks of the run.

The first night he was off, Patterson came to me and asked me to go on. He argued that I knew the dynamic of the performance better than a young cover could. I agreed. It was a horrible experience. Apart from the fact that my playing the part gave a whole new meaning to Othello's 'Ancient', I just didn't have the vocal technique to carry it. I knew it the moment I opened my mouth. It is one of the longest roles in Shakespeare and is played, especially in my production, at an incredible pitch of intensity. When Iago said at the end of the evening 'From this time forth I never will speak word' there never was such a relieved actor. Coming off stage, I immediately told Patterson that if Andy wasn't back the next night the cover was going on. I wasn't up to it. He didn't come back; day by day we hoped he would but he didn't. We were desolate. The houses were packed but the heart had been ripped out of the production.

There was one other bright spot: as a parting gift Marianne had chosen an assistant director for the year, Jo Combes. She was my assistant on *Othello* and she was excellent. Indeed, it was she who rehearsed me the day I went on. It was a good leaving present.

CHAPTER 79

Appraisal

I have not written much about the Arts Council because I have thought it too arcane for the layman. Let me confine myself to saying I am one hundred per cent for its retention. There has to be a buffer between the government and artists. In this philistine country no government really cares for the arts, so artists need a champion. The Arts Council must perform that role.

As a body, it doesn't like me very much. The arts in this country are pathetically underfunded, as if no government understood their medicinal and educative potential, and I have always campaigned for more, more, more, and sometimes very publicly. I, on the other hand, have generally been lucky with the individual officers assigned to the Exchange, both at the metropolitan and the local level. From Ruth Mackenzie and Charles Hart in the early days to Patrick Gilchrist, Keith Halsall, Ian Tabbron, Nicola Thorold and Michael Eakin more recently, they have been genuinely supportive and understanding. I suspect they are as suspicious as I am of the inevitable bureaucracy that constrains them.

This is by way of introduction to the important appraisal we were now to face. These take place roughly every five years and are conducted by Arts Council officers and a peer group from the profession.

Ours seemed to have three sides to it. There was genuine praise for the achievements of the company, both in its artistic output and the way it was run. On the other hand, Matthew had done his best to poison the team against me with his charge of nepotism. This threatened to dominate the proceedings. My point was, and is, simple. Nepotism is not in itself good or bad. It is only bad if the appointment is undeserved. If it is made on merit, what can there be against it? Further, in this case it was made by four people including Matthew. Fortunately the proof of the pudding is in the eating. Sarah and Jacob had turned round the fortunes of the studio in one season and have made it into a great success story. They are both now directing with considerable success in the main house.

It was the third aspect of the appraisal that was most worrying, what the

Arts Council called 'the succession'. It was common knowledge that I wanted to step back from my responsibilities administratively. They were far less than they had been as Pat Weller, the first Executive Director I had ever completely trusted, had taken over huge areas from me, but it was true that for several years the buck had stopped with me and I wanted to pass it on.

The Arts Council took stepping back to mean leaving the company and wanted the Board to set in motion a mechanism for choosing the succession. My argument was that we were a group theatre and, when I did finally leave, there was no succession problem as the group would simply continue as it had when Michael died. I knew that, with Marianne's resignation, we were in a weak position, since Greg would not step into any vacuum but I had given my word to Casper and I was going to do all in my power to keep the company going.

The Arts Council, and not just they, had always had trouble understanding the group as a way of running a theatre. Surely there had to be one boss? It was the way of the world. I have already tried to show what a powerful alternative to the usual structure a group could be. There must be one place in England where this undeniably successful experiment could continue.

Admittedly, we were trying to do something no other group had ever done in the theatre. We were the longest-running group theatre, certainly in England, probably in the world, and we were trying to renew ourselves into the future. It was no wonder that we had initially made mistakes. We were learning, or I was, not to try to reproduce but let the thing happen organically if it wanted to. Marianne's going had, contrary to what I had feared, brought everyone together in greater harmony than had existed for years and the fruits were beginning to show, more quickly than any of us had hoped, although there was still a long way to go.

Trees are extraordinary things. I planted a lot in Dunes where I am writing this. Every year they appear to die and every year they are reborn. The deeper the roots go, the higher the tree grows and the more impressive the crown. If we can achieve the transition, the rewards will be considerable. As I write, after a long debate that has lasted since the appraisal, I believe we are going to be allowed to try. I do not know whether we shall succeed. It may be that this impulse has run its course after all this time. If that is so, so be it.

Clearly the group is now in play, so I am not going to write much about them individually. Equally clearly at the age of sixty-three my function in the organisation will, over the next while, undergo a fundamental change. By the time I finally cease to be directly connected to the company there will certainly have been an augmentation of the group. We now have a host of young directors working with us. It will be clear who that person, or persons, will be. At any rate, it is worth the trial and if we fail then someone else will learn from our mistakes and do it better. I am certain that one way or another the group will become an increasingly common phenomenon and not just in theatre.

CHAPTER 80

More Brad

The day Brad flew back to Toronto after the opening of *Snake in Fridge* he was already hotting up for another one. This was to be a farce about a group of friends who come together in a hotel for the funeral of one of their mutual friends and for a wedding from among them. He also wanted to reverse the 'coming out of the closet' play and make it about a gay man apparently going straight. It was to be called *Cold Meat Party*.

It was unveiled about nine months later, appropriately, when Marianne and I went over with our writers, Johnny Moore, Abigail Morgan and Debbie Horsfield, to workshop at CanStage on our co-commissions. Brad finished his first draft the night we arrived and the next morning it was presented in a reading.

First drafts are not perfect but this was clearly mature Brad. As a genre, it was less a farce than a sitcom, but it broke new ground. Not only was it about the forty-something crisis but it was a generational play. The younger generation ranged from late teens to early thirties and there was a mother–daughter relationship.

Its form was a radical departure. Brad had written a conventional play: one composite set, no swear words, no soliloquies and long scenes (one scene lasted fourteen pages). It was, however, unmistakably Brad. The forty-somethings were a fading rock star, an independent feminist film director and a right-wing politician. In addition to his ever deeper exploration of human sexuality, the added spice was castration, voluntary desired castration with a beautiful vocational castrator in the cast list. That last ingredient seemed to freak Marty Bragg. He hadn't presented *Snake in Fridge*, now he was apprehensive as to what his audience would make of *Cold Meat Party*. I had no such doubts – the Exchange would do it.

There followed, over the next year, two workshops. The first was held in Manchester with the cast of *Time and the Conways*. The public performance of this caused Brad temporarily to lose his nerve. After a tense meeting with him he agreed to leave the script alone for a few months and then come back to it. He flew back to Toronto and had done what was nearly the final version in a week.

The second workshop was in Toronto. Brad had set *Cold Meat Party* in an upmarket Manchester bedsit, where the dead writer friend, Keith, whose funeral the Canadians were attending, had holed up with a young Manchester girlfriend who was pregnant by him. What we hoped was that we could therefore have a cast drawn from both companies and the production would play in both cities. The workshop was to be followed by a public performance, which we hoped would convince Marty Bragg to go further with it.

The performance was an undoubted success. It was a great cast, which included Brent Carver and Ron White. They gave it their all.

CanStage had three auditoria, one very small of about ninety seats, one rather larger of about 250 seats and a very large one in downtown Toronto's theatre district. All the commissions were for the large auditoria in both cities. Marty proposed that *Cold Meat Party* would not play the big auditorium but the 250 seater. Now I had just seen a play in the big one for the first time and had hated it. Intimate playing was not possible, the relationship with the audience was plain awful, so I wasn't unhappy with the suggestion. Added to this, CanStage's production of Judith Thompson's *Habitat* had not gone well there, as far as I could gather in large part due to the dreadfulness of the theatre. Brad was furious. To him the big auditorium meant a hike in status and this was a slap in the face. I hadn't quite realised that until the Exchange had done *Unidentified*, he had always been played in studio theatres. No mediation was possible. *Cold Meat Party* would not be done at CanStage. Brad was famous for his rows with the very people who might be able to help him; I had experienced it on *Snake*. It was obviously how he was.

Back in England, Greg suggested extending our theming experiment by twinning *Cold Meat Party* with *The Seagull*, and forming a company for six months to present the plays in the main house. He would direct *The Seagull*. I thought this a brilliant idea. Both plays were about artists going through their forty-year crisis and the effect it had on the younger generation. Brad seemed not to mind the idea.

He was, by now, one of the scriptwriting team on the American version of *Queer as Folk*, so couldn't be included in the casting process. In fact, he couldn't get to England till the last week of rehearsal, but having been through the workshops with him neither of us found that a problem.

Cross-casting two plays is always demanding and we didn't expect to get star names for a six-month engagement. We found a very fine cast led by Colin Tierney, Geraldine Alexander and Tom Hodgkins, together with

Kellie Bright who had been in *Snake*, Joe Millson, Emma Lowndes and, in *The Seagull* only, a startlingly good new young actor, Steve Robertson.

Rehearsals were spread over eight weeks as the two plays were due to open on the same day. Things went well. This was Brad's most profound work, which merited deep exploration, and the cast were as good as I had hoped.

Brad finally arrived in the middle of the last week and we put on a special run-through for him. The cast was nervous – he is a very imposing figure and his reputation is fearsome – and it wasn't a great account of the play. I retired with him to get his notes. There were a lot of them but they all seemed very justified. I could tell he hadn't been delighted. The next day we broke the rhythm of the final week and went through the notes in rehearsal with Brad present. All seemed well.

The day after was the last run before production weekend. This, we hoped, would consolidate the progress made the day before. Brad did not attend the run-through, he left a message at the stage door pleading the extreme after-effects of jet lag. This was peculiar and we all thought it odd that a playwright would miss such a crucial run-through, but there it was.

Monday was the technical with the dress rehearsal afterwards. It's a tiring day and everyone knows that the dress rehearsal is often all about actors getting used to their clothes and the set. It is invariably awful.

Brad confronted me when it was over. The cast were a load of shit and the set was the worst he had ever seen. I arrived for rehearsals the next day to be told by my PA that Brad had left a message to say that he had re-booked his flight and wouldn't be staying for the first night.

This was shattering. I had to rehearse the cast prior to the first preview, and the man I deeply admired and was very fond of had basically told me that my production was a crock of shit. Somewhere deep down inside me I knew he was wrong, so I managed to take the rehearsals by remaining faithful to Brad the playwright.

The first preview was a great success but to my utter astonishment Brad didn't turn up for it, the first public performance of his play. I was determined to keep the circumstances from the cast who were now becoming bewildered by his actions. I simply told them he had given me notes and gone off jet-lagged to bed.

I phoned him the next day and said irrespective of what he felt about the production, I needed him as an author to look at certain things in the script. He came that night, after the play had started, and even he must have seen how much the audience were enjoying themselves. Afterwards we had a civilised discussion but when he asked if he should attend the cast's notes session I told him that I thought it would be counter-productive. Off he went. I told the cast that he and I had had a row that didn't concern them. Since the previews were clearly successful, they managed just about to process that.

Seagull went into its preview sequence and Brad went off down to London. Unfortunately his face now appeared on the cover of *City Life*, Manchester's equivalent of *Time Out*. His was the lead interview and in it he criticised the Exchange for pairing his play with Chekhov, whom he dismissed as boring. He was telling the actors who were in his play that their other work was not worth doing and he was slamming the company who were presenting their fifth Brad production and second commission. The theatre was in uproar. Normally placid people were hopping mad. Everyone expected me to read the riot act.

There were two Brads. One was the highly talented, intelligent, kind and perceptive author; the other was the Alberta redneck with an apparently uncontrollable urge both to destroy and self-destruct. Nothing could have been more calculated to wreck his own play. But I still loved the man, or rather one of him, so I couldn't do that.

Through the mediation of his agent, I had dinner with him when he came back to Manchester, prior to flying home. I didn't pull any punches, either about the article or the way he had treated the cast. I supposed that what had happened was that, like any committed author (he was also a director), he had conceived his play in totality, especially the characters and particularly the lead character, Marcus, who was a self-portrayal up to a point. He had arrived at the run-through and nothing was how he had imagined it. Why would it be, since he had been totally disconnected from the casting and production process? By the end of this and a subsequent second meal we had reached a sort of reconciliation, and off he went.

The play opened to very good reviews, which I made sure travelled across the Atlantic. Over the next few months I received the odd friendly e-mail and even an appreciative article about the play and production by some German writer. Then, about a year later, Brad phoned me. A company in Toronto called Factory Theatre wanted to produce the play in the autumn and would I direct it? I couldn't believe it but I knew I had to do it and indeed I wanted to; I believed in the play. My proviso was that when I came to Toronto to cast the play, we would sit down and talk through what had happened.

The meeting took place over a Sunday brunch, with me the jet-lagged one. I asked for chapter and verse on my production, because I didn't want to go into rehearsal not understanding what exactly he had hated about it. I wanted to know what adjustments to make.

He told me he had no criticisms of my production whatsoever. I learnt my

Brad lesson. There were, as I've said, two of him and the only way to deal with it was to wait until the positive one reappeared. I later found out he was a Gemini. During rehearsals there were one or two squalls, which I called Bradsides, but in the main he was impeccable and appreciative.

Factory Theatre had about the same status as the Hampstead Theatre Club. It was run by Ken Gass who, like me at the Exchange, had been there since the flood and was one of the fathers of modern Canadian writing, George Walker being his particular creative partnership. Factory Theatre was run on a shoestring – I caught Ken hoovering the foyer and cleaning the toilets – and in terms of organisation and technical back-up the experience was a bit of a nightmare, but it had one huge compensation.

It was like working in England twenty years ago before television broke the acting tradition. These actors were stage animals. They had worked with each other in various different companies and rehearsing with them was unalloyed joy. Ron White, Sarah Orenstein, Ross Manson were the older generation and they were superb.

Factory Theatre had an odd auditorium and Ken gave me a designer who was experienced at working there. I was back on an end stage for the first time since Houston and I put myself in her hands. The set had two locations, the living room of the B&B, and a bedroom, which served for all the bedrooms in the hotel. In Manchester, being in the round, the two rooms existed side by side on the stage floor; on an end stage one would be above the other, on a two-level set.

When I flew over to complete the audition process, Ken had had a mock-up of the set arranged on stage for me to OK. I was worried that not all the audience would be able to see the upper level. They assured me it would be all right. I naturally bowed to their experience.

Cold Meat Party was to be the opening production of the new season so they could build the set on stage for us to rehearse on. I was called in to look at it. Half the audience couldn't see the upper level. I called Ken who arrived with the designer. His reaction was simple: 'Oh fuck!' The only solution was to lower the ceiling of the living room. This solved the problem, but created another one. Any actor who was over five foot ten inches couldn't move up stage.

The day of the technical arrived. I had been asked, and made it clear that I wanted everything there: costumes, props, lights, sound, everything, as I was used to. I turned up to start the rehearsal. My excellent stage manager, Fiona Jones, was there. 'Astrid says you can't have costumes for the tech.'

'Send her to me.'

'She's not in the building, she's teaching.'

'Send me the wardrobe mistress.'

'She's not in the building.'

'Send me the production manager.'

'He's not here.'

'Is there anyone here?'

'Me and the lighting operator.'

The cast were on stage listening to this. 'Don't worry,' I told them. 'I'll go down to the offices and sort it out.' I did and there was no one there except a secretary. 'Where is everyone?'

'They're out.'

Eventually, midway through the afternoon Ken Gass turned up. 'See, Braham, this is the problem. We didn't have everything for you, so it was either start the technical or send everyone out to get what you need.'

Having struggled through the vicissitudes of the production week – at one stage the frustrated company put up masking flats themselves – we started the previews. Our practical problems weren't over. One night the sofa collapsed in the middle of a scene, another night the bed collapsed. It was like being back in Plymouth with Century Theatre. Actually, it was worse and I wasn't used to it. Fortunately the previews went well. The reception was fantastic. I asked if Canadians always cheered. I was told this was exceptional. The first night was heady. The reviews were lousy. To me this was inexplicable. I'm very honest about my own work. This was a better production than the English one and Brad had done excellent rewrites, improving an already fine play.

Brad had never had good reviews in Toronto. He has, as a result, waged open war against the critics, even satirising them on his website. In many people's view we were always going to get bad reviews, irrespective of the quality of the production – very disheartening if you've put your heart and soul into it as all of us had done. I flew home the next day; the cast had to put up with it for another five weeks.

The worst thing about it is that it threatens to stop Brad writing for the theatre. Actually, he is now working on a rather remarkable Broadway musical and I think theatre is too much in his blood. He may desert it for a while but he won't be able to keep away for long. The attitude of the Toronto critics towards him is a disgrace. It can only be personal.

CHAPTER 81

The Home Team Play

Manchester doesn't take to Chekhov and *The Seagull*, in spite of its reviews, lost a lot of money. *Hobson's Choice* made it back again. This is the quintessential Manchester play and I had always thought it worth doing if you could cast Hobson. He is a comic King Lear and there are not many actors of that age who can carry that off. It occurred to me that my old friend Trevor Peacock could, and to my delight he agreed to do it. John Thomson had been a very good Bob Acres in Maureen Lipman's *Rivals* and I asked him to play Willie Mossop. It was good timing because he had had a lot of bad publicity about his private life and this would be a good move for him. For us *The Vicar of Dibley* meets *Cold Feet* had to be good box office. I thought Maggie would be difficult. Lorraine Ashbourne was the perfect choice but motherhood made it impossible. I knew Jo Riding only from musicals and that made me suspicious when she came to audition. That lasted five minutes. She was another one of those gifts from the gods.

If Vanessa Redgrave has a complex hidden acting process, John Thomson appears to have none at all. Rehearsals seem to bore him, especially if he isn't speaking, and this can drive the other actors to distraction. It drove Jo Riding to distraction. She is about as professional as you can get. Their rehearsals, which were key to the play, were not easy. What John has for free is a God-given intuitive sense of how to do things. Once he gets the hang of an idea that might be fun he just does it with no visible effort. It is uncanny. In front of an audience he can do no wrong. He has an extraordinary relationship with them. They love him.

We were looking forward to the first preview. In spite of the tensions, we knew we had a good show. At 6 p.m. Katie Vine, our Company Manager, came to my office. Trevor had collapsed. He was in his dressing room. No one knew if it was a heart attack or what; he would have to go to hospital. I rushed down to see him. He was in a dreadful state; he didn't want to let anyone down. I told him there was no question of his going on that night. We would cancel the preview and he would go to hospital.

301

I called our staff together and told them to cancel. Sophie Marshall spoke: 'Are you sure, Braham?'

'What do you mean? We don't have any covers ready to go on.'

'You were rather good in auditions.'

'Me?'

'I think the actors will be very upset not to do the previews.'

That night Colin Prockter called it *Hobstein's Choice*. Actually, unlike Iago, I was rather good. It was a schizophrenic experience. I was playing a leading role in my own first preview. The first preview is the moment when you pretty well know what you've got. It also tells you what you have left to do, particularly in a comedy where you find out where the laughs are for the first time. Playing the part and suddenly finding myself listening to the audience's reaction as a director was bizarre.

At the end of the show, which was a great success, I had no idea what to say to the cast. The good news as I came off stage was that the hospital had given Trevor the all clear and he would be on tomorrow night.

Managements queued up to take the show to London. After making sure the cast, especially the three principals and most of all John Thomson, who was big box office, wanted to go, I met with them and after a few weeks opted to go with Bill Kenwright because we had got on well over *Lady Windermere* and also he could deliver the Garrick.

I called a company meeting to tell them the good news and got a peculiarly muted response. After the meeting was over one of them said, 'I don't think John will go to London.' She was right. Having played the part for a month, John was bored stiff. He invented some guff about uprooting his family, when in fact he had a house in London, but that was that. I was absolutely livid. He had made a fool of me. Bill was absolutely livid, he had booked the Garrick. The rest of the cast were distraught. He had denied them plum jobs.

John's drink problem had had some bad effects on certain nights. On one occasion he decided to do a stand-up after the show. It was a sell-out audience. He was so drunk he had to leave the stage. I have never witnessed such an angry house. Now, with this added tension, the problem grew. On the last day he was found slumped in the dressing-room corridor with an empty bottle of some spirit by his side. The company's ostracising him had got to him. Somehow by pouring pints of coffee into him they got him on for the last two performances. What a waste of a great talent.

Later that summer Duncan Weldon called me in France. What did I think about doing *Zack* with John? I thought it was great casting but that he'd never work with me again. 'Yes he will,' said Duncan. 'I've just had lunch with him.' I knew that John would never do a long enough run for Duncan and he didn't. A year later the idea of John doing *Zack* grew on me. Rather like what women say about childbirth, I'd forgotten how painful it had been to rehearse him. I asked him to do it only for Manchester. He agreed, then just before the season was to be announced he decided he'd rather be in LA for the pilot season. The cancellation cost us a lot of money.

Amanda Donohoe had done the same thing. We had agreed to do *A Month in the Country* together. We had even changed the dates at the eleventh hour to accommodate a new television series. Even later than John, she pulled out. This shocked and upset me. Not only had we worked successfully together but I regarded her as a friend. In spite of her agent's efforts she didn't even have the decency to call me. That cost the company a lot of money too and both betrayals happened within a couple of months of each other.

From what I hear from other directors, this sort of behaviour is getting more and more frequent. The old traditions, which were good ones, are dying.

However, *Hobson* was an extraordinary success. Each performance was like being at Wembley watching Manchester United win the Cup Final. It was the most at-home audience I have ever experienced. You couldn't get a seat and we extended the run, postponing the Emil Wolk extravaganza, *Sherlock Holmes in Trouble*.

CHAPTER 82

Coming Together

According to the critics – and who am I to disagree with them? – I was going through the best period of my career as a director. *Peer Gynt* appeared to herald a new confidence in me. There were various reasons.

The main one is that I was now very experienced. I assume that, like me, all directors are in a state of panic from the first rehearsal to opening night. You have planned your production in meticulous detail and you have imagined every moment of it. Then you come to the first read-through and they're all saying the words wrongly. You've got four weeks and you don't know most of them. How are you going to get it all together?

As you do more work, you get more used to the ups and downs of the process. You expect very little from the actors for the first two weeks; you don't panic at a very bad run-through, or dress rehearsal, or first preview; and you don't regard every opening night as a gut-wrenching disaster. That means you don't push the actors in the wrong way at the wrong time. You are utterly reliant on your actors, so you learn to imagine what they are feeling. They are as frightened as you are, hence you give them what they need to gain confidence and fly.

You also know that you are by now technically proficient, so you don't have to worry about that; your job is to bring your creative imagination into play. By now I wasn't differentiating between the various genres. Comedy, farce, straight, classical, new: all plays went through the same rigorous mill. Take them seriously, break them down, see where they really touch common humanity and you will create a common goal for the actors and a communal experience for the audience.

The two productions in 2004 illustrate this perfectly. I have referred to *The Happiest Days of Your Life* early on in this book in connection with my prep school days. Until recently I would simply have regarded it as a farce. Make 'em laugh. However, partly because of my own personal connection to the material and partly because John Dighton had also written *Kind Hearts and Coronets* and *The Man in the White Suit*, I knew that underneath this text there was a serious intention. He was charting the moment when the old relationship between the sexes started to come apart. It is a play about the end of the war, when a girls' boarding school is mistakenly billeted on a boys' boarding school and the chaos that ensues. I knew from my own experience the fear masters felt when confronted with the opposite sex and vice versa. I also knew that there were exceptions to that rule. I had met the frightful parents, too, who had sent their children away and was familiar with the schools' blinkered insistence on the disciplined, healthy regime that was the bane of their young victims.

Thus the play was done seriously. The gags grew out of genuine panic and therefore it was very, very funny. Philip Madoc, Janet Henfrey, Simon Robson and the unrecognisable Jo Riding as the frustrated Gossage, were the leaders of a superb cast who took the acting seriously. Emil Wolk created a proper ending to the play, which peters out unconvincingly in the original, as the outside world besieges the school; you know the barriers are coming down and love blossoms at the last.

The same went for *The Importance of Being Earnest*. I had always thought the play was undoable because it was so perfect, but we needed a summer show and I took a deep breath and did it. It's like no other play in the English language, nor like any other Wilde wrote. As I gazed at the text it seemed impossible, almost every line appeared to come from the *Oxford Dictionary of Quotations*. Eventually I thought, having done *Lady Windermere's Fan*, I'd better put it through the Stanislavsky analysis because Wilde was a master playwright and wouldn't have thrown out all the rules. The play revealed itself as meticulously written for actors, a brilliant satire on the empty forms of behaviour and criteria that rule any society, and above all the opposition of society to love and union. Then the stakes became very high, the witticisms stopped being only that and turned into words uttered for a purpose.

It was an expert cast, as it had to be. Gabrielle Drake again excelled herself as the beautiful basilisk-like Lady Bracknell, Joanna David was actually perfect as Miss Prism, everything that is special about English acting. John Watts as Chasuble, Ian Shaw, Jamie de Courcey, Anna Hewson, Laura Rees, John Conroy. I have to name them all.

One of the drawbacks of working north of Watford is that if you do *The Importance* no critic comes to see it. They regard you as doing a filler, a potboiler. Do the same production at the National and everyone does a radical re-evaluation of the play. Only one national critic came to the production but it was sold out and its run extended. You might think this was predictable but what wasn't predictable was that it was a predominantly young audience, discovering the piece for the first time, and they loved it. It was very gratifying.

I was having a good time but the company was still putting in very uneven work. I was worried. Then suddenly, in 2005, it all came together. From the first production of that year, which was Sarah's of *Rutherford and Son* by Githa Sowerby, right up to the moment that I am writing this in the summer of 2006, every show has been out of the top drawer. There hasn't been a dud and that gives me great pleasure, not only because it is good to sit in the auditorium and be proud of our performances, but because it means to me that the new group has come together and are feeding off each other, sometimes in emulation, sometimes in rivalry. It bodes well for the future, but my goodness it has been a long time coming.

CHAPTER 83

The Serpent of Old Nile

My production for 2005, and the last one I shall write about in any detail, was *Antony and Cleopatra*. Ever since I had played Antony at Clifton I had been in love with the play and harboured a yen to do it. I was, however, scared of it. It is famously unmanageable and, since the Helen Mirren–Michael Gambon version, had failed critically. I had put it on the back burner. Then Jacob suggested that Josette Bushell-Mingo would be a great Cleopatra. I knew he was right but fear welled up in me. For all my newfound confidence this would be a real test. Jacob e-mailed Josette to see if she would be interested. She immediately said she would and I was on the path. There was a stumbling block. Who would play Antony? Alas, I had a good idea. Tom Mannion had done great work at the Exchange, and had been a wonderful Dmitri in *Karamazov*. He had the look, he had the talent, he was an experienced Shakespearean actor and he was the right age. I met him first, then had him meet Josette. It was a match. They both agreed to go ahead. This was in 2003. We set the production dates for eighteen months hence, partly because Josette was living in Sweden and partly because there was a hell of a lot of preparation to do. Johanna, of course, would design.

I spent a heady summer of 2003 in Dunes, working on the cutting of the text and immersing myself in the play. I knew this was Katherine's last gift. If it had not been for my relationship with her, I could never have approached the play. I believed and understood the obsessional nature of the love, and finally that it could transcend death. The end was not tragic, it was triumphant. Both lovers knew they would meet again.

During 2004 I used to rehearse Josette and Tom in my London flat. It was very exciting. All the energies were flowing. Johanna's design was exactly apropos. The Exchange was the epic space par excellence. *Antony and Cleopatra* is a bit like a Brad Fraser play: endless scenes, some only a few lines, requiring instant location changes. Johanna created the two worlds of Rome and Egypt on opposite sides of the stage and the action flowed without pause. Here was the Apollo–Dionysus polarity again, beautifully realised in her costumes.

The battles in *Antony and Cleopatra* – and there are three of them – all take place off stage. Fine for Shakespeare's audience, but what to do in 2005? I knew that dramatically the three battles represented three different stages of the lovers' relationship, so instead of having a conventional fight director I asked Mark Bruce to stage the scenes as being interior to Antony's and Cleopatra's minds. His solutions were theatrical, integral and wonderfully inventive.

There were a whole list of fine actors in the cast, some playing very small but crucial roles. I had thought it would be difficult to cast but it was done in record time. Terry Wilton was a heart-rending Enobarbus, Steve Robertson a terrific Octavius, and Sarah Paul and Gugu Mbatha-Raw perfect as Charmian and Iras. I wish I could name them all.

The production got the best reviews I have ever received, but there was one discordant and distressing note. Some time early on in rehearsal Tom lost confidence in himself in the part. He said he hated the role and the play. After spending over a year preparing it with him this was astonishing and it created major problems. Josette was obviously distressed and Tom even blamed her, the most generous of actresses, for his problem. Antony is a hard part. He is a fading superstar who has what is effectively a breakdown and is responsible for the death of thousands. It is the male in vulnerable crisis . . . and he's not in the fifth act.

I somehow had to do enough to convince the audience that they really did love each other. Fortunately they don't have many actual love scenes, but it was a huge task. The hell of it was that despite the play's critical success – and Tom got very good reviews – the centre of the play couldn't flower properly. The great thing about the run of the play is that if everything has been planted properly, once the opening night and its attendant reviews are over, the cast will grow and grow. The production couldn't mature and that was awful to watch. Tom shouldn't have taken the part, it was not fair on the other actors.

Nothing should distract from the astounding performance of Josette. This was pure life force, mesmerising, magnetic, sensual, regal, everything that is conjured up by 'infinite variety'. From my point of view it is one of the greatest performances I have been associated with.

CHAPTER 84

Uncle Max

That's it. It's the summer of 2006, this September is the thirtieth anniversary of the company and I am not scheduled to direct a play in the season. To my surprise, I'm quite happy about that. My projects didn't bear fruit; they will at some other time. It's a good sign. It means that the theatre has a future and that a proper gear change is taking place. It gives me space to make my own transition.

This is the last chapter and it's time to talk about Uncle Max, or more accurately Great-uncle Max. My mother's paternal family name was Prevezer. Originally there were seven sons and four of them escaped from the Nazis to England. They came over on the onion boats with nothing. My grandparents, Sam and Fay, waited outside stocking factories where each night the rejects were thrown out. They matched these up and sold them off their barrow in the East End. Eventually they made enough to buy a proper shop, S. Prevezer Hosiery, in Whitechapel High Street. They moved to Finchley; Uncle Jack, the richest, to Brighton; Uncle Barney to Mayfair; and Uncle Max to Regent's Park.

The sins of the fathers are not just visited upon the sons for four or five generations, but for ever until someone says the curse stops with me. The curse of the Prevezers was total emotional constipation. Inside they were cauldrons of feeling but none of it could be expressed. No one ever hugged my mother and she didn't hug me; it was left to a nanny to do that. No Prevezer could ever appear vulnerable or moved. If you gave my grandfather a present, he'd look at it with worry on his face and say, 'How much costs such a thing?' Inside he was delighted. A Prevezer never called for help. One Friday night, shortly after my stepfather Philip had joined the family, my grandfather went into the kitchen carrying dishes to start on the washing up. 'Would you like some help?' asked Philip.

'No,' said my grandfather.

I waited for a few seconds. 'You'd better go and help him,' I advised Philip.

'But he said no.'

'That means yes.'

Uncle Max was the most extreme example of the Prevezer curse. He had a shop about twenty yards from my grandfather's, M. Prevezer Hosiery. Whenever I visited him my grandfather always sent me to say 'hello' to Uncle Max. This I did and always got some pocket money for my pains.

One day Uncle Max simply stopped talking. When I went to say hello, he merely grunted. 'Hello, Uncle Max.'

Grunt.

'How are you?'

Grunt.

'How's Auntie Bertha?'

Grunt.

'I've got to go now, Uncle Max.'

Grunt, and some pocket money.

Uncle Max retreated from the world. It was a tendency in all the brothers and it is a tendency in me. I hope and pray I have stopped the curse with me. When I look at my sons I think I have, in the main. What I must hope for in this next cycle of my life is to lift it a little for myself.

I won't go the way of Uncle Max now, theatre has saved me from that. At least in the rehearsal room I can express all those passions, desires and yearnings that the Prevezer curse prevented me from doing in real life. I believe that curse did for my cousin Gillian. She became a remarkable philosopher but that also led her inwards. Theatre has taken me outwards, which is why I have no intention of following in Casper's or Max's footsteps and leaving it. My great wish is to see the Exchange through this transition so that it will carry on when I can no longer be part of it, but I do intend to go on directing. There are still plays I want to do, including, of course, one day *Brand*, and I still crave the adrenalin rush the theatre gives me. What I want to do is to extend that raising of the portcullis from theatre into actually living.

Everything that seems to have been negative in my life, viewed from a different angle, can be seen as positive. Without the so-called negatives I would never have been spurred to do what I have done. I have no idea what is to come and that is exciting. I have been rescuing spiders from my pool here in France. I hope Armund is proud of me. I am not afraid of my destiny at last. I'm ready to let go and see where it leads me. As Joe Orton said, 'Just when you least expect it, the unexpected always happens.'

Index